IT CAME TO PASS

IT CAME TO PASS

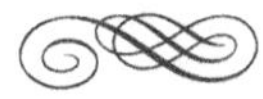

TAMMY EMINETH

Contents

PART 2

PART 3

PART 4

Dedication

Dedicated to my family; to those that carry on legacies in their
own families and to all that will come after us.
To my husband and children.
To my friends that inspire and edit me.
To the Lord for all His goodness, grace, and forgiveness.
Never forget what God has done.
Contributors:
Carol Weiler
Dolores Easley
Richard Byrd

Part 1

Prologue

Mama had died. I was left to care for my two younger siblings while daddy went to work. There wasn't much time for grieving. There were dishes to wash, beds to make, groceries to buy, but only when absolutely needed. The outside world knew we lived in a rural, isolated part of the county but I didn't realize that at the time. It was home and we didn't have the luxury of moving when someone died to avoid the constant reminders of what used to be. My life didn't change all that much, Mama just wasn't there. Daddy shut down and just went to work. It was 1939 and there was something on the radio about Poland and the Nazis but in my small, isolated world, World War II seemed far away, at least for now. There were too many other things that occupied my mind. Getting through the day with the kids fed was the most important thing. That superseded anything else that might be happening in the world.

I had no idea how my life would go, and I didn't even think about it when I was young. I had enough to think about at the present than what my life would look like 5 years or even 10 years down the line. We had moved a couple of times because of the depression and we needed to go where there was work. Eventually, my brother and sister came along so there were even more mouths to feed.

I had to quit school to care for Vern and Mitzi when Mama died and that kept me busy enough until we really didn't have much extra around the house. I didn't make my life happen; life happened to me, but it's not an excuse, it just is. Sure, I made some of my own choices and decisions, but I always felt there was something else out there making most of them for me, be it good or bad. But, I think I truly felt like my life began, and not in a good way, when Mama died.

I

What's Wrong?

"It came to pass, as her soul was in departing, for she died..." Genesis 35:18

Mama had been complaining of stomach pains for a few months, but no one ever thought it was anything serious. Was she pregnant again? Was she eating something that was upsetting her stomach? There wasn't time or money to go to the doctor, so when it became so unbearable that she doubled over in the kitchen one Tuesday afternoon and we went rushing to her side, only then did daddy do something. Four hours later they returned from the doctor with disheartening news. The type of news that didn't really give you answers but was not comforting either.

"We need to do exploratory surgery", said the doctor. They couldn't put a finger on why she was having these excruciating pains and bouts of nausea and vomiting. The appointment was made for Thursday.

I was 17 and helped care for my two younger siblings, Mitzi and

Vern. It was spring in 1939. Ruby, my Mama, had the most beautiful auburn hair I had ever seen. For me and Mitzi, the gene had turned our hair a vivid strawberry blonde, which I hated. I often wrapped my head in a scarf when I went to town so as not to draw too much attention to it. It was a short bob; I didn't need any more of it than necessary. Daddy loved it and called me his firecracker. We shared the fiery red hair. But, I would just shrug and give him an eye roll when he called me that but deep down it made me feel special. No one else had a pet name.

They named me Virginia. It means maiden or virgin, although that sounded more like a virtuous city girl than me. I had been helping out more and more now that Mama spent longer mornings in bed and went to sleep early. She got tired more often throughout the day and just couldn't lift things like she used to.

When Mama and Daddy returned from the doctor, I had unemotionally asked what I needed to do. Mama tenderly put a hand on my cheek and just smiled. She slowly turned away without really looking anywhere else and shuffled off to bed. She stayed there for two days and didn't come out except to ask for help getting to the privy. She didn't eat either. I heard Mama and Daddy talking late one night about the appointment. How were they going to pay for it? What good would it actually do?

The morning of the procedure, I got up early, as I always did, washed Mitzi's face who was only seven at the time, and commanded Vern to finish his bread and wash his face as it was going to be a busy day. Vern was 12 and alternated between being helpful and troublesome depending on the day. Mitzi went along with whatever anyone was doing but sometimes whined when she was forced to have cabbage soup for the third time in a week. This was the day the doctors were going to operate on Mama in anticipation of finding more concrete answers to the stomach pain.

Daddy got up early as well and helped Mama dress. I was instructed to have supper ready should they come home the same day. As she went out the door, Mama longingly looked at us as if she was screaming, 'if I never see you again, I want to remember you just as you are this morning'. But there was no screaming. There was only softness and peace.

I felt uneasy as they prepared for the ride, like the feeling you get when the wind starts slowly dancing through the trees and the sky turns a dark grey and you know a storm is on the horizon. But I didn't know what kind of storm. Were they coming back? Daddy was preoccupied with helping Mama into our 1933 Buick that really didn't fit us all, but it was all we had.

Then they left. I watched until the rear bumper rounded the curve in our driveway. I turned, looked up at the sky, which was now the dusty gray of an early morning in spring, and went in the house to wait.

The air felt heavy all day. No doubt a storm really was on the horizon. I kept checking out the window - maybe for Mama and Daddy, maybe for the storm, maybe for any answer that just wouldn't come that day.

Regardless of the situation, work still had to be done. I helped Mitzi dress and told Vern to brush off his shoes outside so as to not kick dirt in the house. Home was a 3-bedroom house with a small living area, kitchen, and privy out back. Mitzi and I shared a room, Vern had his own and Mama and Daddy occupied the other.

Mitzi and I shared a bed but it was her job to make it every morning since I did so many other things around the house. Our humble little abode didn't seem small at the time even though when we all were seated around the supper table not even Mitzi could squeeze by a pulled-out chair. We all waited until everything was on the table and sat at once.

Behind the table was a meager fireplace but it kept the house warm in the winter so long as we all did our job and brought in the wood that Daddy had chopped and split throughout the year. There was a rocking chair to the right of the stone fireplace and a small table where Mama kept her mending basket.

I shooed the kids off to school and swept the floor, cleaned up from breakfast, and went to see if our eight miserable chickens had laid any eggs that morning. They hadn't. The weather was still cooler and the time of year wasn't giving them enough light to produce on a regular basis. We'd only get one or two a week if we were lucky. I opened the pen and let them roam around for small mice, worms, and June bugs. Hopefully, the chickens kept the pests away from our garden, which hadn't been fully planted yet now that Mama had turned ill.

Mama and Daddy didn't come home that day. Mitzi and Vern walked home together in the afternoon as they did nearly every day after school. I had milk and biscuits waiting for them. They argued slightly when they walked through the door followed by my curt scolding to "hold your tongue". The evening dragged on with no sound of a beeping horn or raggedy car, even though I frequently told the two younger children to "be quiet!" thinking I'd heard something. But there was nothing. No sound. I pulled out *The Secret of the Old Clock*, a Nancy Drew mystery, and read until Mitzi couldn't keep her eyes open any longer. I then ordered Vern to go to bed and carried Mitzi to our own bed.

2

Waiting

"It came to pass in the sixth year, in the sixth month, in the fifth day of the month, I sat in mine house..." Ezekiel 8:1

After a restless night of wondering and waiting, Friday seemed to come early. I got up before Mitzi and Vern and tended to the fire, which had died down some but was easy to get going again.

Our small, humble home was set at the end of a long, dirt, rural road just outside Kansas City, Missouri. We moved here from Simmons, Missouri after the depression hit when there wasn't any work for Daddy. He was able to get a job at a machine factory in the city, which kept food on the table and a meager roof over our heads.

We were luckier than a lot of folks in the area because we had actual wood floors, not hard dirt like a lot of the settlers in Jackson County. Daddy had worked hard on getting the house in a state that pleased Mama. He loved his wife deeply and I could see that in the way he worked tirelessly at the factory and at home, sacrificing time with his children. But as long as Mama and Daddy were okay, everything else seemed acceptable.

Vern was still in bed when I called to get his lazy butt up and Mitzi ran out of the bedroom with her hair pointing in all directions. I smoothed it and tied it back with a blue ribbon Mitzi had found on the way to school one day.

The circumstances of the day didn't matter; the two younger children had to go to school. I, on the other hand, had not been in over a year. Daddy said that common sense and tending a house was more important than conjugating vowels, or whatever that meant. Vern dressed quickly and rushed to the table for cheese and honey while Mitzi dawdled and flopped back on her bed playing with her paper dolls. I gave a stern call and Mitzi jumped slightly, tucking the dolls under her pillow and scooting out the door to the table.

The water for coffee steamed and whistled and I poured the boiling water over a filter full of coarse coffee grounds. I drizzled a little honey in for sweetness and then quickly flicked the honey stick over Mitzi and Vern's bread and cheese.

"Eat up quick. Gotta get going", I mindlessly demanded. There was not a hint of love or tenderness in this statement but there wasn't anger either. Just a matter-of-fact statement clearly emphasizing facts and that my mind was somewhere else.

Daddy was not there, which was not unusual, but the absence of Mama was unnerving. Did she make it? Did they know some answers? What happens now? Mama's presence in the house was gravely missed even though Vern tried to pretend he was the man of the house now. This was the boy that was tough and forceful until he stubbed a toe or was made fun of in school. He quickly folded and would often bury himself in Mama's apron for a good dose of care and reassurance before wiping his eyes and standing up straight saying he didn't need anyone.

"Go on, let's git", I motioned to Vern and Mitzi. They grabbed their hats, coats, and boots and headed out the door. I stood on the porch watching them as Mitzi danced around Vern waving ferociously back at the house. I simply raised a hand from my folded arms position.

Where were they? How long was this going to take? Will they ever come back? Of course, they would come back. I knew Daddy would never leave us. But would Mama? Not of her own free will, for sure. Maybe the doctor was really an evil person looking to do harm. Maybe those doctors and nurses were really in the business of hurting people and not helping? No, I couldn't think like that. I knew that this procedure, whatever "exploratory" meant, was going to cost a lot and it was the last resort. That meant there was nothing else they could have done.

But maybe it was something simple? Maybe she had just swallowed a piece of hardtack wrong and got it lodged somewhere unpleasant and it had to be surgically removed. Yes, that was it. Something silly and simple. She would be fine.

I busied myself by feeding the chickens, gathering the eggs, and picking a few radishes from the garden to eat with butter for lunch. I made sure the beds were made and the kitchen was clean. Gotta be ready in case Mama came home today.

But she didn't.

She didn't come home Saturday either.

3

The Time Will Come

"It came to pass, that when Jesus had finished these sayings, he departed..." Matthew 19:1

Sunday morning came with a bright sun piercing through the linen curtains in our room. The slit between the curtains was in direct line with my eyeballs and forced me to either roll over or get up. I did the latter.

Although Sundays were lazier than other days, work still had to be done. I had already done the washing the day before so fresh sheets and clothes were getting a good dose of sunshine out on the line. It hadn't looked like rain the night before, so I had taken the chance. The fabric was slightly damp from the dew but would quickly dry in what looked like was going to be a warm day.

Water on, fire stoked, cheese sliced. We were running low. I decided to make a loaf of bread and quickly kneaded and puffed up a soft, heavy mound of flour, yeast, salt, and water. I put it in the oven and soon the most amazing smell wafted through the house. Mitzi laughed over something funny she made her dolls do and Vern was running by the front porch chasing a cicada. For a brief second, I forgot the uncertainty of life, until I heard the chatter and bang of the Buick rumbling down the drive.

The car stopped in front of the house and Daddy told Vern to get the bags from the backseat. Mama was frail and looked hollow. She had deep, dark circles under her eyes and looked as if she'd lost 20 pounds since she'd left just a few days earlier. She looked at me on the porch and one corner of her mouth went up in a half-smile, but she didn't look like she had the energy for a full one.

I ran to the car to help Daddy get Mama out. "Be careful with her, she's still very weak," Daddy said. Mitzi came running out when she heard Daddy's voice and screamed, "Mama!" I threw a hand up at her and yelled, "stop!" Mitzi halted in her tracks. "What's wrong with her? What's wrong Mama?"

No one answered Mitzi. Daddy and I each had one of Mama's arms helping her up and out. Her weight was heavier than I would have thought but assumed it was due to weakness and fatigue.

We helped her up the front porch stairs and into the house. We carefully moved her to her room and lowered her on her bed. She let out a long sigh of relief and said, "thank you, dear". She sat still for a minute while Daddy rushed out of the room to get water for her pills. "What can I do, Mama?" I said.

"I just need to sit here a minute," she said. She closed her eyes and breathed deep. Then, opening them, she said, "help me to lie down, won't you dear?"

I gently held Mama by the shoulders and lowered her back onto her pillow. I picked up each leg one at a time and carefully removed her shoe and tucked her legs under the blanket. I adjusted her pillow, tucked in the blankets like you would for a baby and Mama let out another long sigh as she closed her eyes again.

Daddy came in with a cup of water and 2 white pills. He told Mama to take them, which required her to sit up again slightly. She winced in pain when she did so but took the medicine and water and slowly lowered herself back down, looking relieved to be home, still and quiet.

Mitzi was standing at the door looking worried. "Mama," she said sheepishly. Ruby turned toward her daughter and smiled. She reached a hand out to motion for her. Mitzi came in fast and was quickly halted by Daddy. "She's tired. Go slow," he said. She stopped and tiptoed in further to the bed as if she was trying to be quiet.

"Mama, what's wrong?" Mitzi said. I too wondered the same thing but thought it was inappropriate to ask.

Daddy paused and looked down and around the bed as if he were searching for the words somewhere in the blankets. He swallowed hard. "Get your brother," he nodded upward toward Mitzi with just a hint of a glance at her.

She bolted out of the room with a start and yelled, "Vern!" at the top of her lungs. Mama's eyes squinted at the shrill sound and Daddy winced as if he had been hurt by it as well. Mitzi yelled again and then we heard Vern shouting, "what?" in the same decibels.

Daddy didn't want to say anything without the other two in the room but looked at me with a pitying smile and then looked down again. Mama still had her eyes closed but she was not asleep. She shifted slightly to alleviate an uncomfortable position just as my siblings bounded into the room.

"What? I wanted to put the car away," he said perturbed to be interrupted. But his face softened when he saw Mama on the bed.

Daddy swallowed again and looked at all three of us one at a time before speaking. "She has cancer", he said. "Stomach cancer, and it's pretty advanced. There wasn't really anything they could do."

My brain felt like a bullet just went through right between my eyes. A sharp pain hit my forehead and I winced at it. I swallowed hard trying to comprehend what my father had just said.

"They don't think she has much time," he said mournfully and hopelessly. Mama opened her eyes and just looked at me with a Mona Lisa smile. There was really nothing more for her to add. That was it and that was all.

Mitzi's mouth curved to a frown and her eyes got glassy and wet. Vern looked like he might put a hole in the wall. I sat stunned, unable to process this. This can't be right. Go back, I thought. Ask them again. Maybe they did surgery on the wrong person. Maybe the results were wrong. Mitzi came closer to Mama and sprawled out across her legs and started sobbing. "No Mama...no", she whimpered in the bedsheets.

Vern tightened his jaw and clenched his fists. He quickly spun around and ran out of the room with my father calling after him, "Vern!" He was gone through the front door and bounded off the porch with one solid stomp and jump of his foot. "Let him go," Mama said.

We sat there in silence for what seemed like an hour. Daddy put his head down toward Mama and I touched her leg in comfort, but I didn't know if it was more for me or her. Daddy pulled Mitzi away saying Mama needed her rest, but he left me. Mitzi wrapped her arms around Daddy's waist, and he guided her out of the room.

I scooted a little closer up the bed towards her and gently reached for her hand and laid it in mine. She squeezed it slightly and gave that half-smile again. She opened her eyes and just looked at me. She looked at me more deeply than I've ever had someone before as if she was trying to communicate with me or really "see" me for the first time; I couldn't tell which.

"What can I do, Mama?" I said with a quiver in my voice that I didn't expect.

"Take care of them. They need you," she said softly. My eyes were now getting wet and I couldn't deny the hard lump in my own throat, which was making it hard to speak any longer. I put my other hand on top of hers and as I blinked away the tears, all I could do was nod, completely forgetting about the bread in the oven.

4

Without Her

*"It came to pass, that in process of time, after the end of two years...
he died of sore diseases." 2 Chronicles 21:19*

Things were so different after Mama died. She died on a Monday in April. We had barely known about the cancer and she was gone. There was no time to process, only grieve and plan. That's what Daddy did up until she died. Mama stayed in bed all day, every day. She didn't want to go to a hospital to face the inevitable. She wanted to be with her family. We were her whole world. Nothing would ever be the same now.

It was raining in the cemetery. Fitting, if you ask me. No funeral should be performed on a sunny, cheery day. The atmosphere matched our moods. It was painful watching her go. The last couple of days were the worse. She didn't open her eyes, didn't speak, just gurgled and breathed sporadically. Then she was gone. It looked as if life just left her. This was her body, but she was no longer there. I don't know where she went, but she wasn't in her bed any longer.

We had to make the 250-mile trek to Oakdale Cemetery just outside Cabool, Missouri because that's where all the relatives were buried. It was a dinky place with only about 30 graves and a small, white church. The funeral directors transported Mama's body because we couldn't very well haul it in our car. Just a couple of friends followed along to express their condolences, but I'm sure they had better things to do.

I was born just a few miles from this cemetery and was afraid that I too may not have the chance to go very far from my final resting place, just like Mama.

After staying a couple of days with relatives I really didn't know, we made the long journey back home, mostly in silence. Daddy was the most silent of all. Mitzi cried a little here and there, Vern still seemed angry, and I racked my brain about what to do next. Who would take care of the kids? Me, I suppose. I'd been doing that for a while now and it didn't seem like too much was changing in that regard.

Days after the funeral turned into weeks. I'd hear Daddy sobbing late at night and longed to wrap my arms around him for comfort but didn't know how to let him know I knew. So, we both just cried in lonely silence. I could hug and comfort Mitzi and she would often curl up next to me at night asking for stories about Mama and all the good times she had before Mitzi came along.

I would talk about summer afternoons with watermelons straight from the garden, ripe, sweet and juicy running down your chin and arms and how Mama would cut the slices into hearts and diamonds and we'd spit the seeds at each other.

The year we went to the city pool and Daddy was shocked at our swimming suits saying, "no daughters of mine are wearing barely-there pieces of clothing". And how Mama would purse her lips together in an apathetic way and wave her hand at Daddy as if he was being silly and he should just let it go.

Daddy was so good to us, but he loved Mama so much more. What would he do without her?

5

How to Keep Going

"It came to pass, when they had eaten up the corn which they had brought out of Egypt, their father said, go again, buy us a little food."
Genesis 43:2

Daddy was a strong man, and not just in the way most daughters may think of their dads. He was really strong. He had to be. He worked in a machine factory in downtown Kansas City. Everyone called him "Red" because of his fiery red hair, so thick it was like the unthatched lawns in the springtime where you can't even get to the dirt. Mama and Daddy both had red hair, so we were basically doomed to follow, although Vern had more of an auburn color, like Mama. He was lucky. You could spot Mitzi and me a mile away, which made it nice in crowds – for others, anyway.

Daddy's name was Richard Cunningham, but most people called him Dick or Red. People at work called him Red or those that wanted to tease him. Friends and relatives called him Dick. But he

21

was always just Daddy to us. But after Mama died, he wasn't the same.

He would come home from work more tired than I had ever seen him. He would sit in front of the fireplace and light up a cigarette and not talk for a good 20 minutes while I made dinner. He would saunter over to the table when called and eat in silence. Eventually, he started talking more and would ask the other kids about their day at school.

"How was *your* day, Daddy?" I boldly asked.

He looked up from his stew as if no one had ever asked him that before or with a look that said, *how do you think my day was?* But he quickly brushed the awkward glance aside and with a half-smile nodded and said, "it was just okay."

Vern and Mitzi didn't look up. Vern plunged his bread back into his stew bowl and took such a big bite the stew dribbled down his chin onto the table.

"Vern, stop that! You're spilling onto the table," I scolded. He gave me a shrug and refocused on the stew.

Mitzi spoke, "Daddy's crying". She stopped eating; we all did and looked up at him. One gigantic tear was halfway down his face, but he didn't look up.

"I don't know what I'm going to do without her," he said solemnly.

"We'll manage, Daddy. I'm almost 18 and I can take care of the kids," I promptly stated.

"We're not kids!" stammered Vern.

"Yes, you are," I said sternly and brushed him off with a hand in the air. "Daddy, I can do this. I know what to do."

"I know you do, Firecracker," he plainly said. He got up from the table. His stew was almost gone anyway. "Creth will be by later in the week with some groceries. He wants to help out."

Creth was Daddy's friend at the factory. They were similar in age and he had become a good pal to my dad. They would often sit out on the porch smoking and talking about how awful a certain foreman was or how the new receptionist was attractive. They weren't crass and I was grateful for that. Too many of my friends had fathers that were just plain awful. I always said I didn't care how poor we were as long as my Daddy kept us safe. And he did... for as long as he could.

6

✥

Creth

"It came to pass, when I Daniel had seen the vision, and sought for the meaning, then behold, there stood before me as the appearance of a man." Daniel 8:15

Creth was an average man, a little shorter than Daddy. But what he lacked in size he made up for in personality. When he entered the room, you knew it. Everyone sat up and took notice. He was kind of a show-off. Every time he came in the house, he told Mitzi and me something funny he'd done or seen or would tell us a new joke or show us a magic trick.

Creth didn't have red hair and I liked that. He had a jovial smile that lit up a room and he really looked at you in the eye when he entered. He never just pretended you weren't there or that you weren't that important. Even Mitzi knew he had a kind heart because she would run up to him when he came over and he'd swoop her up in his arms and give her what he called a "bear hug". I don't know if bears really hugged but that's probably what they looked like if they did.

Creth was married to Nell but he didn't seem to like her very much. They didn't have any children but the way Creth talked, he wished he had. Creth would bring groceries from the corner market about once a week. Milk, cheese, ketchup, flour, and a few canned goods, and pretty much anything we asked for. Our meager farm supplied eggs and some vegetables from the garden. He would stay at least once a week for supper. Then eventually I noticed he was coming over more than once a week and staying longer into the night.

Creth would come over to the house and sit on the porch with Daddy, nursing a beer and talking late into the night. My bedroom window faced the porch so I could hear their conversations. Mitzi would fall asleep fast, but I couldn't sleep, not until they left the porch anyway.

One night he mentioned that he was leaving Nell. "We want to go in different directions," he said. Daddy didn't say anything. "She wants to go off and travel and I'd really like to settle down and have a family. I'm not getting any younger, you know." The squeak of the rockers on the porch was the only sound for a long minute.

"I understand, Creth. There's nothing better than those three in there. I'd die for them. But I can't seem to shake this feeling. I can't seem to get over it," Daddy said sadly. "I wish I knew how people get over things like this."

"I feel real bad for you, Dick, I do. If there's anything else I can do to help, you let me know, alright?" Creth got up from the chair and tipped his hat to Daddy before lumbering off the porch and into his car. Daddy sat out there until I fell asleep. I didn't hear him come in.

7

The Garment Factory

"It came to pass when they had made an end of eating the grass of the land, I said, by whom shall Jacob arise, for he is small?" Amos 7:2

Things were getting tight and Creth could only do so much, especially since Nell had thrown most of his things out the front door when he told her he was leaving her. He stopped coming by for a while and Daddy said he had moved into an apartment in the city, closer to work. We missed his weekly visits but we really missed the food.

Daddy's paycheck supplied the mortgage and basics, but we were getting thinner on supplies all the time.

One evening over a poached rabbit that Vern had caught that day I asked Daddy if I could get a job.

"A job?" he replied. "I'm doing the best I can, here, Firecracker."

"Oh, I know that Daddy and we are ever so grateful. But if I'm to pull my weight around here I need to be doing as much as I can and when the kids go off to school and my chores are done, I just sit here twiddling my thumbs until dinner." I said emphatically. "The garment factory is hiring. I thought I could go work there?" I said in a questioning tone wondering if it really was a question or request for approval?

"Well, I don't know. I suppose I can't keep ya down. You are practically a grown woman," he said looking down at his rabbit. "As long as dinner is ready on time and the kids have help with their homework and you don't slack on your chores here at the house... I suppose it's alright, if you're really sure you want to do this?" He sheepishly replied seeming a little downtrodden.

"I think it would really help, Daddy," I said hopefully.

He nodded and continued to eat his rabbit smiling a little at Vern as if to say, good job on catching dinner.

The next morning, I walked Vern and Mitzi to school and kept going on to the garment factory on 10th Street. It was a big building with large, square metal boxes on top and symmetrical windows on every level of the 4-story building. It seemed large and intimidating. My willpower was stronger than my fear though and I marched into the front of the building where a woman behind a desk was looking down until I arrived.

She raised her head higher than it needed to go and her perfectly round spectacles flashed a glare at me from the low-hanging light. "Yes, dear?" she said kindly.

"I'm here about the job?" I mentioned boldly yet respectfully.

"Oh, yes, dear. Right this way," she said as she got up and motioned for me to follow her around the desk to the door directly behind her.

It smelled like textiles and the laundry after it had sat in the drawers a couple of weeks. Not a bad smell, but not the fresh-from-the-line scent either. Behind the door were dozens of women and men at desks leaning over sewing machines, heads down and knees pumping fiercely. The sound was almost deafening, and I was surprised how I didn't notice it from the reception area.

I followed the lady as we weaved between the desks and dodged limp and lifeless fabrics strewn on the floor. "Mind the fabrics and don't slip," she said curtly.

At the back of the room was another door. She tapped on it lightly and leaned her ear in but then turned the knob and went in anyway. A man with similar spectacles looked up with an inquisitive stare at both her and me. "She's here about the job."

"Great, great, come in, come in," he said copying himself. I wondered if he talked like this all the time. "Now, now, you're here about the job?"

The receptionist smiled at me and pointed to a chair and quickly exited the room, closing the door behind her.

"Yes," I said. I sat down and took my gloves off. I laid them neatly in my lap and sat up straight and tall.

"Wonderful, Wonderful! Have you ever made clothes before?" He asked.

"Yes, I have made almost all my own clothes as well as for my brother and sister and mended many things for my father," I stated proudly.

"Do you own a sewing machine?" He inquired.

"Er, no, sir I don't but I am a quick wit and learn fast and I've done everything by hand so a machine will probably make it even easier," I spoke fast as if I was trying to convince him I was the best person for the job.

"Hmmm, I see, I see," he said running his tongue over his front top teeth and furrowing his brow as if he was trying to size me up.

"It's $.42 an hour unless this war heats things up. We might go up, we might go down. You good with that?" He said.

"Yes, sir." I politely responded. Anything was better than nothing.

"You get a 15-minute lunch break at 1 pm. You must be here by 9 am and you may leave at 5. I'll show you to your station." He didn't hesitate or even ask for further reply but got up straight away and bounded around the desk for the door. He swung it wide open and I hastily jumped up and hustled out the door into the large, noisy room.

He walked fast with wide steps around a couple of desks to an empty seat between a man and a woman. He took both arms and brushed off all the contents onto the floor. He then pointed to the chair with his whole hand and said, "Mary will be right over. She will give you some direction. You are welcome to keep your coat, hat, and purse under your desk or in the lady's locker room, which I would prefer anyway. What's your name?" He said as if he completely forgot to ask in the office.

"Virginia. Virginia Cunningham, sir" I said in a noble tone as if people "knew" me.

"Well, good to meet you, Miss Cunningham. Mary will get your information and you can fill out a card so you get paid," he said quickly as if he had to be somewhere else. "I'm Mr. Tillington, your foreman. Mary is your supervisor. You will address any issues with her first." He then took a quick bow and shuffled off back to the office.

I sat there with a dumbfounded look on my face. What now? I still had my gloves in my hand, and I looked to the right and the left. Both employees were hard at work with their heads down but the lady on my right turned to me when I looked at her.

"Hello." She said with a kind smile. "I'm Estelle. What's your name, again?"

"Virginia," I said politely.

"Well, good to meet you. Guess you'll be my seat partner. Ever done this before?" She said as she whipped another long piece of fabric up to her machine.

"Well, not professionally, but I make clothes all the time at home," I said.

"This is different. Don't sew your thumb to the drapes. Mr. Tillington doesn't like blood on the textiles." She stated very matter-of-factly.

My polite smile disappeared to a horrified look when she said the word 'blood'. I had pricked my fingers at home before and quickly shoved them into my mouth until the iron taste dissipated but had never sewed a body part to a pair of trousers.

8

Merchant Marines

"It came to pass that the children of Israel asked the Lord, saying, who shall go up for us against the Canaanites first to fight against them?" Judges 1:1

I liked working in the factory or I liked the idea of a job, I couldn't tell which. Vern and Mitzi were always home before anyone else so I had to give them a new list of chores to complete by the time I got home so they wouldn't get into trouble. It was fairly easy though as they took over a few of my chores and by the time I got home most of the supper was ready. Daddy got home about 30 minutes after I did and by 7 o'clock dishes were done, the kitchen was clean, and we could sit around the fire and either listen to the radio or listen to Daddy read a newspaper article while Mitzi colored and I mended clothes.

I got so good at sewing that Creth would come by often to have a shirt or torn jacket mended now that Nell wasn't doing it anymore.

Even though he moved into the city, he started coming around more and he and Daddy would return to sitting on the porch smoking and drinking.

That evening after Vern and Mitzi went to bed and it was just Daddy and me, he threw another piece of oak on the fire and shuffled his weight to pull the pack of cigarettes from his back pocket. I was always amazed at how they still seemed round after being hauled in a back pocket all day.

He shook the pack and took one out then another and handed it to me. I stared blankly at it and then at him. He nodded up and blinked his eyes, "come on, you know you want one."

Did I? So many of the girls at the garment factory smoked on their lunch break and only once had they offered me one. After looking like an idiot and coughing up a storm, they never offered me one again. They just laughed at me as they retold the story nearly every day.

I took the cigarette and Daddy reached down and pulled out a half-burnt, narrow stick from the fire and lit his cigarette then leaned the stick toward me to light mine. Again, I really didn't know what I was doing but I had watched Daddy and the garment girls enough to know how to light one.

I coughed a little again and daddy said not to inhale so deeply. "Just a little puff then blow it out", he said. I put the unlit end to my lips again and sucked ever so slightly and then quickly blew it out before it probably even had a chance to reach my lungs. It tasted good. Like the way Mama smelled after she had hugged Daddy in a long embrace when he came home from work.

Mama... there she was again in my mind. When I wasn't working, making supper, doing chores, or helping with homework, there she was. It was like she was just waiting to pop up in my memory at the first chance of boredom.

"It's been hard on me, Firecracker," Daddy said looking down and taking a long drag on his cigarette. "You're doing pretty well here."

"What do you mean, Daddy?" I said furrowing my brow.

"You got things pretty well under control here at the house and with work and all," he said, still not looking at me, "I might take a break."

I had no idea what that meant. Was he quitting his job? Were we moving? Still, I said nothing. There had to be more.

"I've joined the Merchant Marines," he said in a tone that seemed final as if there was no way of getting out of it and no arguing about it either.

"What does that mean, Daddy?" I said confused.

"The war needs help and I'm too damn old to actually fight in this war but it would get me out of here," he said flicking his cigarette toward the fire. It was then I realized my own had burned down quite a ways and was at risk of dropping an inch of ash on the floor. I followed suit and copied Daddy.

"But what will you do? Where will you go?" I said with a fervent tone of worry in my voice. "What about us?"

"You don't need me. You have a job, the kids are fine, and it won't be like I'll be gone forever... at least I don't think. They just need more supplies for this war business," he said, flicking his cigarette into the fire and getting up from his chair. He faced the fireplace and put one hand on the strong, wooden beam of the mantle. He was looking at a picture of Mama holding Vern when he was a baby sitting in a rocking chair. She had a white shift dress on with pockets in the front and was smiling. It looked like Vern was trying to wiggle off her lap but she kept a firm hold on his arms. Daddy ran his finger down the frame but didn't speak.

I swallowed hard, stood up and threw my half-burnt cigarette into the fire around his legs. I put a hand the back of his shoulder and he turned around. "Creth will look in on ya, he's a good man,"

Daddy said, putting both hands on my shoulders and looking me in the face. "You're a strong woman, Virginia. Don't let anyone tell you different." He hardly ever called me Virginia unless it was around other people or if he was mad. But it wasn't either of those things. He was serious.

"I'll miss you, Daddy," I said softly and bent my head in toward his shoulder turning my face so my cheek was against his lapel. He let go of my arms and wrapped his around my shoulders with one hand against my face and the other firmly on my back. He gave me a few squeezes and I returned the embrace and really didn't want to let go. I could feel my face getting hot and the tears starting to form behind my eyeballs. I blinked hard and swallowed.

9

Marriage?

"It came to pass when Jacob saw Rachel ... he went near and watered the flock of her fathers." Genesis 29:10

The future seemed so cloudy. I couldn't tell what it looked like. Daddy didn't leave for a couple of weeks, so it gave us some time to get things in order both physically and emotionally. Daddy put a couple of accounts in my name and put me on the title to the house "just in case", he had said. I didn't want to think about what that really meant.

Two days before Daddy was set to leave, Creth came over for dinner. It was a weekly occurrence again and it brought a different life to the house whenever he came. I had made chicken paprika with a few root vegetables and a can of string beans from the cellar. Creth loved my biscuits so I quickly whipped up a batch. They were the easiest things to make and Mitzi would love to watch me get my fingers all doughy. You couldn't mix the dough too much or the biscuits would be tough. Flatten out the lard into disks the size of a dime and add just a little milk in to bring it all together. Pat out the dough on the floured, wooden board and cut into circles with a floured, rimmed glass. Tenderest biscuits you've ever tasted.

Creth poured the honey on after slathering his in butter. "Man, Virginia, best biscuits this side of the Missouri," he said scooping up his 3rd biscuit.

"You always say that," I said with a nonchalant smile.

"How'd you like to make them for me every night?" He said.

I laughed and disregarded the compliment.

"I'm serious. Your dad and I have been talking," Creth said. "I'd really like to take care of you and the kids. How'd you feel about making it legal?"

All commotion at the table stopped as did I. Vern popped up, "marry her? But aren't you related?"

"Hush up, Vern," I said sternly. I looked at Daddy who was still waiting for me to respond.

Daddy let out a deep breath, "Creth's taken a shine to you and the kids. I honestly don't know how long I'll be gone and he can really take care of you all."

"But... Daddy... he's old," I said leaning into him as if I could shield the words from Creth himself.

"I'm not that old," He perked up taking another bite of his biscuit. "I love you all. You're my family. I'd do anything for you and I just thought why not make it easier on everyone. I always wanted kids and now you have a household you can manage. You don't have to work at that garment place anymore neither. My welding job at the machine shop does pretty well and if I move in here, I don't have to keep the apartment in the city."

There was too much in that statement to digest. Move here? Marry me? Live here? "But I'm just a kid," I stammered.

"You'll be 18 in December, Firecracker," Daddy said.

"And you're okay with this?" I questioned Daddy.

"If you get married to anyone else Vern and Mitzi could be homeless. This way I'll know everyone's safe," he nodded.

"But you don't have to leave!" I pleaded.

"You don't know what it's like!" He cried in a higher and more pronounced tone, firm and yet desperate. "I can't be here. She's everywhere; in the house, in the pictures, even in you. This is too hard." His voice dropped and he got up from the table and turned to the fireplace. He pulled a Pall Mall from his back pocket and lit it with a match from the mantle.

The kids turned and looked at me as if I was a balloon ready to pop. Creth stood up and walked over to me.

"This is a family. I want to keep that family together. I love you, Virginia. Will you marry me?" Creth said tenderly taking my hand from off the table and holding it in his as he put his other hand over the top.

"Does it mean you'll be here all the time?" Mitzi jumped and clapped her hands.

"It does if your sister will have me," he said turning to Mitzi then back to me.

"Have him, have him V!" Mitzi cheered.

"Shush," I shouted, trying to gather my thoughts. "If you're done, leave the table and take your plates with you." Both kids got up and gathered their items from the table. Creth let go of my hand and sat down in Vern's chair that was adjacent to mine.

"I know this is quite a shock, Virginia. I didn't want you to think I was trying to be underhanded or devious in any way. Your pop knew and he's agreed to this," he said trying to convince me this was everyone's idea but mine.

"Do you want more kids?" I said sheepishly, but that's really the only thing I could think about, sharing my bed with a man; a man I wasn't in love with.

"Maybe, but that's nothing we need to talk about now. I want to help you with your siblings and help raise them for your dad. When he comes back, if they're not old enough, they can go live with him in a new place." Creth nodded toward Dick at the mantle and he turned around and nodded his head as he took a deep drag off his cigarette.

"Do I get to think about it?" I said inquisitively but really just trying to buy some time.

"Of course, of course, I wouldn't want you to think you had to make a decision this big at the drop of a hat. Your dad leaves in a couple days. If he knew you were well taken care of before he left, that's good enough, I 'spec. Right, Red?" Creth looked at Daddy for acknowledgment.

"Sure, Firecracker. Think on it. It's a good proposition," Daddy said with just a hint of disappointment in his voice, as if he wished he could find another way. "We'll leave you to the wash'n up. Come on Creth," Daddy motioned to him and they sauntered outside to sit on the porch.

I didn't leave the table for what felt like an eternity. I could hear Vern and Mitzi in their rooms arguing and Creth and daddy's low voices muffled from the distance yet I felt frozen to the chair. I didn't know people married for reasons other than love.

10

Time to Buy a Dress

"It came to pass that Esther put on her royal apparel and stood in the inner court of the king's house..." Esther 5:1

Daddy left on Monday. We said goodbye at the train station. He had been dressed so nice and dapper, ready for whatever lay ahead. He didn't really know any more than we did. He just knew he was headed out to the closest ship, which was at the mouth of the Mississippi River in Louisiana.

"I'm sorry I won't be there to give you away, Firecracker. I think I feel worse about that," he said, holding my hand and looking sheepishly into my eyes.

"Me too, Daddy," I said, looking down. He hugged me tight, tighter than I had ever been hugged.

I honestly didn't know if I would see him again. We'd heard that the Merchant Marines were being killed more often than our own military.

The U.S. wasn't prepared as well as they had liked when they entered World War II so civilians were called in to volunteer to transport supplies to the Naval ships off the coast of South Carolina, Virginia, and Florida. Daddy knew he would be moving cargo and passengers between nations and within the country but he had no idea for how long or where he'd end up.

I agreed to marry Creth, primarily because I couldn't think of another solution. Working in the garment factory without the financial help of Daddy was almost impossible. We probably would have lost the farm, the meager plot that it was.

We had planned on June 6th in the courthouse. He told me to go buy a dress and handed me $5. What did one wear to a wedding they weren't particularly excited about? Woolworth was having a sale that week so I walked the kids to school and got the trolley into the city. It dropped me right out front, which I was glad for because it had started to get a little drizzly. The air felt wet so I tugged at my headscarf a little tighter to avoid getting my hair frizzy, although it was frizzy almost all the time regardless of the weather.

I shook off my scarf just inside the store. People were bustling around me in all directions and the noise of the chaos so early in the morning was a little startling. I looked up at the expansive building. I had only been here one other time with Mama. Daddy told her to take me to get new gloves when I was 9. I had never seen a larger building. I felt so tiny. I didn't feel as small now but rather like an adult. I was almost 18 now and even though I didn't feel like I should have been an adult, I clearly was, legally and to anyone who might have thought to look at me.

I had let my hair grow a little longer since Mama died but it still irritated me how frizzy and bright red it was. Mama said that it might mellow out as I got older but I was not seeing any evidence of that so far.

I was so lost in the size of the room that I forgot I was standing in the doorway. An older woman with a child of about 2 pushed by me with a glare. "I'm so sorry," I said and ducked off to the side.

I had no idea where to go. There were shoes on the left, hats and coats on the right. Straight ahead were mirrors and glass cases. I didn't see the dresses anywhere. I must have looked lost because an attractive woman came up to me with a big smile, too big and too fake. "Can I help you, dear?" She said tilting her head to the side and staring at me with her fake smile.

"Um, yes. Where are women's dresses?" I asked.

"Oh, right this way," She said and turned tightly on her heels and urged me to follow her. She walked quickly through the crowd and I skipped a little to keep up. She led me through the rows of glass cases and mirrors to a wide set of grand stairs that went up, turned to both the left and the right, and went up again. "Right up that way, dear," she pointed.

"Thank you," I said with a nod.

I did a fast little tiptoe up the stairs, turned to the right, and finished my ascent. There was a completely new level of products and items up here. One whole side of the 2nd floor was women's dresses. I was glad I didn't have to go far and now I could remember how to get out too.

White? Should I go with white? I suppose so. People usually got married in white, well women did anyway. I quickly spotted a few racks of white and cream-colored dresses. I fingered through them quickly. What exactly was I looking for? Price.

Yes, that was it. It needed to be under $5. Before even looking at the size I looked at the price. $3.25, $2.89, $4.56... What about tax? I tried to do that math in my head but what was the local sales tax? I couldn't go over because that's all the money I had.

I pulled out one with a square bodice and ruffles around the neck and held it out to get a better look. I really had no idea what size I was but it looked decent enough. "Do you need some help, miss?" A kind voice startled me from behind.

I spun my head around with alarm. "Oh, um, I need a dress," I said hesitantly.

"Oh, wonderful! For a special occasion?" She said with a plastic smile.

"Um, a wedding," I said a little apprehensively.

"Fabulous," she said clasping her hands together as if I just gave her the most anticipated and honored task of all. "What're the bride's colors? You don't want to clash."

"Well, I guess white, you see, it's me," I said narrowing my brows looking for some approval or maybe just non-judgment.

"Oh! Honey, it's for you? Well, then, let's go all out!" She said with way more excitement than I could even pretend to muster.

"Well, I only have $5," I said trailing after her as she seemed to instantly be in this 'bridal' world all to herself.

"Oh, we can do that! Come dear, let me show you our bridal collection," she said motioning me to another section of the store.

I followed her to a department that was full of fancy dresses and top hats, garters, stockings, and gloves. She thumbed through the dresses faster than I ever could and whipped one out holding it up to me. "A size 4, I think," she said, not confirming, just assuming and looking at me with an approving look. "You like?"

It had ruffles around the neck like the first one I had procured, a narrow waist with buttons running down the front and pleats protruding from the waist out into additional ruffles that cascaded to the floor.

"How much?" I asked.

"Let's see if you love it first," she said and held it up to me and she spun us both around to look in the mirror behind us. "Oh, I think this is just lovely!"

"But, how much?" I said.

"Well, it's $6.29, but I'm sure your beau or father would want you to have the best!" She tried to keep things positive and encouraging.

"Ma'am, I only have $5," I said solidly.

"Alright, let's look over here," she said and put the dress back, and walked a little slower to another section.

She pulled a simpler dress without a long train out from a sea of white ruffles, taffeta, and silk. She didn't say anything but held it up to me and put it back, shuffled through a couple more, and pulled another out. "Here, try this one," she said and pushed it toward me.

"Is it under $5?" I asked.

"Yes, yes. I think it's about $4.59," she said. I took the dress even though I really didn't think much of it. "Here, dear, you can try it on here," she said putting her hand on my back and pointing to the fitting room.

I took the dress and went in. I stood in front of the mirror for a minute or two just looking at myself. *You're going to get married. To Creth. Do you even love him? No, but you like him. Yeah, you can like him. Does he really love you? What will happen when the younger kids are grown? Do I still have to be married to him? I suppose so. What if you ever fall in love with someone else? No, you can't now. You can't ever fall in love. This is what you have to do now. And he likes you, red hair and all. A million freckles and everything.*

I took off my clothes and tried on the dress. She was right, it fit like a glove. I bought it that day and left the store.

I I

And Just Like That...

"It came to pass when the priests blew with the trumpets, Joshua said, Shout; for the Lord hath given you the city." Joshua 6:16

The morning came. Gail, my friend from school, was helping me get ready. She and Creth's friend Tom were to be our witnesses. Mitzi and Vern argued and played in the house even though I told Vern to take care of the outside chores before we left. Creth said he would meet us at the courthouse. Gail helped me dress and curled my hair so it wouldn't be frizzy and scattered. I pinched my cheeks to draw out the color and Gail put deep brown colored powder on the top of my eyelids. She handed me a deep rose-colored lipstick and told me men like that sort of thing. The less attractive I felt the better, honestly, but this was the way it was done and I had to live up to it.

We got in the Buick and Gail drove the four of us to the court-house in town. Simmons was small but it did have a courthouse. We

44

had to get married on a weekday so they'd be open. It was a Monday and it was sunny, yet surprisingly chilly for June. I had a small shawl around my shoulders because the dress the woman picked out, although it had long sleeves, was very thin and the chill of the wind whipped across my exposed chest just under my collarbone. The dress came with a veil, which Gail affixed in my hair after we entered the front courthouse doors so it wouldn't be swept away with the wind.

We all shook off a little when we entered and looked around. A woman behind a barred desk with thick horn-rimmed glasses looked up, saw the sight of us and said, "weddings, down the hall, Room 2."

We made our way to Room 2 and the door was already open. I was shocked to see pews, like a church on either side of the aisle and couples, dressed in similar attire to my own seated in pairs in various places throughout the room. My eyes scanned the room and caught sight of a waving hand in the front off to the left. It was Creth, seated next to Tom. I shifted around the back of the room and went down the left side quietly as there was already a wedding being performed at the front of the room.

I slid in next to Creth, who scooted over a little to make room for our little entourage. "We're next," he whispered in my ear. A chill shot through my body when I felt his breath so close to my ear. His lips even brushed my ear lobe slightly and a tingling sensation went through me. I swallowed hard thinking of the rest of the day and what was to come. I sat rigid. Creth reached over and grabbed my hand on my leg and squeezed it and gave a reassuring glance.

He looked so pleased, so excited. So much so, I wish I could share in this emotion but I was just not in the same place as he was. He'd done this before. There was no fear with him. He had a satisfactory smile on his face, yet it wasn't prideful. I didn't pull my hand away but I didn't respond with a squeeze either. I just left it and turned my attention to what was happening up front.

"Do you take Margaret to be your lawfully wedded wife, to love, honor and cherish..." said the Justice of the Peace and all the traditional things you say to the betrothed. And before you knew it, it was our turn.

"Virginia Cunningham and Creth Lamb," said the recorder. I snapped out of my trance and looked at Creth. He still had my hand and stood up prompting me to follow. I did. We made our way to the front of the room and Gail, Tom, Mitzi, and Vern followed taking their place on the front row. Mitzi had a silly grin on her face and Vern looked bored. Gail had a kind and empathetic smile and Tom just grinned and nodded. We turned toward the Justice of the Peace and with a couple of 'I Do's' it was done. I looked up at Creth, my husband, and knew this was a whole new adventure, for one I was very apprehensive, yet I felt I had to be positive. The sun was still shining when we left the courthouse so I thought that couldn't be a bad sign.

Part 2

12

First Date

"It came to pass, when the sun did arise, that God prepared a vehement east wind [to ease Jonah]." Jonah 4:8

After the clinical and rigid ceremony, Creth leaned down and kissed me on the cheek. Appropriate, if you ask me. I didn't know this person romantically at all and I appreciated the platonic gesture. Gail drove Mitzi and Vern home, Tom shook Creth's hand and patted his shoulder with his free hand and said his goodbyes in the lobby of the courthouse.

Creth turned to me and asked if I wanted to go out. "You're all dressed up so nice, how about a fancy dinner out?" He said lovingly. He paused and watched my reaction, not wanting to ruffle my feathers.

"I suppose. Might as well get as much out of this dress as we can. Thanks, by the way, for the money for the dress. I don't think

I thanked you. I really like it," I lied; not about being thankful, but about the dress. I swore after tonight I would never wear it again.

He held his arm out for me to take and led me down the steps of the courthouse to his '35 Plymouth, which was just a two-seater. He opened the passenger door and I got in collecting up my dress as to not snag it on the running boards or let it get dirty hanging out the door. I sat frozen in the seat as he went around and climbed in the other side.

We fit nicely in the car, like two married people should, If was as if we were a picture in some *My Home* women's magazine you'd find at the doctor's office. He started the car and turned toward me before putting it in gear.

"Thanks, Virginia. Thank you for marrying me. I'll treat you real good and make ya a good life," he vowed.

"I guess I'm the one that should be thanking you. After all, you didn't have to marry me and take care of all of us," I said appreciatively yet still hesitant.

"I know, but I'm serious. I love you, Virginia. I just hope that one day you can come to love me too," he gave a small, closed-mouth smile and lingered his gaze just a second longer than was comfortable and turned toward the windshield and started the car.

We ate at Prosecco's, an Italian place down on 6th. I thought that maybe if I could stand a man slurping spaghetti, I could handle him the rest of the time as well. We talked about our lives when we were kids, his marriage to Nell, how much we both loved Daddy and things of the past. There was no talk of the future, and I appreciated that. I just wanted to get to know him for someone other than 'Uncle' Creth. We were married now and I had to start acting like it. We laughed a couple of times and I got to see a side of Creth I had never seen before. When he looked at me between bites, when there was a lull in the conversation, he lingered that half-second more than was normal, and I felt he was studying my face and really taking me in too for the first time.

He asked if I'd like to stay in a hotel downtown. I said I'd rather go home if it was okay. He nodded and we drove home in silence, both of us wondering what was to come next.

When we got to the farm Vern and Mitzi were already asleep and Gail was reading in the rocker by the fireplace. She looked up and smiled when we came in. "Well, how-do, Mr. and Mrs. Lamb!" She said with a proud and teasing grin. "Guess I better get going now."

Gail grabbed her coat and hat and headed out the door as Creth closed it behind her. He breathed deep and looked shy.

"I'd like to go to bed now if that's okay?" I asked.

"Yes!" He said emphatically. But when I walked over to mine and Mitzi's room he let out a disappointed, "oh."

"Can I just stay here one more night, please?" I asked. I was not quite courageous enough to take Mama and Daddy's room, especially not with a 'stranger'.

"Yes, of course. I understand. I'll be waiting, whenever you feel comfortable," he said, yet there was just a hint of irritation in his voice with the over-arching feeling of trying to control himself.

I went into my room and closed the door behind me. I leaned against the back of the door and pulled the veil off my head that had somehow managed to stay on through the entire evening and meal. I unbuttoned my dress and slid it over my hips. I hung it up in the very back of the closet so I didn't have to see it every day. I thought I'd eventually have to move my clothes into Mama and Daddy's room but I'd leave the dress here. I removed my slip, girdle, and bra and slid my night shift over my head. I crawled into bed next to Mitzi and snuggled up next to her back. I inhaled her sweet, musty hair deeply and wondered if I would be here tomorrow night.

13

New Normal

"And it came to pass on the day when the Lord spake unto Moses in the land of Egypt" - Exodus 6:28

The day came upon us like any other day although it was not an ordinary day. This was a new day as Mrs. Lamb. Vern asked if we should call Creth 'Daddy' now and I glowered at him, "Of course not!" I scolded. "You still have a Daddy and it ain't Creth!"

Vern looked scared and ashamed and turned back to his bowl of oatmeal. Creth came out of Daddy's room all dressed to the nines and ready for work. "Good morning, all," he said with a hearty smile. He reached down and pinched Mitzi's cheek and patted Vern on the shoulder. He leaned over to me as I was pouring a cup of coffee and kissed me politely on the cheek. I forced myself to lean in slightly to him. His hand touched my back in a gesture of gentle reassurance and sat down at the head of the table. "What's for breakfast," he inquired.

"Oatmeal," said Mitzi, "with raisins and brown sugar."

"Wonderful. Gotta keep our strength up, don't we?" he said.

I set a bowl of oatmeal in front of him and pushed the butter, sugar, and raisins in his direction. "Thank you, Virginia," he said with that lingering stare again.

He sure was trying, I could tell. But every fiber in my body wanted to reject the kindness. My red-headed stubbornness was wanting to come out in full force. Daddy said it might get me into trouble if I wasn't careful. Was I just being stubborn for the sake of it? What did this man do? Nothing but try and help out our family. He hadn't forced himself on me and for that I was grateful. Come on, Virginia, get it together. You gotta start acting like a married woman at some point.

I poured Creth a cup of black coffee and set it next to the cream and butter. He thanked me and I smiled. The kids were done eating and I told them to get ready for school. Creth ate fast and drained his coffee as he was getting up from the table.

"Gotta go, too, V," he said and leaned over to kiss me on the cheek again before grabbing his hat and coat by the door. "Maybe we can have a picnic as a family this weekend?" He asked.

"Yay, a picnic!" shouted Mitzi jumping with excitment and bouncing off to her room.

"Get your coat," I said shutting her excitement down.

"Are you going into work today, too?" Creth asked me.

"I need to at least tell them I'm quitting," I mentioned as I cleaned up the breakfast dishes. "I can take better care of the farm with more time around here."

"Good," He said, nodded and pressed his lips together in approval. "Okay then, well I'll see everyone at supper time." And he threw open the door and bounded out.

**Creth and Virginia close to the wedding
date with Mitzi in the background**

~

I walked to the garment factory by myself after everyone else had
gone ahead. It gave me time to think. I assumed I was going to have
to sleep with Creth even though the thought of how much older he
was than I was a little disturbing, but it wasn't as if I was a little
girl. I was an adult, after all. I would need to buck up. There was
a lot of digging my heels in and doing what had to be done for the
good of the family and I suppose this was just one of those things. As
I was walking I seemed to hear my own thoughts answer me back,
you're going to be okay, Virginia, they said. Or maybe I was just trying
to convince myself. I missed Daddy terribly and Mama even more. I
felt like I was violently thrust into a parental role that I didn't ask
for and now I had to manage a household. Not like I hadn't been do-

ing that already for a while now, but this was different... new. And I'm not sure I liked it. But again, I really didn't have a choice. It was this or potential homelessness.

By the time I reached the garment factory, it was just before 9 am. Mr. Tillington was just getting to his office and I followed him to the door and knocked before he had a chance to close it. I told him I needed to quit and he unemotionally told me to wait out front for my last paycheck. Mary could write it out while I waited.

I stopped at the bank on the way home and cashed my check for $16.80 for a week's wages and tucked it into my pocketbook. When I got home, I put that money in an empty soup can with the label torn off and stuffed it in the back of the cupboard with the spices.

I did my usual chores, cleaned the chicken coop, weeded our humble garden and prepped for dinner. The kids showed up around 5 and potato soup and biscuits were ready by 6:30 when Creth walked in the door. He didn't knock, he just came in. He had a couple of suitcases with him and an unmarked box.

"Just some of my things from the apartment. I'll clean out the rest on Friday," he said as he sauntered into the bedroom and I jumped a little hearing the clunk of the suitcases on the hardwood floor. "What's for supper?" he asked.

"Potato soup," I said ladling the creamy, white liquid into bowls and handing them to Mitzi to put on the table.

"Oooo, with leeks and biscuits?" said Creth rubbing his hands together as if this was a meal for a king.

"Yep," I said unemotionally.

We sat and ate and didn't talk much except for Vern and Mitzi talking about some kid at school that got expelled because he put a cherry bomb down the outhouse and blew excrement all over the schoolyard. I looked up at Creth and raised one eyebrow with a smirk I was trying to hide with a biscuit.

He smiled back when he saw the softness in my face and scooped another spoonful of soup into his mouth keeping the smile as long as he could.

After supper and things were washed Vern and Mitzi did their homework at the table and I darned a hole in my stocking with light pink thread so it wouldn't be as noticeable.

"I think you make those stockings look good, V," Creth said with that lingering stare.

I did have nice legs. Some of the girls at school told me so a few years back as well as a naughty boy or two. It was pretty much the only feature I liked about myself. My lips curled up in a half smile but I didn't take my eyes off my work.

Creth read the newspaper and eventually it was time to retire. Mitzi and Vern went to bed and I followed Mitzi in the bedroom. "I'm gonna stay with Creth tonight. You alright with that?"

She yawned and shrugged her shoulders, crawled into bed and I kissed her cheek and smoothed her hair. I grabbed my night shift from the end of the bed and a robe and quietly left the room closing the door behind me.

Creth was still reading by the fire and the way he fit so nicely in Daddy's chair made him look as if he always belonged here. I stopped just outside Mitzi's room and he looked up from his paper.

"I'm going to go to bed now," I said confidently yet with a hint of fear behind it.

"Alright, goodnight," he said and looked back at the paper.

"In our room," I said apprehensively.

He turned the paper down again and just stared at me like I'd spoken a different language. He looked as if he was desperately try-ing to decipher it. "Okay," he said with that questioning tone that raises your voice at the end of the word.

I walked over to Daddy's room, my room now, and opened the door and walked in. He didn't follow at first. I left the door open as I stood off to one side and took my dress off. He still didn't come in so I kept removing clothes. I pulled the nightgown over my head and crawled under the covers.

I pulled the blankets up around my chest and under my armpits. I still didn't hear him move. I swallowed and then I heard the paper rustle and land on the table and the squeak of the rocking chair as it was left rocking in place slowly stopping after he got up. He walked to the open door frame and looked in. There was a small candle on the nightstand next to me flickering just enough so I could see his silhouette at the door.

"You want me to come to bed too?" he asked.

"That'd be alright," I said.

He came in slowly and sat in a low chair by the door and took off his boots. He unbuttoned his shirt to expose his undershirt and stood again to undo his large belt buckle. He unzipped his work trousers and pulled them off one leg at a time. Then he just stood there; undershirt and knickers. I think we were both waiting for the other to make the first move.

He decided it was going to be him.

He walked to the bed and got in. I had no idea if we had a 'side' or not. He pulled the covers up around him and we both laid there on our backs not saying a word.

"Goodnight," I said, waiting to see if that was okay.

"Goodnight," he said and then I didn't hear anything else until morning.

14

So This Is What This Is

"And it came to pass at midnight, that the man was afraid, and turned himself; and behold, a woman lay at his feet." - Ruth 3:8

When I woke, Creth was already gone. I wandered out of the bedroom and the house was empty and quiet. Creth's boots and clothes were gone off the chair and his hat and coat were missing too.

I opened Mitzi's room and she was still asleep so I assumed Vern was as well. I went in and shook her lightly to wake her until she moaned and moved. Then I went and knocked on Vern's door. I heard another moan of acknowledgment and turned to change my clothes for the day.

Over by the kettle was a small note.

Went to work early. Thank you for staying with me last night. I can't wait to see you tonight. - C

To my surprise, I was relieved that I hadn't scared him away or upset him last night. I folded the note and tucked it into my front apron pocket and got to work on breakfast and coffee.

After everyone left, the house felt empty but it also felt a little liberating. For the first time since Daddy left, I felt in control, like really in control of the house. This was my house. My name was on the deed now and I could do with it as I wanted. I was the 'lady of the house' and there was no one to tell me how to run it. I lit up a Pall Mall and sucked hard. I had gotten good at smoking by now. They tasted salty and sweet and the perfect after-anything treat.

I moved the table so it faced a different direction and moved the rocker to allow more space around the fireplace. I reorganized a few things on the mantle and went outside. It was a warm and bright morning with a slight breeze and the tomatoes were already starting to turn from a dull green to a yellowish pigment and strawberries were a vivid crimson on the vine.

I walked down the drive a bit to our mailbox and looked at the name, 'Cunninghams' it said. I hunted around for a sharp rock and scratched 'Lamb' underneath, just in case Creth changed his address and the mailman didn't know.

That evening developed the same as the previous evening. Creth came through the door and immediately walked over to me by the stove and kissed my cheek. The kids were reading by the fireplace and I spooned the chipped beef on toast onto each plate. The oven had roasted the turnips until they were brown and sweet and perfect for dragging through the cream.

After dinner, Creth read a few funny stories to the kids from the paper and the routine went on as planned. Off to bed, kisses on the cheek from the kids and even Mitzi hugged Creth around his neck before bounding off to bed.

The two of us sat staring at the fire until he held out his hand to me. I paused long enough to make it awkward then took his hand with a relinquishing smile. He stood up and tugged slightly on my hand leading me to the bedroom. I followed suit but my nerves were now building in my stomach and throat. I was so scared this was going to hurt.

He took me in the bedroom and closed the door. He put the small chair in front of the doorknob. "Just so we don't get any unwanted visitors," he said as he started unbuttoning his shirt. I didn't move. All the hairs on my arm stood up and I was instantly cold. He walked over to me and wrapped his arms around me, untying my apron. He pulled it off over my head and threw it on the chair. He took my head in both hands, one on each side of my face and looked me dead in the eyes. "I love you," he said squarely. Then he kissed me.

The feeling of someone else's lips on mine was an odd sensation. His lips were soft, warm, and sweet from the clove cigarette he liked to suck on before bed. I moved my lips in rhythm with his, trying to keep up, and then he just stopped.

"We don't have to do this yet if you're not ready," he said backing away slightly.

I felt like there was a tornado going on in the room around us and we were the eye. I swallowed hard. "I'm okay," I said, even though I wasn't exactly sure that was true. He unbuttoned my blouse and slid it over my shoulders and I didn't resist. The skirt came off easy. He took off his trousers and kissed me again, gently pushing me toward the bed. I sat down when my legs hit the bed.

"Let's get in, it's cold," he said with a little giggle. I was so thankful for that giggle. It was way too serious. I swung my legs up and tucked them under the covers and he practically jumped in after me. We were almost like two little kids playing hide-and-seek, scared to reveal ourselves.

He pulled his arm outside of the covers and pulled me into his chest. I smelled welding metal and sweat but it wasn't a bad scent. He kissed the top of my head and I buried my head just under his chin. I could feel his body heat starting to warm me up and not just physically but emotionally as well. I felt secure and safe, right now in this place - in this tiny little spot in the world. Whatever happened, I felt that right now we would be okay. His kisses made their way down the side of my head to my cheek and then my mouth and wave of electricity went through my body as it involuntarily moved into his. He was kissing me passionately now and I knew this was it. Be brave, Virginia, but a little part of me inside said I didn't have to try very hard.

15

Getting to Know You

"It came to pass that Ishmael came unto Gedaliah and they did eat bread together in Mizpah." Jeremiah 41:1

It had been a few weeks since we'd been married and our daily routine had become just that. Vern was almost 14 and was looking at joining the Marines full-time as soon as he could. He kept saying things like, "well, if Daddy can do it," and "I won't let him be out there by himself," and we would just roll our eyes and tell him to hold his horses until school was done. But we knew he wouldn't listen. You could join when you were 16 and he was itching to go.

Mitzi was almost 9 now and doing well in school. We'd heard from Daddy about once every couple of months. He was doing well although he had mentioned that a few of his mates had died after being transferred to other boats and that made him a little worried although he never actually said so in his letters.

We had been getting along fine at the farm with Creth making decent money welding at the machine shop. It was a skilled profession not many shared so when someone needed a particular piece, he was their man.

The days were full of tending to an instant household so I didn't have much time to think about my new life. I had taken Daddy's place on the porch next to Creth many an evening and we would get to know each other in a more 'husband and wife' sort of way. Creth would talk about opening a cafe one day as he didn't like the welding work so much. We'd laugh and find real joy in each other's company.

"Your biscuits would be the talk of the town," he said as if he could taste them while he puffed on his cigarette and sipped his Kentucky Bourbon.

"What else could we serve?" I asked as we fantasized.

"What else do ya need? Them biscuits will draw 'em in from all over," he said proudly.

I chuckled a little and took a drag off my Pall Mall. "Well, we have to serve something else. Whoever heard of just a biscuit shop?"

"You could put something on them? Like that chocolate gravy or honey butter. Maybe make a meal of it with some ham and eggs," he said, his mouth starting to water.

"Like a breakfast cafe? I suppose. Although Mama did make a wonderful chicken pot pie," I said remembering how she'd cook a chicken for a couple hours in a pot with carrots, celery, and onions, until the thing would just fall apart. She'd mix up a stew pot of vegetables, throw in a little flour and the chicken and ladle it into a big cast iron skillet then top it with those biscuits. Man, now my mouth was watering. There was nothing as good as Mama's chicken pot pie. "I could use the biscuits for that too," I said as if we were seriously working on the menu.

"Well, now you have to make that tomorrow," Creth said. "Do

you have enough money for a chicken, or do I need to take care of an old one we got around here?"

"I can get one tomorrow," I beamed and poked his growing tummy. "But you better lay off those biscuits," I joked.

He grabbed my hand before I could pull it back and leaned into me, "Ain't nothing keeping me from those biscuits... or you." He kissed me sweetly on the nose and crinkled his own before letting me go. We both sat back in our rockers. I thought about my girlfriends and how they always said they wanted to grow old with someone sitting on their front porch in rockers. Well, here I was, getting older by the minute.

16

Christmas

"It came to pass when the time was come about after Hannah had conceived, that she bare a son..." 1 Samuel 1:20

1940

Christmas was coming and it was our first Christmas as a married couple. The winter was already on top of us with the temperature, but it still hadn't snowed. Vern and Creth had piled enough wood along the side of the house to last at least 2-3 months and I had canned all the turnips, carrots, string beans, peppers, and stone fruits from the trees as well as pickled the cucumbers and radishes. We were set. I'm so thankful Mama taught me how to can and pickle and now I was teaching Mitzi. Preserving vegetables for the winter was a mandatory skill one must learn or you could go broke buying fresh from the store. They shipped in all sorts of exotic fruits and vegetables from around the county but the farther away it came from the more expensive it was. We couldn't afford fancy produce and the war had rationed jams and dried fruit, which made me even more thankful we could supply our own.

Meat was even scarce so we had switched to eating it only once a week and tried to extend it out with beans or in a soup as long as we could. As a growing teenager, Vern would often complain that he didn't get enough to eat but I told him he could eat again tomorrow, and he eventually stopped arguing with me.

For Christmas, Creth bargained with a farmer down the lane and got us a ham in exchange for Vern and him cleaning out a couple of stalls. It was the saltiest, sweetest ham I'd ever tasted. I poured a little raspberry jam over the top as it cooked in the oven and before long the rich, succulent smell of roasted pork was wafting out the house and down the lane, drawing those boys back home.

The four of us sat down to a feast on Christmas Eve. Sweet ham, potatoes that roasted alongside the pork soaking up the cooking liquid making them juicy and tender, pickled beets with homemade sour cream, savory stuffing from the stale bread I hoarded all week for this occasion and sweet potato pie for dessert. It was delicious. Vern ate as if he hadn't eaten in a month and Mitzi would take a bite, stop, close her eyes and just smile. I grinned and looked at Creth and he nodded in silent reply putting a hand on mine. We had a lot to be thankful for.

I had almost finished cleaning up the kitchen after the fabulous dinner when my stomach turned upside down and a wave of nausea and heat swept over the top of my head and ran down my spine. I barely made it to the sink before that amazing meal came right back up.

Creth shot up from his rocker by the fire and threw down his paper. "What in the Sam-Hill?" He cried.

I leaned over the sink and sat there for a minute. I pumped the handle on the water pump to wash away my vomit but didn't stand up straight yet.

"You alright, V?" Creth questioned with a concerning twinge in his voice.

"No, I don't know," I said partly still nauseated and partly upset I'd lost such an extravagant meal. "I think I need to lie down," I said and stood up, shifted over to the bedroom and went straight for the bed, apron, and house shoes still on. I heard Creth order Vern and Mitzi to finish cleaning up the kitchen and he followed me into the room lighting a candle on the nightstand.

"What's going on?" He asked.

I let out a deep breath. "I don't know. It just came on me so suddenly, I need to just lie here a minute. I'll be okay," I said, although I wasn't so sure. He touched my forehead which was cool and then clutched my wrist looking for a pulse, I assume, although I'm not sure he knew what he was feeling for.

"I'm still alive," I said with a little snicker. I smiled at him and closed my eyes.

"Well, you just rest. You've been on your feet all day making this wonderful meal. It's about time you get some Christmas rest," he said to me and stood up, walked out of the room and closed the door behind him. I didn't know another thing until the morning.

I woke with my dress still on but my shoes had been removed. It was early, probably around 5 am and now I was wide awake since I had fallen asleep so early. Creth was still asleep next to me so I quietly tip-toed out of the room and started the coffee. While the water boiled I slipped my shoes on and went to the window. I wanted to go sit on the porch but it had to have been 10° out there today and finally, there was a skiff of snow on the ground. Merry Christmas, I thought to myself. I grabbed a Pall Mall from the mantle and fired up the end. The first drag of the morning felt so good, almost as good as that first cup of coffee.

I felt better too. I was worried we had opened a bad jar of beets or the ham wasn't cooked all the way through but no one else seemed to be any worse for wear. I thumbed through the newspaper on the table waiting for the whistle to sound letting me know coffee was ready. After pouring myself a cup and taking that first blessed sip, the queasiness returned. I set down the coffee and put out my cigarette. I sat in the rocker and closed my eyes trying to breathe deep and calm my wavy stomach. It seemed to work but I didn't want to push it so I sat there a while longer and eventually drifted back to sleep for a bit.

The day progressed and the kids were just excited they didn't have to go to school. We bundled them up in as much clothing as they could bear and sent them out in the cold to play in the skiff of snow. When they came in with their teeth chattering we gave them a half cup of coffee with a couple of chocolate shavings on top, rationed by the government but kept for a special occasion. Everyone should have chocolate on Christmas.

The new year rolled around and the snow finally became more fierce. With the cold temperatures it didn't melt or go away very quickly and it would snow again on top of the old snow making it hard as a rock underneath.

Creth had been worried about me for a few weeks so I finally made an appointment with a doctor we really couldn't afford. After an easy blood test, it was revealed I was pregnant. I knew how these things happened but I didn't want to admit that's what it could be just yet. I didn't know if I was ready to have a baby since I had only just learned how to be a wife. But Creth was overjoyed when I came home with the news that cold January day. Mitzi was just as excited but Vern just shrugged his shoulders and said he had homework to do.

Creth wrapped me up in his bear hug and looked deep into my soul, "You've made me so happy, Virginia." Then he smiled and kissed me on the mouth then the cheek and continued to kiss me all over my face until I shoved him playfully away from me.

"Well, don't be expecting fancy meals and a lot of work around here. This kid's doing a number on my insides," I said and threw my apron over my head and tied it around my waist in one fluid movement.

"Baby, you can do whatever you want," he said in a tone that sounded like someone just handed him the moon. "I hope it's a girl," he said dreamily.

"Why a girl?" I inquired.

"Well, don't get me wrong, I don't mind what it is, but girls are just so fun," he said jovial-like.

"You're too much, Creth Lamb," I said lovingly, shaking my head and getting to work on supper.

"I want a little sister to play with," Mitzi piped up.

"She wouldn't be your sister, Mitzi, she'd be your niece. You'd be her aunt." I corrected.

"Well, could I still play with her?" Mitzi asked concerned.

"Well, sure, but you're going to be 10 by the time she *or he* is born and you might not want to play with baby dolls anymore," I said pulling a skillet from underneath the sink.

"Oh, I will. Or I can at least help you take care of her," Mitzi said confidently.

"You can," I said with a smile. "But in the meantime, come help me with supper."

17

And Baby Makes Five

"We told you before that we should suffer tribulation; even as it came to pass, ye know." 1 Thessalonians 3:4

1942

Being pregnant during the hot, summer months in Missouri is about as pleasant as shoving a bag over your head and being asked to 'breath normally' for 4 months. For as cold as it got in the winter, it got just as hot in the summer. I swear there was a good 120° difference between the two seasons, and I couldn't imagine how any animal survived either.

But fall was one of my favorite seasons. Pumpkins dotted fields, the leaves were turning vibrant shades of crimson, scarlet, flaxen, fire and orange and it just blanketed the countryside with an image no artist could ever paint. It had cooled slightly although we were still having days here or there that broke the 80° mark, which was still more comfortable than the 110° just a month earlier.

The morning sickness somewhat subsided around month four and I started to feel good again until what the doctor called the third trimester hit. I became not nauseated but tired and sore. More tired than I ever thought possible. I would get up to pour a glass of water and have to sit back down again. I couldn't believe I didn't have the energy to make myself a cup of tea in the afternoon. Mitzi had to pull her weight even more so when it came to making supper. She had gotten good at it too. She could truss a chicken, boil a stew and pickle a beet all faster than I had been able to at her age. I was so grateful for her and for Creth being so gracious of my condition.

I could have burned the house down around him and I don't think he'd care so long as he was having his girl. He still assumed it was a girl and no one could tell him otherwise. At this point, I desperately hoped it was a girl otherwise I might have to drop a boy off at the orphanage due to neglect.

The morning of September 15th came like any other day so far. It was a Wednesday and the kids left for school. Creth kissed me on the cheek as he grabbed his coat and hat and headed out. A strange tightening was happening in my belly but that had been going on for a week now so I didn't think too much of it. As the morning went on, the tightening got worse. I was wondering if this was it when all of a sudden I felt as if I had wet myself. As soon as the clear liquid hit the floor the tightening got worse and I had to lean on the table to steady myself.

I grabbed a towel and sopped up the mess on the wooden floor, thankful I didn't have another contraction while down there as I might have not been able to get up. I braced myself between the rocker and the table and reached for my coat and hat. I walked out of the house to the closest neighbor to see if someone was home. They were.

Our neighbors Jack and Marie had been faithful acquaintances for years and they knew our family and our history and still loved us all the same. I cut through a short cut in the woods that popped out at their back porch. Marie was hanging up sheets on the line.

"Marie.." I hollered, as another wave of contractions came over me and my voice was cut short. I stopped on the trail and waited for it to pass. She turned and instantly knew.

"Should I get the doctor?" She yelled back.

All I could do was nod.

Marie helped me back to the house as Jack went for the doctor. Marie laid me in bed and tucked extra blankets and towels underneath my bottom and around the bed. She tried to make me as comfortable as possible, which is an impossible task for a woman about to give birth.

The contractions were coming strong and consistent now. Doctor Baker came through the door around 3 pm followed by Jack. Marie ordered Jack to go find Creth. He didn't respond but turned quick and jetted back out the door. I was glad the kids weren't home yet. This might scare them. It scared me.

The doctor came into the room, took off his jacket and rolled up his sleeves. "Well, Virginia, are we going to have a baby today?" He said in a good-natured tone.

All I could think was, *well, I'M having a baby, I don't know what you'll be doing...* but I didn't say anything coherent because all that would come out was a wailing yell as I braced through the next contraction.

Doctor Baker washed his hands and situated the towels around my bottom. He pulled up my skirt and investigated his workspace. He didn't say anything but looked a bit concerned.

"Is everything alright?" I managed to get out between contractions.

"Yes, yes. You're doing fine. Are you ready to push?" He said assuredly.

I nodded. The feeling of wanting whatever was inside me out was so overwhelming that I thought even if he told me I couldn't push I don't think I could have obeyed.

I gave one big push and felt like my insides were trying to rip themselves from my abdomen.

"Wait, wait," the doctor said as he feverishly conducted some medical business on *my* business end. But I couldn't wait, the feeling was building again and I had to push.

I felt as if worms were trying to kick their way out of me. Doctor Baker looked worried, the little I could see of him between my squinting and shutting my eyes tight because of the pain and the need to push.

"Virginia, it's a footling breech," he said with a determined yet very concerned voice. "We have to deliver now. I'll help you through it but it will be tough and painful."

My body wanted to push again but I felt I was not getting any relief from it, unlike the feeling after having a bowel movement. I kept pushing but nothing was moving. Just then another spasm of pain ripped through my abdomen and I cried out as sweat beaded up on my forehead and my back felt hot and sticky.

I sat up a little on my elbows and rocked back and forth a bit and a little more came out. A knee. "I see the hips, Virginia, keep going. We have to get the baby out quick," he said. I didn't know at the time that most footling breech babies strangled themselves on their own umbilical cords before they are born due to the time it takes to get the baby out. It's probably a good thing I didn't know.

When the hips ripped out of me I felt a burning sensation and hot, wet liquid came rushing onto the bed. I was squeezing this child in half. I had to get it out. The shoulders were next. This was one tear at a time. When the shoulders tore through I blacked out.

It was only for a couple of seconds but I felt like I wasn't in the room any longer; like I was looking over myself assuming I had died, yet I was still moving and pushing.

"Just one more push, Virginia, you can do it," the doctor said, staring at the three-quarters of a baby in his arms. "Just one more and I think we got it,"

I couldn't. I didn't have it in me. I didn't have a shred of energy left. "Come on, Virginia, you can do this, just one more push."

From somewhere deep down inside me, I felt a wave building. It seemed to be the only strength I had left. I sat up on my elbows again, pulled my knees back and pushed again with all my might.

I had seen a baby foal being born once and it seemed like the head had been sticking out of the back end of the horse for way too long like it was stuck. Then all of a sudden the entire thing came sliding out, liquid, blood, everything. That image shot into my head as I felt what the mare must have felt getting all that out, even though it had come out backward.

I didn't even care that I had just had a baby, I was just so glad it was over. I felt better right then than I had felt in 9 months. I breathed deep and basked in the feeling that it was over. I didn't even feel the searing, burning pain at the site where I had just birthed a human being.

Creth burst into the room only to have the doctor order him out. "Baby, I'm sorry I wasn't here. Are you okay?" He tried to speak as Marie ushered him out.

"Yes, yes, she's fine and so is your daughter," Marie said.

His eyes got big and bright as he was pushed through the door. "I knew it! My girl!" he said followed by a little 'yippee'.

Marie took the baby and wrapped her up in a blanket after Doctor Baker inspected her and cleaned her up a bit. "Can I see her?" I said.

"Of course," the doctor said but ordered me to keep my legs

spread. I really didn't care what was happening down there right now, it was over and I had a baby girl and everything was right in the world again.

She was wrinkly and red. She looked like someone from a different planet. I had been with Mama when Mitzi was born but I don't remember her looking like this. But this baby was mine, and she was perfect. She wouldn't open her eyes yet and seemed mad we tore her from her cozy, warm environment. I kissed her forehead and said, "Well, don't keep her from him any longer or he'll tear the room down around us." Marie smiled and took our daughter to meet her daddy.

I laid back and felt dizzy. The doctor was still at the end of the bed and my legs were still in the air even though I didn't know what was keeping them up. The room was spinning and I closed my eyes to steady myself. The next thing I knew it was the next morning.

18

Birds Fly the Coop

"It came to pass, when she was in hard labor, that the midwife said unto her, Fear not; though shalt have this son also." Genesis 35:17

It had been three days since the birth and I still couldn't sit up. Doctor Baker tried to sew me up but he said I had torn more than just about anyone he'd seen before. That didn't help. When I woke my breasts were swollen and ached something awful. I didn't know what was worse, though, the ache in my breasts or the pain between my legs. They brought the baby and luckily, she nursed right away.

I hadn't left the bed since she was born. Creth wanted to name her Dolores after Dolores del Rio, the first Latin American crossover star in Hollywood and I agreed. Dolores was healthy despite her rude entrance into the world. I, on the other hand, had lost a lot of blood and needed iron and water. Doctor Baker had been by every day since the delivery to check on both of us, although Dolores seemed to be as healthy as a horse. Mitzi was having fun playing 'babysitter' and would bring Dolores to me for nursing as often as possible. She would also make dinner with me shouting instructions from the bedroom.

After four days in bed, I was tired of peeing in a bowl and seeing only the inside of my room, so I carefully swung my legs over the side of the bed and sat up. Throbbing pain went through my thighs and groin, so I sat there for a minute until the pain subsided some. I then planted both feet firmly on the cold floor and braced myself. I stood up and promptly lost my balance and sat back down. My legs were so wobbly they wouldn't hold my weight.

It was Sunday and everyone was home so I thought that if I fell, there would be plenty of people to help me up. I squared my feet again and imagined them being tree trunks firmly rooted in the floor and slowly stood. My legs wobbled some, but I regained control of them and pursed my lips together in a stubborn move as if to make them straighten up. I stood up straight and waited. My feet were still planted and wouldn't move. My nightgown fell around me, and I felt like I was wearing a diaper with all the gauze and wrapping around my hips.

I shifted my weight forward a little and my foot scooted on the floor. I did the same with the opposite foot and eventually, I was to the door. It was open and Mitzi was making biscuits at the table. Vern and Creth were outside chopping wood. I stood in the doorway with the frame supporting me for a minute.

"Hi, V!" Mitzi said when she noticed me. "You're up!" she exclaimed excitedly.

"Yes. I'm tired of being in that bed all the time. Where's Dolores?" I asked.

"In her bassinet over there," she said, pointing by the rocker. "She's asleep and making funny little gurgly noises."

I braced myself for the walk and shuffled over to the bassinet. I looked over the hood to her peaceful and sweet little face and smiled. Maybe this was worth it. She was pretty cute. I sat down in the rocker with a sigh that sounded as if I'd just run a marathon. I closed my eyes and rocked the chair holding onto her bassinet, which rocked in rhythm with me.

Creth came bounding in the house, not knowing I was up. "Hey, look at you!" He declared. "How ya feeling, V?"

"Sore, tired, but also tired of that room. It's time I got up," I concluded.

"Well, alright. Doc said you can when you felt like it but take it easy. This little cutie-pie practically tore you in half," He said with a casual, matter-of-fact tone.

He said it so inadvertently that I thought that he wouldn't be saying it like that if it was his muff this thing clawed out of. He washed his hands and came back to the bassinet to stare at Dolores. "I don't think she's going anywhere," I said.

"Oh, she better not. This little one's already got daddy wrapped around her little finger. Doesn't she, now?" he said making googly eyes and baby talk at someone that was clearly fast asleep.

I rolled my eyes and leaned my head back on the rocker closing them slightly. It was just nice to get out of that bed.

~

Several weeks had gone by and the addition of a new person in the household was a fun and sleepless adventure. I had almost healed completely by now and was feeling somewhat back to normal even though my body was clearly still a breakfast, lunch, and dinner producer for this little 13-pound subordinate.

Creth celebrated with his family any chance he got. Being from a family of 15 siblings, there was always someone around to celebrate with. Aunt Maud and Aunt Meryle came by every couple of weeks with baby clothes and fresh cloth diapers and Creth would spend most Saturday afternoons with his brothers drinking and smoking and shooting the breeze.

Vern had already signed up to go to war and Creth allowed him to go early, so, as soon as he could, we put him on a train for North Carolina where he was to spend 6 weeks in boot camp and then board a ship.

Daddy still wrote often and was hoping to come home in a year or two. He talked about leaving Kansas City and starting a new life with Mitzi, maybe in California or Oregon. That was too far away for me to even think about, geographically and chronologically. My whole life was here. Creth, Dolores, and me, three little peas in a pod. I liked the simple, little life we had built and now that I was on the mend I was feeling more positive about things every day.

Until Creth came home drunker than a skunk one night. I knew he liked to drink, heck, we'd both sit on the porch nursing a whiskey from time to time but he started coming home late and heading out with the boys from work a little too often. I had casually mentioned that it bothered me over dinner one night and I got a talking to.

"Don't talk about things you don't understand, Virginia, it's just the way it is," he'd say. "You do fine here at home and I'll support you. Isn't that how it was supposed to be? Have you had to beg for bread once since you married me? No. I did that for you."

But he would say these things after being at the bar for a couple of hours so there was really no point to try and reason with him then. He was still so hungover in the morning that it was useless to carry on a conversation then either.

One night he didn't come home for supper. I made chili and cornbread and Mitzi and I ate it in silence at the table. She cleaned up and I helped her with some homework and by the time she went to bed he still wasn't home. I opened the front door and peered out into the darkness. *You better come home or I swear...* I said under my breath.

I closed the door and locked it. I got ready for bed and crawled in under the covers. Dolores slept peacefully at the foot of the bed in her bassinet and soon I drifted off. I awoke with a jerk to a blow that sounded like someone had thrown a sledgehammer against the house. I sat straight up with a start and spun around when the bedroom door flew open. Creth came in and growled, "who locked me out?"

"I didn't know if you'd be coming home," I said rubbing the sleep from my eyes.

"Well, I'm home now," he said and took off his clothes and flopped into bed. The smell of whiskey and musty cigarette smoke was permeating every pore and I turned my nose up and rolled over. "Hey, you, don't you be turning away from me," he said pulling at my nightgown and urging me to roll over.

"You're drunk, Creth, go to sleep," I said muffled in the pillow.

"I ain't drunk, I want my woman," he said softening his tone a bit, trying to get on my good side maybe. "I'm sorry, I didn't mean to be so late. The boys got to talking and..."

"I know, the boys got to talking and one thing led to another and now it's 1 o'clock in the morning. I know how these things go," I said turning my face to the ceiling to talk to him.

He tried to compose himself with a more comforting tone. "Forgive me. You know I love you," he said, still pulling at my nightgown. I rolled over to face him, the faint flicker from the fireplace in the other room casting shadows across the ceiling. I couldn't really tell but his face seemed to have calmed down and he was getting tired but still handsy. I think his eyes were closed but his hands were not asleep. They reached under my gown and ran the full length of me all the way up to my shoulders. He slipped the gown off my head with resistance and pressed his body against mine.

Fine, I thought.

19

Log Cabins

"And it came to pass when men began to multiply on the face of the earth, and daughters were born unto them..." Genesis 6:1

1943

1943 came and things were steadily getting worse. We hadn't even been married 2 years yet and we had one child and another on the way. When I found out I was pregnant again at the end of January my heart sank. Dolores had come so violently that when my doctor confirmed the pregnancy I broke down in the office. I can't have another baby, I thought, not now. Fear gripped me and Doctor Baker said he would check up on me more often to see if the baby had turned right. Still, I didn't want another baby nor was my body ready.

Our relationship had gone from one of convenience to one of inconvenience. His drinking was getting worse and although he was never a mean drunk, the money spent on whiskey, nights out with his family or friends, and loss of time together was really taking its toll. Dolores had just barely turned one when I started feeling the onset of contractions. This pregnancy hadn't been as tough as the first one. I didn't have as much morning sickness and food wasn't the distasteful gruel it had been with Dolores. But still, the thought of another delivery on the horizon kept me up at night. I couldn't sleep. I kept dreaming of legs kicking their way out of me. The doctor had said that this baby had turned right and all seemed well, but again, *he* didn't have to push this thing out.

Creth had been working at R.L. Faubion, welding skirts on tanker trucks during the war when he met George Lord. George was a tall, lanky man of about 50 with a salt and pepper mustache, green eyes, and thinning hair. He was the supervisor over Creth's position as head welder. George had been working at the factory for over 20 years and wanted to retire and do something fun. A good-natured man, George and his wife Helen had joined us for dinner occasionally and talked about going into business together owning and managing a dance hall.

"Virginia's a good cook," Creth said one evening over coffee and apple pie after dinner. "She'd be good in the kitchen. I can manage the rooms and liquor store."

"We're building up by Sugar Creek," George said, separating a bite of pie from the slice and scooping it into his mouth. He sat back in his chair and let out a sigh that implied he couldn't eat another bite. "I'd like you all to run it," He said with a chipper tone.

I was refilling the coffee in Creth's cup when and looked up. "All of us?" I asked, forgetting I was pouring the coffee until it had almost run onto the table cloth.

"Virginia, watch what you're doing," Creth stammered and let out a quick huff of irritation.

"I'm sorry, sorry," I startled and regained my composure.

"That's right," George said, "All of you. The *Log Cabins* is almost complete. A few more cabins need to be built and the building codes need to be approved and we can open for business."

The *Log Cabins* was to be a dancehall/diner/liquor store/motel northeast of Kansas City in Sugar Creek. It was just off the Missouri River at the mouth of Rock Creek. It was far enough out of town for folks to feel like they were on vacation but not so far that locals wouldn't travel to the diner for Sunday supper or a mid-week breakfast.

"I have your house all ready to go too," George said. "Everything should be ready to go by next spring. You can take the time to settle your things here and gather your family. We're glad to have you, Creth," George said in a jovial tone as he leaned forward and patted Creth on the arm by his shoulder. Creth nodded and I sat back down not saying a word.

When George left that evening and Mitzi and Dolores had gone to bed, I thought about probing Creth more on the dancehall idea. "Is this what you want?" I asked. He hadn't drunk a lot at dinner so I thought this would be a good time to have a serious conversation.

"What do you mean? I think this will be a great opportunity. We can get out of the farm and maybe make some real money. It's what we've talked about, V," he said, with the air of irritation again as if this was obviously the right direction and I should stop talking nonsense and just go along with it. "You can make your food and I'll run things. George trusts us. He's put in a lot of money on this and we can't let him down. Says he'd like to open 3 more in the next 10 years, although I don't know how profitable that will be with this war goin' on."

He leaned back again and grabbed the newspaper. I sat at the table rotating my coffee cup on the table and staring into the black abyss. Was I ready to leave the farm? I guess I had no other choice. Sitting there still and quiet for a minute I felt a small turning in my belly. A dull ache came from somewhere deep within and I thought this might be the start of it.

I slept surprisingly well that night; some of the best sleep I'd had in a month. A stronger contraction is what woke me, though not enough to produce a sound. I rolled over pushed myself up with my elbow. Another one came quickly with the instant movement. I twisted around and looked at Creth still completely passed out next to me. Here we go again, I thought.

I reached my hand for his shoulder and shook him gently. He moaned and hunkered into the blankets. I gave up quickly and stood to face the day. My side of the bed faced the window and it looked like it was going to be a drizzly start to October.

~

Gratefully, Carol came in the normal fashion although the general mechanics of childbirth is never an easy ordeal. Keeping with tradition, Carol was named after Carol Lombard, a prominent actress in the 1930s and again, one of Creth's favorites.

Creth was always good at naming things. He'd named our hound dogs, stray cats, and of course, our daughters, not that I had any say in it. He insisted on calling them by certain actresses and if I objected, he shut me down right quick. "I won't be having any daughter of mine named after a poodle or hound," he'd say. "Girls need proper names from proper women."

I just hoped they turned into 'proper' women. I spent more and more time at home with them, not that I had anything else to do. Since I'd quit at the garment factory my life had been changing diapers, making supper, cleaning bedsheets, weeding the garden, and making sure Dolores and Carol stayed out of each other's hair... literally. They would pull and bite at each other something fierce, so much so I had to build a makeshift partition between them in their crib just so they would ignore one another and get some sleep. Not that they disliked each other, it's just that they only had each other to entertain and it usually came about in painful, violent behaviors.

When Dolores turned two in September and Carol was just about one, we finally moved from the farm into the caretaker's house at Log Cabins. It was even smaller than the farm. I had sold the farm to Jack and Marie who decided to turn it into a half-way house for folks returning from the war. We got a little bit of money from the sale and Creth took all of it and sunk it into the Log Cabins as an 'investment'. Daddy was clean tired of the place and said whenever he returned, he would take Mitzi and find a place in the city, at least for a while.

The house at Log Cabins was new but cramped. We only had two rooms for the five of us and the main bedroom only had a double bed. Dolores and Carol had to sleep in the room with Mitzi, who was 12 now and not so keen on 'playing' with the girls as she had been just a year prior. The girls shared a crib and Mitzi had the twin bed. The living space had a small stove, table, couch, and chair. We were amazed at the fact that there was no fireplace but instead, electricity kept the place warm with a loud, monstrous-looking machine in the corner by the stove. It would groan and squeal when it kicked on but the heat that emitted from it was a welcome exchange for keeping a fire going. The furniture was older but sturdy and we were able to bring our beds and bedding from the farm so it felt a little more like home.

Creth went right to work managing the Log Cabins. There were 12 cabins in all folks could rent, not including ours, a pool hall, which had a dance floor adjacent to it, and a cafe, which doubled as a liquor store for those that wanted to take their libations home. The cafe and dance hall were two separate buildings even though they were next to each other with a little breezeway connecting the two for folks wanting fresh air or to converse without the noise of either establishment. Our house was about 200 feet from the dancehall so we could hear the music last long into the night but not so close that it didn't lull us to sleep most nights. On occasion, there was a ruffian that caused trouble and Creth was always out there to keep the peace, so long as he wasn't drunk himself. Most nights I fell asleep to the honky-tonk of the piano and girl's voices hollering in delight.

20

Things Are Not Good

"It came to pass, when Rehoboam had established the kingdom and had strengthened himself, he forsook the law of the Lord..." 2 Chronicles
12:1

1944

It was 1944 and things were going well, for the business end of things anyway. We had been doing well at Log Cabins and George Lord seemed to approve of the way Creth ran things. However, I was not approving of the way Creth ran his household. Nearly every night he'd come home drunk and while he was not abusive, he was not himself.

Janell said that's what husbands do after a while and you just get used to it, but I didn't think this was the way it had to be. I saw Mama and Daddy always loving and kind to each other and wondered why this wasn't the case in my marriage.

Janell was a young woman that lived down the lane from Log Cabins. She had also married young and was about 25 when I met her. We had met when I was out on a walk to get the mail and she'd just driven by in her sporty 1940s Plymouth Roadking. It was teal blue and the snazziest thing on the strip. She waved with her gloved hand from the driver's seat and I was amazed that she knew how to drive at all.

"Well, hi, y'all," She'd said as she pulled over to the likes of our motley crew. "You're the new caretakers of the Cabins, right?" She was chewing gum and had large, circular sunglasses. She flicked them up with one finger and smiled broadly as she cracked her gum. She had the look of an affluent woman from a summer wives camp if there was such a thing. Her dress was dotted with cherries against a stark white background. I staggered my troop off to the side of the road and tried to behave in a composed manner.

"Ye, yes," I stammered, hoping the girls wouldn't act up and start screaming. I had Carol in the stroller and Mitzi had a hold on Dolores's hand and all were getting a bit antsy.

"Well, I'm Janell. I live just up there," She pointed behind her in a nonchalant fashion. "If you need anything, you just let me know." She smiled big again and snapped her jaw.

"Thank you. I'm sure we'll maybe call on you at some point," I said with a little hesitation hoping that wouldn't scare her away. I figured if she wants to be our friend she should know what she's getting into right away. "I'm Virginia, and this is Carol," pointing to the stroller, "Mitzi and Dolores," motioning in their direction.

"I have an excellent babysitter too if you should need one. She's cheap and really good with the kids. I have two myself, a boy and a girl and my goodness I need my space," she said laughing in a high pitch tone that I thought sounded fake. "I'm sure she'd love to help anytime."

"Thank you. I might take you up on that. Going to the market with three little ones is a job," I said, trying to connect with something we had in common.

Mitzi immediately spoke up, "I'm not a little one," she said, stomping her foot on the ground and looking indignant. "I'm almost 13!"

"I know, I know," I said, trying to make her hush, "just when you are in school." And I shoed her off with a wave of my hand.

"Well then, I'll get you her name," said Janell. "I can come by later today or tomorrow if you're home?"

"That'd be swell," I said, almost relieved our conversation was nearly over. My pretense in the situation was making me irritated and hot.

She drove off with a small puff of dust in our faces and skidded away from the edge of the road. I gave a little cough and continued our walk, wondering what it could possibly be like to have a babysitter watching the girls all afternoon while I shopped. The thought made me giddy.

The next day, true to her word, Janell came by. She drove up fast and stopped with a jerk in her fancy, teal car. I heard her coming, or someone coming anyway and looked out the window. Creth was already somewhere else on site working so I went out to meet her. Mitzi was at school, which had started on September 1 in the new school district. It was a fancier district where the kids were required to wear certain outfits or at least certain colors and styles so there was no arguing over dress or teasing. We had to buy a black blouse and plaid skirt for Mitzi with white stockings and black Mary-Janes. She actually loved them and felt so fancy. I was glad the 'fancy' hadn't rubbed off a month in already.

It was October and luckily the sun was still shining, and it was unusually warm, although Missouri was hit and miss when it came to winter. It could be 20° when you woke up and 80° by 5 pm. You just never knew what you were going to get.

Janell got out and waved a big 'hello' to me as I came out onto the porch. The girls were on the floor in the house playing with some boxes we had received with business cards in them advertising the Cabins.

"Well, hello there Virginia!" She said. Had I told her my name yesterday? I must have completely forgotten.

"Hi, Janell," I said cheerfully, a little relieved for the break and a little concerned at what Creth might think.

"How the heck are ya?" She asked.

"Um, just fine, I think," I said, wondering what she was fishing for. She came around the back of the car and popped the trunk. "Need a little afternoon delight?" She asked flipping up a bottle of some alcoholic drink.

"I suppose it could always be better," I said with a smile. This was instantly a welcome retreat. I was no longer being judged but invited. Someone wanted to help me escape. Someone understood the lonely, long days of screaming children and tired husbands. I don't know if she understood everything she was offering but it was an oasis nevertheless.

We laughed over her bottle of 1940 Bordeaux as it neared the bottom. The girls had passed out on the rug and we tried to stifle our giggles over things like men's trousers, the way they tried to keep it up on a drunk night, and how they didn't have a clue when we burnt the roast. I had had so much wine our conversations started getting quite a bit more personal. I didn't even hesitate when I asked her about contraception. "Can I ask you something? How do you not get pregnant all the time?" I asked jokingly then much more serious as I finished the question.

"Oh, that's easy. Just don't let him in your bed around that time," she said, pouring the last few drops of the deep red liquor into my glass.

"What does that mean?" I asked in a slurred tone.

"I mean, if you know you're going to get pregnant, just don't let him into bed with you." She said as she drained the last of her wine.

"But how do you know?" I asked, suddenly completely intrigued by the idea that there was a way to tell.

"Honey, don't you know?" She said setting her glass down and looking at me dumbfounded.

"Well, no, not really," I said lowering my eyes and hiding behind my glass.

"Honey, you can only get pregnant a couple of times a month, don't you know that? You know your cycle, right?" She asked but at this point, I just felt stupider the more she talked.

I took a sip of my wine and looked worried but didn't say anything.

"Baby girl, you can only get pregnant about 2 weeks after you start your cycle." She put her glass down and leaned in resting her palm flat on the table. "Just steer clear during those days and you should be good."

"Oh, that's good to know," I said. My insides did a little turn. So there was a way. Mama never shared this with me, understandably so as I was just a girl with no inkling of marriage on the horizon.

"Yes, child, there is a way," she said as if she was responding to my thoughts.

I was getting a little dizzy and needed a cigarette. The girls were still passed out on the rug and I didn't see no harm leaving them there. We stepped out on the porch and I lit up a Pall Mall breathing in deep to clear my foggy head.

Janell and I talked for a good hour or so about our lives and it felt good to laugh with someone that really seemed to understand me. Janell had been married since she was 19 to Bob, a now 29-year-old accountant in Excelsior Springs. She complained about him non-stop yet would always follow up a complaint with 'but God love him'. I didn't know if that meant she loved him too. She had raven

black hair that she tied up in a dog-tooth hairband with curls top-
ping her head in the front and clips holding it in the back. Her skin
was smooth and glossy and she wore bright red lipstick. She said
men liked it but I didn't know if it was for her husband or other
men.

She gave me the telephone number of her babysitter and I
thanked her as she hopped back in her car and bounced off down
the driveway with her gloved hand waving out the window back at
me.

Katie Stevens was the babysitter and she was 15 years old trying
to save up money for school, should she ever go in the future. I called
her and asked her to come by for a couple of hours during the day
to watch the girls while I went into town. The thought of shopping
on my own was practically heaven. Katie was thin and pale and had
dirty blonde hair that she tied in a ponytail. She was extremely polite and I asked her a couple of questions about caring for young'uns
and she answered them all without hesitation. She had 4 small siblings of her own so she was well versed in changing diapers, keeping
small objects away from their mouths and getting them to lie down
and take naps. I gave her the number to the dancehall should she
have an emergency, although I prayed she wouldn't have to involve
Creth at all. I put my gloves and hat on and headed out.

I was able to take the car since Creth was somewhere on site although I never asked if I could. I figured he would be off managing
the liquor store or emptying it, one of the two and wouldn't give a
lick where I was.

I had a glorious afternoon just window shopping, browsing for
coats and hats, looking at jewelry, and eyeing fancy dresses in Wool-
worth's windows. On my way home I stopped at the store and
picked up a few necessities but even a market trip was dreamy without two screaming kids in tow.

When I pulled up to the house about 2 hours later I heard a

ruckus going on inside. Creth was home. Oh, God. I quickly threw the car in park and flicked the key. I jumped out and darted up the stairs.

"Well, where the hell is she?" Creth yelled throwing up a hand at poor Katie. She cowered in the corner and the girls were crying on the floor. I could tell he had been drinking this afternoon and there was no reasoning with him.

When I came in the open door Katie shot a glance at me and Creth spun around. "There you are! What's the meaning of leaving our children with some stranger?" He spouted, turning his anger on me.

"She's not a stranger. She was recommended by a neighbor and I had to go to town for groceries," I said in a casual tone, hopefully prompting a more casual response. I went over to Katie and handed her $.50 and thanked her as I guided her out of the house quickly. I didn't know where this was going to go so the sooner she was out the better.

Katie quickly scurried out the door and down the steps at a sort of half trot to get away faster. I shut the door behind her and Creth turned around to look at me but didn't say anything.

"What?" I said like there was nothing to be concerned about.

"What?" he said copying my nonchalant tone. "That's all you have to say?"

"What is there to say? I had to go out and got a babysitter. What's the big deal?" I said taking off my gloves and making my way to the kitchen.

He grabbed my arm as I went by him. "I thought we talked about no babysitters? I don't want some stranger raisin' my girls," he said still clutching my arm and leaning into my face.

"She's not raising your daughters," I said. "She was here for a couple of hours at most. I hardly think that's raising your daughters."

"I don't care. You're here all day. What the hell else do you do?

Why couldn't you have taken them with you?" He demanded, letting go of my arm with a flick.

"Because it's easier without them!" I argued back. "You have no idea what it's like to be with a 1 and 2-year old all day without a break. I'm going crazy here," I barked, grabbing my apron and tying it around my waist. "That's all I do around here. Take care of your kids," I emphasized the 'your'. "I'm tired and I get no time to myself."

"Oh, so I suppose I get all the luxury, huh? I get to relax and do nothing all day, right?" He said sarcastically. "Don't you know who brings in the food and money around here? What do you do? Nothing. I can't even keep you at home for one day," he said, tone getting louder and angrier.

I clenched my teeth and scowled at him then turned and stomped into the kitchen. The girls were still whimpering on the floor but looking at both of us with wide eyes. "I do more around here than you'll ever know. I *have done* more than anyone should have to," I said. I could feel the tears welling up behind my eyes but I quickly blinked them away. I turned and stared at the sink waiting for his rebuttal.

"I have done more for you than anyone would," he said not moving but standing his ground in the middle of the living room. The girls had scooted off to the corner and Dolores had grabbed her Raggedy Ann doll and clutched it tightly pulling Carol into her lap a bit. "How dare you not be grateful," Creth said in a calm, even tone.

I didn't turn around. I looked down and saw a meat cleaver on the counter to the right of the sink. I could see the girls off to the side in the corner of my eye. My anger swelled in me from my stomach and I felt hot rising up over my head. Without thinking too much more about it I grabbed the cleaver and swung around hurling it across the living room.

Creth ducked unusually fast considering he was probably drunk. The cleaver stuck in the wooden door with a gong.

"What the hell, Virginia?" He exclaimed with a shocked look, slowly rising up with his hands over his head. His wide eyes stared at me and mine bore right back into his. "You could have killed me!"

"Don't tempt me," I said but I didn't move.

"There's something wrong with you," he said and grabbed his hat off the rack and backed out of the door leaving the cleaver where it landed. He slammed the door behind him and I let out a breath that felt as if I was holding it the whole time. I put my hands on the counter behind me and looked around the room. I'd had it. I couldn't do this anymore.

I took off my apron and went to the bedroom. I grabbed the suitcase from under the bed and threw it on top violenting opening it and laying it out flat. I grabbed some dresses from the closet and a few undergarments. Then I ran to the girl's room and scooped up a load of clothes and diapers and rushed back into the bedroom and stuffed them in the suitcase. I could barely close the suitcase so I turned around and sat on it bouncing up and down to smash the clothes down even more. I locked it and went back to the kitchen. I phoned Janell and asked if she could take me to the train station. She didn't even ask any questions but she just said 'sure' without question.

Two minutes later I was loading the girls, the suitcase and me into Janell's car. I quickly looked around for a sign of Creth. I had no idea where he ran off to, probably the bar. I got in the front and said 'go'. She hit the gas pedal and we flew out of the driveway in a puff of dust.

21

Mrs. Gentry

"It came to pass when Jeroboam who was in Egypt, whither he fled from the presence of Solomon the king..." 2 Chronicles 10:2

We grabbed Mitzi from school on the way out of town and Janell dropped us at the train station. With a hoard of children, I trudged up to the ticket counter. "4 tickets to Colorado please," I begged the ticket taker.

"Where in Colorado, ma'am?" He said scanning our clan.

"Nederland," I said.

Nederland was just outside Denver and the home of Mrs. Gentry. We had met Mrs. Gentry when and Mama were still living on the farm. She was the midwife in the county and was called out to many a home in those days. She delivered Mitzi and we all loved her so. Mrs. Gentry moved just after Mitzi turned five to be a governess for a family in Nederland. We were all sad to see her go. She had become a pillar in the community and a trusted friend when needed.

"The closest I can get you is Boulder," the ticket man said.

"Fine," I said, shifting Carol on my hip.

"I got 4 tickets for Thursday for $19 a ticket," he said nonchalantly.

"Thursday? I can't do that. Don't you have anything sooner... and cheaper?" I asked pleading. Mitzi started to pull at me and Dolores had to go to the bathroom.

"I'm sorry, ma'am, I don't," he said with a concerned look in his eyes.

"Please, sir. Anything? I gotta get out of here quick," I said, hoping he could feel the desperation in my voice.

"Well, I do have a troop train leaving in about 30 minutes. They're going to Denver but you might be able to get something from there," he said, looking over his schedule sheet.

"How much is that?" I asked.

"Well, you'd be with the men, but I can get you on for $4.25 a person," he said confirming the price.

"I'll take it," I said, shifting Carol to the other hip. I put my bag strap in my mouth while I rifled through the pockets for the cash I'd been stowing away for a year. I handed him $17 and he responded with 4 tickets.

~

I boarded the troop train with the three kids in tow a little haphazardly and apprehensively not really knowing what I was getting into. I had never ridden on a train before so my expectations were low.

A troop train, or troop sleeper as they were sometimes referred to, was a railroad passenger car constructed to serve as a mobile barracks for transporting troops. They were not fancy and were equipped with bunks stacked 3-high and each car accommodated up to 30 men. Troop kitchens, or rolling galleys, also joined the train to provide meal service en route. Most trains had a medical department kitchen car, which aided wounded servicemen and transported these men back home if you were lucky enough to get on a train going the right direction.

We were quite a sight lugging ourselves up into the car, but the young men that accompanied us were eager and quick to help. As nervous as I was, I was also a little relieved and yet, still angry at the whole situation. How dare he tell me what to do? I had rights and feelings and deserved some respect. I never saw Daddy treat Mama like this and knew there had to be a better way.

Half of our car was bunkbeds three high and the other half were seats connected at the base three across. Some faced the front; some faced the back and the middle ones faced each other. There was a toilet at one end behind the bunks and doors on either side. We piled in and sat in the middle of the seats taking up no more than we needed to. The stares were palpable, but this wasn't the strangest thing these boys had ever seen. Troop trains often carried citizens here or there when necessary, but this sight was definitely rare; a fire-haired woman and her three kids. Carol started to cry when the train jerked forward, and I felt embarrassed and a little flustered trying to calm her down. Dolores just sat wide-eyed on Mitzi's lap sucking her thumb and staring at all the eyes staring back at her.

They were friendly stares though. No one seemed to be upset by the situation even though the car was clearly crowded and hot. The two end doors were open allowing a little breeze through the car but with the number of bodies in there even a cool October afternoon didn't provide much relief.

A young man with a hard hat and fatigues got up from his seat and cautiously walked over to us sitting down next to me. He looked about 17 and reminded me of Vern.

"Hi, ma'am," he said politely.

"Hello," I nodded, bouncing Carol on my lap trying to quiet her. The rocking of the train had reached a rhythmic motion and most of the men had settled back into their routines, which were really card games or naps.

"I'm Ben," the young man said searching my face for approval. "Do you need some help there?"

The car was full of Privates both first and second class either just getting started or transferring under new orders. All seemed pretty well occupied with their own business after about 20 minutes but a few gave us pitiful, sympathetic looks and seemed awkward to even approach us. Ben, on the other hand, appeared kind and eager to help. He was baby-faced and blonde and had a small scar right between his eyes, possibly from an old chickenpox mark. He had bright blue eyes and I could tell he had not seen the full effects of war yet, not that I had either, but I had seen men who had and it changed them. They were no longer soft and innocent, but hard and had a gaze that they were always seeing something they couldn't get out of their minds; something harsh and disturbing. Ben didn't have that look. I wondered how long he would keep that innocence.

"I must look like a disaster," I said, adjusting Carol and trying to organize my things.

"Not at all. It just looks like you might need an extra hand," he said in a southern drawl even stronger than mine.

"Do we really look that bad?" I said with a defeated look.

"Oh, no, no, " he said waving his hand. "I just thought that if you needed some help, I have nothing else to do."

"Well, thank you. That would be helpful," I said and breathed a little sigh and just sat back. Ben immediately started clapping and tickling Carol to try and get her calmed down. The distraction worked. Dolores was still enthralled with the environment and Mitzi just stared while Carol started to laugh and giggle. I felt myself lean back on the chair and the sounds in the car started to get muffled and distant.

I awoke from my brisk cat nap to singing. The boys had gathered around the girls and were singing "Mairzy Doats". The boys seemed to be having just as much fun as the girls as they all danced around and clapped scooping each other's elbows and twirling around singing:

I know a ditty nutty as a fruitcake
Goofy as a goon and silly as a loon
Some call it pretty, others call it crazy
But they all sing this tune

Mairzy doats and dozy doats and liddle lamzy divey
A kiddley divey too, wouldn't you?
Yes! Mairzy doats and dozy doats and liddle lamzy divey
A kiddley divey too, wouldn't you?

If the words sound queer and funny to your ear, a little bit jumbled and jivey
Sing "Mares eat oats and does eat oats and little lambs eat ivy"

Oh! Mairzy doats and dozy doats and liddle lamzy divey
A kiddley divey too, wouldn't you-oo?
A kiddley divey too, wouldn't you?

The song was a common sound around our house now that we had a radio at the cabin but nothing beat this live version. The girls seemed to love the entertainment and Carol had gone from crying to laughing and clapping her hands imitating her sister and the troops.

It took about a day and a half to get to Denver and the boys on the train had become like family in an instant. A few citizens got off in Tokepa but most went on through. We pulled into Denver on a Saturday night around 7 pm. What little money I had bought us a hostel in town and we curled up in one tiny bed thankful for something other than the hard metal of the train seat.

Sunday morning, I walked to the station and asked about a train to Boulder. It was only $.65 per person and the soonest train was leaving at noon. We collected our belongings and arrived at 11:30 am. The girls were still tired and we all needed a bath. Mrs. Gentry would take us in, I was sure of it. She would do whatever it was we needed. However, it was a bit presumptuous to assume she remembered me and that the family she worked for would take us in. I hadn't really thought about the possibility of rejection until now.

I picked up the telephone at the station and rang the operator. I asked for Mrs. Mattie Gentry. The operator paused for a moment then told me she'd put me through.

"Foster residence," the polite female voice on the opposite end of the phone answered.

"Yes, hello, is Mrs. Gentry at home?" I asked timidly.

"May I ask who's calling, please?"

"My name is Virginia Lamb," I replied. There was a brief pause and some shuffling on the other end. Mitzi laid in the hardwood pews of the station and Carol was playing with the strap on my bag.

"Yes? This is Mrs. Gentry," the voice came on the line, soft, sweet and firm.

"Hello? Mrs. Gentry? Oh, this is Virginia Lamb. Do you remember..." I was cut off by her cry of delight.

"Oh, Virginia! Yes, of course, I remember you! What on earth are you doing calling me?" She asked in a high-pitched, excited tone.

"Well, we're in Boulder and I was wondering if we could come and stay with you a while?" No need to sugarcoat it. We needed a place to stay and Mrs. Gentry would appreciate the forthcomingness of my attitude.

"Oh, I'm sure it would be alright. Let me check with the Mrs. In the meantime, I'll send Boris to get you. He shouldn't be more than an hour. Sound alright?" There was no hesitation in her voice, just a welcoming retreat that felt like a soft pillow after a long, hard day.

Boris was Mrs. Gentry's houseman and arrived about an hour later. We were all sitting on the steps of the train station when this large, broad, black man got out of the car. The entire car moved upward when he stepped out. He came toward us with an intentional stride.

"Miss Virginia?" Boris said in a southern drawl that was low and weak.

"Yes," I said answering. This must be Boris although a little warning on his appearance would have been helpful.

"Miss Gentry send me fo' ya," He said politely, picking up our bags and turning around slowly to put them in the car.

"Thank you," I said gathering up my own troops from around the steps. "Come on, let's go," I said to the girls. Mitzi yawned and dragged her feet a bit and Dolores was getting antsy from sitting for so long. Luckily the afternoon was warm and there was a cool breeze through the oak trees surrounding the now quiet and deserted station.

The road to Nederland was bumpy and quiet and the girls fell asleep on one another. I sat in the front with Boris yet we didn't speak. I too felt myself closing my eyes to the rhythmic motion of the road but was jarred back to life when we rounded the driveway where Mrs. Gentry lived.

The house looked like a Savannah estate I'd seen in magazines. It was stately and grand with columns running down the front, framing the front doors. The circular drive ran directly in front of the grand staircase where we stopped. Boris shut off the car. I didn't get out for a minute but just looked up at the magnitude of the building. This reminded me of the library back in Kansas City that had a clock under the peak centering the entire structure. This, however, didn't have a clock, but I was still amazed that one family lived in this massive home.

Mrs. Gentry must have heard the car because she flung open the front door and came running out the steps to greet us.

Mattie Gentry was born in 1880 and I'm sure had an intriguing past of her own but by the time we got to know her, she was in her 50s and seemed comfortable being a governess. The family she worked for had four children, all under the age of ten, and the parents were always away going to some party or function so she was left to raise the children most days on her own. I thought about what Creth had said. Now, *this* was letting someone else raise your children. But of course, I kept my thoughts to myself, especially under the grace and hospitality of the family we were staying with. I didn't really know why we came here other than there wasn't anywhere else to go.

The Foster family was gracious to put us up for a while, but they were pretty clear that it shouldn't be forever. I couldn't really think about the future, just the immediate present and we were all so grateful to have a hot meal and a warm bed to sleep in that night. I think I might have slept for 3 days.

22

A Voice of Reason

"It came to pass, when Baasha heard it, that he left off building of Ramah and let his work cease." 2 Chronicles 16:5

Mrs. Mattie Gentry was a kindly woman. She was thin, pale but could wallop you if ever you got out of line. Her pursed lips and wire-rim glasses made her look like a schoolmarm but she had a soft, tenderness about her too that no school mistress ever displayed with me.

We'd been staying in the mansion for about a week when Mrs. Gentry came in our room and said she had gotten a letter from Daddy. I thought it was odd that Daddy was corresponding with her but didn't pay a lot of attention to the thought offhand. He had switched from Merchant Marines to contract work for the government after the bombing of Pearl Harbor. The government had sent him over to Honolulu to construct and help build bridges and structures destroyed by the Japanese. Now that his assignment was done and he really didn't have a home anymore in Missouri, he was coming to Colorado. I let my thoughts wander as to why Colorado, but I thought he must have known we were here. He'd be coming into town in a week or so and Mrs. Gentry just thought it was God's timing that we were here at the same time. I didn't know anything about God or His timing but assumed it was a coincidence none the less.

Mrs. Mattie Gentry

Mitzi had taken to helping with chores around the house and Mrs. Gentry assumed the customary position of governess for Carol and Dolores too although I don't know how the lady of the house felt about that. We'd eat leftovers in our room or in the kitchen but never with the family and I was okay with that. I already felt out of place. It was a rainy November afternoon when two strangers were spotted wandering up the long driveway. They looked like vagabonds with suitcases slung over their shoulders and Boris was ready to tell them to be on their way when Mitzi screamed from the gazebo. I heard her from our room on the 3rd floor and flew to the window. I couldn't see who it was through the trees but I saw Mitzi jump off the steps of the gazebo and race down the lane.

I hesitated for just a moment, then hurried down the stairs, more for Mitzi than myself. I threw the dish towel I had been wiping the table with, over my shoulder and ran out the front steps. I stood on the porch squinting my eyes to try and identify the figures. It was Daddy and Vern.

Everything in my soul gave a welcome sigh of relief and I too ran down the steps and along the road faster than I thought I ever could. I could see Daddy's smile 50 feet away and just stared in his eyes as I crashed into him and wrapped my arms around his neck. The tears couldn't help but come streaming from my eyes. I hadn't held my Daddy in almost 5 years. His smell, his back, his strength, his comfort all enveloped me, and I felt like a child again wanting to cower in my Daddy's coat when I was scared of something. I couldn't let go. His hands clutched my back so securely that I felt if I let go, I would feel as I had been before, lost and alone. I didn't want that. But he pulled away and looked at me.

"Ah, Virginia. So good to see you, girl," his voice sounded strong, solid, calming. So much so I hardly remembered Vern was standing right next to him.

I shook off my tears and emotional greeting and turned to Vern. "Hey, boy," I said grabbing him around the shoulders and 'bear hugging' him. "Aren't you all a sight for sore eyes."

"What are you all doing here now?" I said, finding composure as Vern scooped Mitzi up in his arms and swung her around. We all four turned and started walking very slowly toward the house.

"Mattie told me ya'll were here. When we got our orders about the same time, we decided to come be with family," Daddy said putting an arm around me and squeezing me tight.

"Mattie?" I said. "But when did she tell you we were here?"

"We talk," he said casually but with a hint that there was more. "Come on, let's get inside. I want to see those two grandbabies of mine."

That evening was one of the best of my life so far. We sat around the fireplace in Mrs. Gentry's apartment in the attic and laughed, reminisced, cried and caught up. The girls, although shy at first, quickly fell in love with Daddy. He was so warm and funny that you couldn't help find yourself drawn to him. I noticed Mrs. Gentry felt the same. As soon as she put the Foster kids to bed she hastily joined us. The girls fell asleep while Daddy told us stories of Pearl Harbor and Vern entertained us grown-ups with tales of wild women in shady ports.

~

It had been 3 weeks since Log Cabins and I hadn't heard from Creth. I don't know if I was grateful or irritated. Probably both. Daddy and I had some wonderful talks out in the gazebo but life was getting stale and I felt the time here had an expiration date.

"You know, you're married, Virginia," Daddy said one cloudy fall afternoon. Missouri autumns were always my favorite but Colorado got colder sooner than we did. I pulled my shawl a little tighter around my shoulders. "You gotta go back," he said.

"I can't Daddy. You don't know." I warned.

"Oh, I know," he said. "Creth is a drinker but he's not an abuser. You threatened him, remember?" He noted.

"I didn't threaten him," I interrupted.

"Really? Throwing a meat cleaver at a man that didn't lay a finger on you isn't threatening?" He quipped.

"I'm tired of him drinking all the time. He treats me like I'm nothing," I said coming to join him in the lounge seats bordering the interior of the gazebo.

"He loves you. He's already had a woman that didn't have kids and that's all he knows. He thinks you should be as invested in those girls as he is," he contended.

"Oh, I'm invested," I said.

"I know that but I don't think he does. Has he ever been cruel to you?" Daddy asked.

"Well, no, not really. Just rude and drunk. I'm tired of him being drunk all the time," I said crossing my legs and turning away perturbed.

"He loves those girls, Virginia. You gotta go back," he pleaded.

"I can't.... Go back? I just got out!" I exacted, maintaining my stand.

"You can't stay here. You have a family... and so do I," he said hesitantly as if there were more and he was waiting for my response so far.

I turned toward him but didn't say anything.

"I'm heading out to Oregon," he finally stated. "There's a good job out there and I need to get back on my feet before taking Mitzi with me."

"You're leaving?" I asked, trying to wrap my head around the implications of all that was just said.

"Yes," he said. "I'm leaving on Monday."

"That's in two days," I said, stating the obvious.

"Yes. You're going to be alright, Virginia. I know you won't like it, but Creth's coming to get you," he said with just a hint of reluctance in his voice wondering how I'd take that, no doubt.

"What?" I said, my mouth hanging open.

"He knew you were here. I told him. He's coming tomorrow on the train," he said. He knew it was out now.

There was nothing more he could have said about it. I was being hauled back to jail. My escape was over. I sat back in the chair. There was nowhere to run. Not when your closest kin rats you out. My mind was whirling. In reality, what else could I do? I had his kids. I couldn't just start up a new life here knowing he wanted to be with his girls. Maybe this break was a good thing. Maybe it was a really bad thing. Maybe he *would* now beat me for running away. My whole life *was* in Missouri. I had no idea what it was like living somewhere else. And he hadn't actually, ever hit me. I did have all I needed when it came to a roof over my head and food on the table. So what if I had to deal with a little irritation now and then? No. I was just trying to justify Creth's behavior.

But Daddy was honorable. If he thought Creth was a good man, why couldn't I? Did I just not see the quarrels between him and Mama? Were they just like us? Maybe it was me. Maybe I was the unreasonable one. He did ask me not to hire a babysitter and what did I do? Went and got one out of spite, just to have a day to myself. Was I selfish? I didn't know anymore. Daddy's perspective was clouding my own.

"Virginia? Are you hearing me?" Daddy said leaning in.

"Oh, I'm sorry, Daddy, what did you say?" I snapped out of it and realized he'd been talking to me the whole time.

"I said are you going to do the right thing?" he asked. He looked at me as if he was hanging on my answer.

"I... I guess so, Daddy," I said, not really knowing what the right thing was.

I didn't have enough time with Daddy and Vern. I suspected there was something going on with Mrs. Gentry and Daddy but it was none of my business, so I didn't pursue it. Monday came and Boris was to take Daddy and Vern to the train station in Boulder. Mitzi refused to go, saying she was used to us and living in Missouri, so we convinced Daddy to let her stay. She was whimpering and complaining that she didn't want to say goodbye to them again.

Creth was supposed to be coming later in the week and that left me anxious even though all I could really think of was Daddy and Vern leaving me, not knowing if I'd see them again. Oregon was so far away.

Daddy's sister Lela and her husband Martin Bridges lived in Klamath Falls Oregon and they would take Daddy and Vern for a while until Daddy got some money together to have a place of his own again. He had a little saved up from the war but not enough to buy anything permanent. The Martin's owned a 3 story apartment house in Klamath Falls and had a vacant unit that Daddy could rent for a while.

Dolores and Carol really didn't know what was going on but I sure did. I threw my arms around Daddy and held him so tight I thought he might go unconscious. He laughed, coughed and wiped away the tears. I gave Vern a manly hug and patted him on the back. He was his own man and had his own future ahead of him.

But it was Daddy I was having a hard time letting go of. I had barely got a chance to rekindle our relationship now that I was a married woman when he had to go. I didn't know why it had to happen so fast but I was grateful for the time I had with him... without Creth. I hardly remembered a time when it was just he and I. I could see his eyes getting wet and filled with tears when he pulled me in for one last hug. When I squeezed my eyes shut the tears just pushed out of mine. I felt a well of emotion stir in me and actually wept out loud. I didn't know if it was of relief, sorrow, pain, guilt, fear, or sadness. Maybe all of it. I couldn't hold it in any longer. Dolores just stared at me and started to whimper herself when she saw me cry.

Daddy and I both wiped our tears away and smiled trying to be brave. He scooped up Dolores and snuggled her close giving her a warning, "you be good to your Mama, alright?"

Dolores nodded with a dazed grin. He laughed and put her down. He picked up Carol and kissed her sweetly on the forehead. "Dear child," he said closing his eyes.

"Alright, enough of all this. We need to catch a train," he said and turned to get in the car where Boris and Vern were already waiting. Mitzi waved ferociously and Vern looked back through the rear window. Daddy reached a hand out of the car window as it bumped and galloped down the gravel driveway.

~

Later that week Creth showed up. He came into town on Friday and pulled up at the house about 4 pm. Mrs. Gentry, as always, was hospitable and cordial. I met him on the front steps and he greeted me with curious grace. He didn't yell, scream or demand. He just greeted us both kindly and asked to speak to me privately after a formal introduction of Mrs. Gentry and Boris.

I nodded and accepted his invitation to a stroll in the gardens. We walked in silence side by side for some time before he spoke.

"I know why you left me, Virginia," he said solemnly. When I didn't respond he kept talking. "I was drunk and didn't listen to you. I'm sorry for that."

He was always quick to apologize so I didn't know what made this time any different.

"George Lord has offered us a new place. The Spur in Excelsior Springs. He opened it just last week. He found someone else to man-age the Cabins and wants us to run The Spur. We'd have a better house, and you could have some help with the girls." He seemed re-ally excited and hopeful but to me, it only sounded like the first time he had this idea.

"Where would we live?" I asked, still walking beside him looking down at the grass.

"George has a house he's willing to rent to us about a block from the building. It's a real house, not just a cabin or apartment. You can set it up however you want and the girls can be with you in the restaurant. You can cook and be your own boss. I'll run the lounge and dance part of the business." He kept turning toward me as we walked, trying to convince me this was the better option. But better than what? We couldn't stay here much longer anyway.

"Can I get a babysitter every once in a while?" I asked. It was ne-gotiation time.

He turned with a jerk and looked down at his feet while we

walked, contemplating his answer. "I suppose if you have to. But you can have the girls at the restaurant with you," he said.

"I can't have these youngin's around a hot stove when things get busy. I'd step on them or run them over with hot gravy or oil. You want scarred, deformed children?" I questioned, hoping this would persuade him.

"Okay, okay. I understand. We'll work it out. I hear ya." And his tone conveyed to me that he really had.

He swung his arm down next to mine and tried to casually take my hand. At first, I jerked it away, then realizing the harshness of that behavior, softened my stance and smiled at him. I took his hand. "I'm sorry I almost killed you," I said with a blank but guilty, big-eyed look.

"I'm thankful you didn't. The door's a bit upset though..." he smiled.

I smiled and let out a comical huff. I wasn't sure if we should talk about that anymore. I didn't know if any other man would be grateful I didn't impale him with a meat cleaver and come 600 miles to find me and bring me home, not kicking and screaming anyway. We talked a little more about what had been going on in the last few weeks and how the next few months would look like when I came home. By the next Monday, all five of us were boarding the train in Boulder back to Kansas City and our new adventure in Excelsior Springs.

23

Figuring Things Out

"It came to pass at the end of forty days, that Noah opened the window of the ark which he had made:" Genesis 8:6

1946

Another Christmas came and went and as we prepared to move to Excelsior Springs once the snow melted things were getting back to a new normal. Creth was trying not to drink so much and spent most his days planning and prepping for The Spur once we got there. We rented a house about 3 blocks from the joint, which was literally a hole in the ground.

Excelsior Springs was built in a ravine or canyon and most people drove down to get to Main Street where The Spur was located. The building was constructed of concrete blocks that took up the entire block between Crown Hill Rd. and Kearney. The building had two parts, a restaurant on the east and a dancehall/lounge on the west. I would do the cooking for the restaurant and Creth would manage the lounge.

The lounge was a little smaller than the restaurant and had red leather booths lining the walls all the way around except for a small section near the front for the stage and the bar. In the center was the parquet dance floor. There were a couple of beams and poles carefully positioned at the corners next to the booths so they wouldn't get in the way of the dancers. The bar was thick, dark wood with a carved beveled railing around the edge so your drink wouldn't slide off and brass bar stools that squeaked when they swiveled no matter how often Creth oiled them. The wall behind the bar was well-equipped with every type of liquor and cordial imaginable and clean, pristine glasses hung upside down from the ceiling-mounted bar rack.

The restaurant was accessible through the side of the bar or from Kearney Street. It was your typical diner with matching red leather booths in front of the windows, a couple of aluminum tables and chairs in the middle and the diner bar with the same squeaky brass stools affixed to the floor, except these had padded red leather tops that matched the booths. Each table had a napkin dispenser, an ashtray, and salt and pepper shakers. Behind the bar was a wall separating the kitchen from the diners and was well stocked with coffee makers, filters, a soda machine, glasses, plates, bottles of soda and beer, and all the little details a customer might want with their meal. At the end of the bar was a glass case that housed the pies and cakes I would eventually make and serve.

By April everything was ready and we opened on a Friday morning greeting patrons with a large vinyl banner hung across the front of the building welcoming folks to The Spur. News of the opening had been in the paper for a week and when we unlocked the doors at 7 am we already had a line.

We had hired two local girls to help waitress and I was in the back ready for my first order. There was something liberating about it. I liked having something to do other than raise kids and manage a house. I felt like I had a purpose. I liked cooking and got a real delight from seeing the happy faces pleased with their eggs and hash or my *now-famous* biscuits.

The restaurant filled up fast and things were hopping. I got order after order and because I had made the menu easy and minimal to start, turning out plates of food quickly was straightforward. I had already been up since 3 am making sheets of biscuits so a quick warm-up in the oven was all it took before tossing them on the plate next to the corn beef hash, scrambled eggs, seared sausages from the flattop, and crispy potatoes with onions and garlic. The smell permeated the entire block drawing even more patrons in throughout the morning and by noon, we hadn't slowed down, only shifted the menu.

By now it was corn beef sandwiches, hot browns with roasted turkey and gravy, fried chicken from the cast iron skillet Mama had left me, ham steak with red-eye gravy made from the morning's coffee and broiled calf's liver with onions and bacon. Again, I had limited the menu until I got the hang of preparing everything the night before. I wanted to add on some fried catfish at some point but was still perfecting the dredge.

The girls took to the place like white on rice. They ran around the diner and folks didn't even seem to mind. Giddy and Mags, our waitresses, would scoop them up from time to time and carry them around the diner taking orders and delivering plates or refilling coffee. Often Carol and Dolores would sit in a booth and color or look through picture books and sometimes Creth would even come in during the day and take them out for a ride in the car to the park or river.

Mitzi started the 8th grade at Excelsior Springs High School and helped with the girls and at the restaurant as often as she could. She had really become quite a help to us. She was finding some friends at school and would hang out with them when she wasn't at the diner.

Things were going pretty smoothly and we settled into a decent rhythm. George Lord seemed pleased with our work and we were actually saving a little money. Creth's sister Aunt Meryle helped out at the diner when we needed extra hands. The lounge side of The Spur was also going well. It was busy almost every night except Monday when we all took a break. I would work the diner until about 4 and then clean and close up and Creth would take over in the lounge. Bobby Jenkins was the bartender, and he could throw around those bottles so fast you'd think a bullet just whizzed by. People would come in from all over the county for his coffee nudge and Tom Collins. We'd have live music nearly every night from some up-and-comer in the county or even from Kansas City and they would play for tips, so we didn't have to keep them on our books.

The months flew by quickly with so much going on. Before we knew it another year or two had come and gone. By 1948 Mitzi was preparing to graduate in the spring and we had been managing The Spur for 3 years now. George Lord was happy with our employment even though we had gone through about 10 waitresses and 4 bartenders in that time. I expanded the menu to include waffles and pancakes for breakfast with fruit when we could get it cheap and fried fish, chicken soup and shrimp cocktail just to name a few. My sweet potato pie and lemon chiffon were always the first to go.

The girls had started school at the Moore Schoolhouse just outside of town. Mitzi would walk them in the morning and I'd pick them up in the afternoon. It was a two-room schoolhouse. One room was for grades first through fourth and the other for grades fifth through eighth. On Saturday and Sunday, the girls would be at the diner crawling over booths and sliding on the freshly waxed dancefloor in their socks.

It was May and Carol and Dolores had just gotten out of school for the summer. They would race back and forth from the diner to the lounge in the mornings since the dancehall wasn't open yet. By lunchtime, the place was slammed. The girls kept getting caught underfoot and I'd yell at them to be still and go somewhere else. When I came out of the kitchen with a pan full of drippings Dolores ran by me so fast her hand bumped my elbow and the hot juice spilled all over the front of me and the floor. I lost it, right there in front of all the patrons.

"Dammit, Dolores! Get out of here!" I screamed. Meryle rushed over to help clean up the mess. My apron and dress shielded most of me from the hot liquid, but I was still covered. I tore off my apron and threw it on the floor to mop up the mess. The next thing I heard was screaming from the lounge. "Good lord, my blood pressure," I said pushing my hand off of my knee as I got up off the floor. I threw the door of the lounge open to see Dolores screaming on the floor with her hand over her eye and Carol standing over her with a shocked look on her face.

I rushed over to the girls. "What happened?" I hollered. "Move your hand Dolores, let me see."

She screamed again when I tried to pull her hand away but my strength was no match for her will power. She had a cut just to the side of her nose and blood started to cascade down her cheek and onto her dress. "What happened? What did you do?" I said looking at Carol as if she was responsible.

"Nothing Mama," she said sheepishly. "She fell," was all I could get out of her.

"I hit the booth," Dolores said through cries and sobs. Her face was now almost completely red with salty tears and blood. I sat down on the floor with her and took my dress, already ruined from the stock, and held it up to the cut to stop the bleeding.

"Well, if you two wouldn't be so wild around here running everywhere this wouldn't have happened!" I said scornfully with pursed lips and an irritated tone.

"I'm sorry, Mama," Carol said with a frown and big eyes like she was ready to cry.

I pulled Dolores into my lap and rocked her still holding her face firm to stop the bleeding. Her sobs diminished and she snuggled a little closer to my chest. I pulled my dress-covered finger away from her face and inspected the damage. It was a cut only about a half-inch long, but it would probably turn into a black eye. "You're lucky you didn't get your eye," I said firmly. "Now pull yourself together and let's go clean up. "

When the three of us walked into the house Creth was in the kitchen making coffee. "Why didn't you just come to the diner for a cup?" I questioned.

He turned around and saw the sight of us all, wet, bloody, and messy, and ran to Dolores. "What happened? What did you do to my girl?" He demanded.

I cocked my head back and to the side with a wide-eyed, shocked look on my face. I furrowed my brows, "What did *I* do? What makes you think this was my fault?" I inquired. I couldn't believe he was actually accusing me of injuring our daughter.

"Well, what happened?" He asked, still demanding, and turning her head this way and that for a closer inspection. "Are you hurt too, Carol?" He turned toward her and gave her a quick scan.

"No, she's not hurt. Good lord. These two hellions were running in the lounge and ran into a booth." I said irritated that I had to explain it like this. I felt as if I needed to explain even more information than I knew.

"Well, where were you? Why weren't you watching them?" He demanded.

"Are you kiddin' me? What I do all the time! Cooking. I can't cook 13 orders of fried chicken and watch two heathens at the same time," I spat back. "Do you see me? I'm covered cause a' these two!" I left the scene in the living room and headed for the bedroom to change my clothes. I pulled the dress over my head careful not to get the grease in my hair. I left it on the floor while I grabbed another from the closet. Our room was bigger than the one at Log Cabins and this house had three bedrooms instead of two so Mitzi could have her own room. The kitchen and living room were similar but we actually had a dining room, which was ironic now since most every meal was had at the diner. I adjusted the simple floral dress and went back to the living room. Creth now had Dolores on his lap in the rocking chair consoling her although I think she'd had enough coddling at this point.

"She's fine, but now she's your problem," I said. "I gotta get back," I said and headed for the door.

Just before I grabbed the knob, I heard Creth say under his breath, "a good Mama wouldn't let this happen."

I stopped and closed my eyes, my hand still on the doorknob. I thought quick. I could keep walking out or I could turn and confront that statement. I decided on the latter.

"What did you just say?" I turned toward him and put both hands on my hips. "I know you didn't just say that to me."

He looked up still clutching Dolores and rocking. Carol had found something to keep her occupied in her room. "I *didn't* say that to you," he started looking down and rocking more feverishly.

"So, you're telling Dolores I'm a no-good mother, huh?" I paused for an answer that I knew was not coming. "How dare you. I'm doing all of this for you!" I shouted. That was it. Six months of minor irritations had reached their limit. Little jabs here and there about the way I cooked, cleaned, raised our kids, slept with him or not slept with him and even how I talked to diners had reached a boiling point.

"I am *not* your slave!" I exclaimed. "We're supposed to be in this together, you and me. I'm tired of feeling like I'm never good enough and that you're the perfect parent all the time. Well who's there to tuck them into bed at night and who's there to make sure they get up and to school on time?"

I could see his face getting flustered and hot, but he couldn't move with Dolores in his arms. He gently put her down and she ran to the bedroom to avoid the vocal shrapnel.

"I can't be there at those times and you know it!" He stammered back getting up out of the rocker. He came close to me and leaned in. "You never wanted them. I can see it all over you," he accused. "Why should you care what happens to them?"

"How can you say that? I love those girls otherwise I wouldn't have taken them to Colorado," I said, dragging up the past.

"Oh you did that just to hurt me, and while we're still on that subject, I had to go 600 miles to get my family back, so don't tell me I'm not in this." His voice got firmer, ready to continue the fight. He threw his hands up in the air to emphasize the '600 miles'.

"I didn't ask you to come get us," I said.

"Oh, I know. Lucky you got someone else in your family with a brain to try and knock some sense into that thick skull," he said arrogantly, referring to Daddy.

Before he could flinch, I slapped him across the face. He grabbed my arm before it had a chance to fall back to my side. "Hit me," I said, "you know you want to. Just give me an excuse," I taunted.

"You don't need an excuse to walk out," he said sarcastically. He let go of my arm and looked down and around the room. He lumbered with long strides around me and grabbed his hat slamming the door behind him. Dolores and Carol were both crying now.

~

The very next day Creth was outside our house digging post holes and cutting lumber for a fence. I didn't go back to the diner after our fight that day but let Meryle handle the kitchen, which she could if she had to. I slept in Mitzi's room that night and Creth got up early and left before any of us had a chance to stir. He came back an hour later with fence materials and started sawing and digging by 8 am.

I dressed and went to the diner while Mitzi got the girls ready for the day. It was a slow morning, for which I was grateful as it gave me time to think and re-evaluate. By the time I got home that afternoon, Creth had nearly the entire yard fenced. I didn't even ask or talk to him but went inside and started on housework. He left shortly thereafter for the lounge and hadn't gotten home by the time we went to bed.

The next day was Monday and we all had the day off. Creth was up early again finishing the fence. When he had it all connected to the house and completely enclosed he stood back to admire his work. I came out onto the porch with two coffee cups in my hand, a peace offering perhaps. I handed him the cup and he looked at me suspiciously.

"Do I dare?" He asked.

"If I wanted to poison you I would have done it a long time ago," I said with a circumspect grin.

He cautiously gripped the cup and took a sip not taking his eyes off me. I looked away and sipped my own coffee. "What's all this about?" I asked gesturing toward the newly built fence.

"I gotta keep those girls safe this summer and they can't be running in the diner making messes and hurting themselves... or others" He took another drag of his coffee then set it down on the porch railing and pulled out a cigarette. He handed me one and I obliged. We had become experts at this subtle way we made up; not really talking or resolving anything but just going back to normal in a couple of days.

I nodded at his ingenuity and quick work, letting the coffee soak my insides and the nicotine calm my mind. The girls came out on the porch and stopped short when they saw the two of us in close proximity to each other. They seemed to evaluate the situation and saw that there was no war going on between us at the moment so they continued their jumping and dancing off the porch and spun around the yard close to the fence.

I sat down on the porch step and sucked on my cigarette watching them, thinking what it must feel like to be so free and nonchalant. Creth leaned on the porch railing and drained his coffee. The girls ran to the corner of the yard and tried to jump up and reach the top of the fence to no avail. Dolores then grabbed a bucket from the side of the house, her eye now completely engulfed in a purple bruise, and took it to the corner where she climbed on top and reached a hand to Carol. She pulled herself up and together they pushed against one side of the fence while Dolores pushed Carol up toward the other side of the corner far enough that Carol could reach the top of the fence. She hung there a minute and then threw her leg up onto the top and flung herself over.

Creth and I just stood there watching this acrobatic maneuver. When Carol actually made it over I threw my hand over my mouth to stifle the laugh that I couldn't hide. Creth threw his cigarette down in disbelief and just stood there, mouth gaping open. Carol ran around to the gate, which was only accessible from the outside or from a taller grown-up over the fence, opened it and Dolores ran through to join her sister. All that work... for nothing.

I couldn't help it. I laughed out loud and had to set my coffee cup down for fear of spilling it. My laugh turned to a cough and Creth just stood there in amazement. He looked at me, saw I couldn't keep it together and joined in my humor. What could you do? At least the house had a fence now. We both laughed, somehow resetting our relationship and once again we were both on the same side.

2 4

Hilda

"It came to pass, while there was war between the house of Saul and the house of David, that Abner made himself strong for the house of Saul." 2 Samuel 3:6

1948

Mitzi graduated in June when she was just 16 and went to work at the diner full time. A young man named Jim Brassea would come by every week to deliver the fuel for the oil stove in the kitchen. We didn't recognize him at first until he said something

"Hey there, remember me?" Jim asked as he hauled in the fuel one Thursday afternoon. It wasn't busy and I was just wiping off some tables.

"Oh, I'm sorry, no. What's your name again?" I said politely, wiping my hands on my apron to shake his.

"I'm Jim Brassea. My mom and pop ran the grocery store in

Elmira. Pete and Catherine Brassea!" He shook my hand and held it a moment as I thought.

Jim was a large, young man with a long face.

"Oh, why yes! Well, little Jimmy Brassea? How the hell are ya?" I said and pulled him in for a quick hug.

Pete and Catherine ran the grocery store in the small community next to Log Cabins. We would occasionally run over there when we were low on ice or cigarettes. Jimmy, along with his sisters Marie and Lucile, would be running in and out or in the backroom doing homework so I really never got a good look at them.

"How's your folks?" I asked sitting at the diner bar and grabbing a cigarette.

"They're good. Still running the store. I graduated last year and got this job. I'm sharing an apartment in the city with a friend," he said.

Mitzi walked between us with a tub of dirty dishes. Jim's gaze followed her past me and into the kitchen. When I could see he was not interested in my conversation anymore I spoke up with more intriguing topics.

"Mitzi has just graduated too. You remember her?" I asked. He shook his head slightly and snapped back to reality with me.

"Oh, uh, Mitzi?" He questioned.

"Yes. Mitzi dear, come here." I heard her put down the tub of dishes. "Do you remember Jim Brassea? From Elmira? You know, next to Log Cabins?" I kept talking while she came out of the kitchen in a shy, not wanting to talk, sort of way.

"Yeah, I guess so," She said, looking at Jim and then smiling a cool grin when he wouldn't stop staring at her.

"Well," I said. "Thank you, Jim, for the fuel. I'm sure we'll see you next week." I got up and left the conversation to see if they would carry it on alone. They didn't. Jim tipped his hat and muffled a "ma'am" and wheeled his cargo back out the door. Mitzi turned and went back into the kitchen. I snickered and went back to wiping tables.

~

Daddy sent a letter in July saying he had met and married a Hilda Dammand in Klamath Falls, Oregon. We were taken aback but not shocked. It had been nearly a decade since Mama's death, and he had been through war, famine, trial, desertion, and home-lessness. It was time he had some happiness.

He moved to Klamath Falls in 1946 and stayed with his sister Lela and her husband Martin for a couple of weeks in the apartment complex they owned. He got a job as the custodian for the Klamath High School. Hilda worked in the school cafeteria but strangely enough also lived in the same apartment building that Lela and Martin owned. They eventually started walking to school together and one thing led to another.

Hilda was a small woman, smaller than Mama although Mama was not a large woman at all. Mama just had more 'meat on her bones' as they say even though she wasn't fat like some of the women I'd seen hanging around the diner. But Hilda was smaller nonethe-less. She was frail and thin but seemed like she could wallop you if you gave her enough of a reason. She had dirty blonde hair, fair skin and long fingers with perfect nails that looked like she'd come straight from the salon although I never thought she ever spent money on that sort of wastefulness. She always wore floral dresses that hit her about mid-calf with a tight waist and a button-down blouse. She would tie her hair up behind her head in an almost school-marm style. What Daddy saw in her I'll never know but I think he missed the companionship. Daddy talked about their rela-tionship more as if she was a good school friend than a lover. He said they'd married at the courthouse in Multnomah and were plan-ning on moving back to Missouri.

Daddy had saved about $5,000 and wanted to resurrect his idea of a Missouri farm. He said he was planning on moving home in a month or two. He decided on Purdy, where he purchased a small farmhouse and 2 acres. He said he'd be coming into town soon and would love to see me and the girls as soon as possible. I wrote back congratulating him on his nuptials and couldn't wait to see him. Vern, on the other hand, decided to stay in Oregon for a while as he had a good job at a machine shop making welding casings for bulldozers and didn't want to miss out on all the money he was making.

By September Daddy and Hilda had made their way to Missouri and started to settle in. Purdy was about 200 miles from Excelsior Springs so it wasn't like I could pop over anytime I wanted. We had to make a special trip down to see Daddy and when we did it was like a family reunion all over again.

They first came through Excelsior Springs before heading south and we had supper all ready for them. It was nice to have a good meal at home for a change instead of at the diner all the time. Daddy and Creth caught up on 'old times' and the girls drove Daddy crazy crawling all over him while he tried to sit and relax after dinner. I attempted to ignore the annoyance and get to know Hilda. There was a bit of resistance with me in knowing her and I figured it was just because she was not Mama. It was nothing against Hilda I was sure, just the constant reminder that Mama wasn't here anymore.

"Have you ever been to Missouri before?" I asked Hilda, pouring her a cup of coffee and sitting down at the now cleaned off table after dinner. I pulled a cigarette and a lighter from my apron pocket and flicked the flint, sucking in on the fragrant stick filling my lungs with the calming vapors. She took a sip of her coffee watching me inhale a second or two, before she spoke.

"No, not really. I believe we passed through when I was young. My family's from back east and we moved to the west coast when I was 9, so if we did I don't remember it." She took another sip and let her eyes wander around the room.

"Well, I think you'll like it. It gets pretty hot in the summer, not like where you're from I'm sure, but we also have some serious winters. I kinda like it. I feel like we get all four seasons," I paused to take a sip of my coffee and a puff of my cigarette. When she didn't respond to that I continued. "Fall is my favorite, though. And there's about two to three weeks in Spring that's mild. It's a great time to plant winter crops if you're planning on having a garden." She smiled and nodded. It was getting awkward. "I miss our garden. We had one at our first house on the farm but there's not enough space here and I really don't have time to tend to it being at the diner all the time."

"Yes," she said seeming to spark something she could talk about. "Do you like working at the diner? You're the cook, right?" She asked.

"Oh yes. I love cooking. My Mama taught me how to cook all sorts of things and I'm teaching Mitzi." The words came out so fast I wondered if the topic of Mama was uncomfortable for her. I pushed the thought aside. "Do you cook?"

"Yes, some. I'm teaching Nora how to do a few of the things I can do," she said.

I looked confused. "Nora?" I asked.

"My daughter," she said.

Well, this was news. I didn't know she had a daughter. Daddy didn't say anything about Nora, and by the way, where was she? "Where's Nora now?" I asked.

"Oh, she's with her grandparents and will come out on the train when we're settled," she said and looked down at her coffee, swirling her cup.

I assume Daddy knew this. Wow, so I had a stepsister. I wondered what she was like. "How old is she?" I asked.

"Eight," she answered, and nothing more.

Creth and Daddy were having a completely opposite conversation than we were. Between trying to repeat each other over the commotion of the girls and catching up from years of being apart they finally got as much out as they could. Daddy and Hilda wanted to head on down and try and get to Purdy before midnight. We said our goodbyes and I was glad Daddy wasn't so far away anymore even though he belonged to someone else now.

25

A Wedding

"It came to pass, as, in the days of Noah, they did eat, they drank, they married wives, they were given in marriage..." Luke 17:26-27

It was nice having Daddy within a few hours' drive away. He seemed happy with Hilda although I couldn't quite figure her out. Nora came out about a month after they moved in as Hilda had said and I was able to meet her at Christmas time. We all went down in December to spend Christmas with Daddy, Hilda, and Nora. They had fixed up an old farmhouse, but it still had a ways to go. However, it was livable, and we were able to stay with them a couple of nights. The girls slept on the floor and Creth and I took the upstairs loft. The house was small but cozy and seemed just perfect for the three of them.

Daddy said as soon as the ground thawed, they would start on the garden. The plot of land was just shy of an acre but plenty enough for a good-sized garden and a little barn. It was too cold to get chicks yet, but Nora was excited to assume the role of a chicken farmer as soon as spring delivered the first-of-the-season chicks. Daddy spent most days constructing a chicken house and pen and true to his word, as soon as the last frost came and went, he and Hilda started on rototilling the garden. They were making a new home for themselves, a fresh start, Daddy said. But sometimes I thought he was just trying to forget Mama.

We were still doing fine at The Spur and I was cooking up a storm nearly every day. Mitzi and Jim started dating in the fall of 1948 and by the start of 1949 were considering getting married. The new year also brought a shock from Daddy. I got a letter in February saying that Hilda missed Oregon too much and they were moving back. I couldn't believe it. They had just gotten here and were leaving again. Daddy said he was going to come up and get Mitzi and take her too.

When I read this out loud to the family one evening Mitzi jumped up from the table and said, "I'm not going! I'm tired of moving around and Jim and I are getting married! I can't leave now!" She sounded angry at first, yet her voice trailed off in apprehension.

"I'll ask Daddy if you can stay," I said trying to calm her down. "He probably just thinks he's still responsible for you, so he needs to take you with him." I folded the letter and set it back on the mantle.

"It's okay, I'm sure it's fine," I said, tying on my apron to clear and clean the evening dishes. Mitzi wrung her hands and still looked worried. "Look," I said and turned to face her putting both my hands on her shoulders, "If you're going to be married soon you won't be anyone's concern anymore but your husband's." I smiled hoping this would calm her and make her think more about upcoming nuptials than moving across the country.

Creth was reading the newspaper by the fireplace and hadn't even looked up in all the commotion. "Do you have any words of wisdom here, Creth?" I said, trying to get something encouraging out of him.

"I don't care what she does. She's a grown woman," he mumbled not even looking up from his paper. He kept rocking in the chair and flipping the pages of the paper. I turned back to Mitzi and rolled my eyes and smirked. She mirrored my movements to suggest we understood each other. I gave her a gentle hug and said, "Now, help me with the dishes."

~

Daddy was able to sell the farm to a local man and with the money they had, moved back to Klamath Falls. Daddy's nephew Jerry got him a job at Fairhaven elementary school about 5 miles out of town. There was an old parsonage house attached to the school that Daddy and Hilda were able to rent for a while. Nora went to school there and Hilda worked in the small cafeteria. I don't know if Daddy was happy being in Oregon but I knew Hilda was and that was probably enough for him.

Mitzi and Jim were married that fall. They had been dating for almost a year. Every time Jim brought fuel into the restaurant they would chat and visit. Their visits were getting longer every time and eventually, he asked her out on a real date, somewhere away from the restaurant. They spent nearly every moment together when they weren't working. Part of me assumed Mitzi just wanted out of her current lifestyle and the other part considered she wanted to start a life of her own. Either way, she was getting there fast, and I couldn't blame her.

Vern had come out from Oregon for the wedding along with Daddy, Hilda, and Nora. It was good to see him. Although he was just a couple of years older than Mitzi and a few younger than me, he looked like a grown man now. And he was. He had a good job in Klamath Falls and was saving his money. He didn't quite know for what just yet, but I told him that was okay. Having a nest egg set aside is good insurance.

Jim's two sisters, Marie and Lucille, were Mitzi's bridesmaids along with a friend from school. We held the reception at The Spur in the dancehall and as the party dragged on into the night, I noticed Vern spending more and more time with Marie Brassea. I thought about all the young love floating around the dancehall that night and how I never got to experience it myself. My life had been thrust upon me whether I liked it or not. My heart ached for the past before Mama died, when there was so much hope on the horizon. It was a difficult time but at least it was our own. I didn't feel my life was my own now at all and hadn't since I married Creth and took on grown-up responsibilities. Everyone should be able to have that 'young love' feeling at some point. I hadn't married for love but for necessity and convenience. Part of me felt like my life was already over and part of me felt I hadn't even begun to live.

The guests were getting drunker by the minute and with Creth opening up the bar, there was no telling when this party was going to end. But Mitzi looked genuinely happy. Happier than I think I'd ever seen her. Jim swung her around the floor in her long, cream and lace wedding gown with the train trailing behind her. Vern and Marie let the whiskey open their mouths a little more than normal and were talking up a storm in the corner. I don't believe I ever saw Vern interested in something or someone so keenly.

Carol and Dolores held hands and spun around the dancefloor in their pink taffeta gowns. I didn't care that it was 3 hours past their bedtime. Everyone was having such a joyful time I couldn't spoil it even for them. Creth had his arm around the DJ's shoulder swaying with the music, obviously drunk and Daddy and Hilda danced close to each other, seemingly dancing to their own tune. I smiled a little to myself thinking of Daddy. I was glad he was getting his second chance at happiness. A fleeting thought raced through my mind wondering if I would ever have my first chance.

My life had not been easy. Both girls were a challenge and not only coming into this world but being so close together. It was almost like having twins if I could imagine what that must have been like. On one hand, the girls were playmates, entertaining each other on a daily basis but on the other, they were so close in age that they wore me out constantly. They were always conniving and scheming something awful to get away with or getting into something. They would use each other as a distraction while one got into the pie case at the restaurant or manipulated potato pancakes away from the line cook saying they were delivering them to a customer. I had to be on my toes all the time and between that and cooking at the restaurant, I felt like I didn't have a moment to myself.

Maybe everyone feels like this. Maybe I had no right to feel this way. Sometimes I felt selfish and other times justified. I would see lovers come into the restaurant and sit across from each other or sometimes sit on the same side so their shoulders touched, and I watched as they ogled each other and stared into each other's eyes as they intertwined their fingers and giggled. The rational side of me rolled my eyes and huffed in a skeptical fashion. Who does that, I'd think? Who really feels like that? That can't be real. It can't last. It won't. My cynicism was showing through dramatically and I was only 26. I felt myself getting hardened to the idea of real love for me. I didn't deserve it. It wouldn't happen for me. This was my life and I better get used to it, even though I tried hard to resist the gnawing that I needed to just get over it.

But watching Mitzi and Jim twirling on the dancefloor gave me a little hope. Not for me, but for them. I had heard parents say that as long as their kids had a better life than they did, that's all that mattered. Even though Mitzi wasn't my kid, that sense shot through me and I resigned to it. This is your life, Virginia. Get used to it.

That evening after the wedding party drained the last of the keg and we had to get cabs for most of the guests, Creth and I finished cleaning up the bar even though Creth stumbled through most of it and bumped into booths and banged into bar stools. I had had a couple gin and tonics so I too was feeling a bit warm but nothing that couldn't sober me up enough to clean and tidy and lock the place up. The girls had fallen asleep in one of the booths and Creth and I picked up a girl each and headed out the door. We walked the few blocks home and put them into their beds sometime around 2 am. I staggered into the bedroom and removed my dress and slip. As I was unrolling my nylons Creth took off his shirt and knelt at my feet. I sat in the chair by the door and stuck my leg out to unroll the stocking. He stopped me and replaced my hands with his and continued to unroll the stockings while he stared at me with a drunken grin.

I sat back in the chair. The gin had clouded my resistance and I watched him unroll the nylons off my toes. I voluntarily propped the other foot up for him to do the same. His hands then followed the length of my legs up to my girdle. His hands slid around my hips and gripped the top edge of my panties and girdle and in one movement slid them off down my hips and thighs. I didn't resist; probably because of the gin and probably because of the evening. He hadn't irritated me too much today and we weren't fighting at the moment. I needed some connection even if it was Creth.

1951

"George has a new plan for us, V!" Creth said late one afternoon in September. We had been managing the Spur for several years now and the girls were still attending the Moore School, which had grown to 4 classrooms and about 50 students. Vern and Marie got married in 1949 and moved to Higginsville, Missouri. Vern got a job at Southwestern Bell Telephone but only worked there about 4 years when Daddy insisted he should come to live in Oregon. Vern and Marie said they wanted to start a family away from all the drama and chaos he said was in Missouri. I didn't know what he meant by that but it's probably because I was right in the middle of it. Before they moved, Marie got pregnant and had a baby boy. They named him Michael and I just barely got to spend what felt like 5 minutes with the child and they were gone. I, on the other hand, was still in Missouri.

I had just closed up the restaurant and got home in time to welcome the girls from school and start dinner when Creth burst in with his 'great' idea.

"He's building a new place out on 69. Wants you to be the cook. I can manage this and the new place as it's just a diner. But Buddy's got this place covered so you can work out the menu there, all on your own, whatever you want. George loves your cookin' and trusts you to come up with whatever you want. Whatcha say?"

Buddy was our line cook that had been working with us for 3 years. A black man whose Christian name was Nathanial Lyons but everyone called him Buddy. He was about 6'3" with midnight black skin and large lips that looked like a bee had stung him twenty times. He had broad shoulders and bulging muscles from years of hauling logs and timber from his previous job as a logger in the Ozarks. He'd been loyal, a quick learner and an even better teacher to those that had come and gone in his kitchen. He was clearly capable of taking over the kitchen, so long as people didn't get all prejudice of a negro running things back there. People were odd. You never knew who you would upset but as long as he stayed behind the wall in the kitchen, no one would be the wiser.

"So, wait, what's going on?" I said trying to find the common sense in his statements and bring some reality to it. "Another place?" I vexed, in an almost exhausted tone.

"He's going places, V," Creth said, puttering around the house looking for something. He finally found what he was searching for; a scrap of paper and pen to take some notes, I assumed. "We're his right-hand men," he expressed, sitting at the table, licking the end of the pen and scribbling something on the paper he had procured.

"What's this place, then?" I said, tying my apron around my waist and scrubbing carrots under the sink.

"Uh, The Green Diner," Creth exclaimed, not looking up from his paper.

"Green Diner? Why on earth would he call it that?" I asked, not turning from the sink but turning my attention to the potatoes that had to be scrubbed next.

"I don't know. Something about the trees around the area, or something," he said, voice trailing off. I knew this didn't matter and he didn't care why it was called anything only that he was managing yet another hopefully successful business. "I think he wants to paint it green too," Creth said under his breath.

"Well, couldn't he just name it anything he wanted and paint it any other color?" I asked.

"I don't know... maybe he got a good deal on some green paint. Don't bother me with the details, Virginia, goodness." He seemed frustrated. I still didn't know what he was writing on his paper but he quickly stuffed it into his shirt pocket and got up. I kept scrubbing the vegetables and tossed them into a pot. I filled it with water and set it on the stove. I opened the refrigerator for something that resembled protein but there was just an old chicken carcass wrapped in wax paper. I took it out and dumped it into the pot. At least the broth would be flavorful.

Part 3

26

The Green Diner

"It came to pass that when Abram was come into Egypt, the Egyptians beheld the woman that she was very fair." Genesis 12:14

I was very fair. You couldn't really tell what color my skin was because I had so many freckles on my milky skin that I looked like one of those drawings you'd see in a comic book where the red dots almost completely covered women's skin tone. I was just fair, so fair that 20 minutes in the direct sun would toast me like a marshmallow and I didn't get that golden-brown tan either like other women with olive skin. I got as red as a lobster. Avon made a decent cover-up that helped me work in the garden for a little longer than 20-minute sprints, but nothing helped as much as just staying out of the sun. Missouri summers were hot, and it was torture not joining the girls at the local swimming hole but instead shielding myself under the largest shade tree I could find, donned with a large, brimmed hat and oversized sunglasses.

My hair had not muted in the slightest either as I entered my late 20s and I gave up trying to hide it anymore. I kept it in a short bob with curls around my face. My wire-rimmed glasses hid a lot of my face but without them, I was as blind as a bat.

The announcement of the Green Diner proposition seemed exhausting, what with two little girls still running rampant through the restaurant but it was easier now that they were in school. The Green Diner was up on Hwy 69 just outside the city limits of Excelsior Springs Missouri. It was a great location that George had procured, right where the highway split into two directions around the town so folks coming and going could easily pull in for a bite. People had to be quick too because the diner only had 12 bar stools and 4 tables, half of which could only seat 2 people. The diner opened May 11, 1951, and George and I had been going over the menu for the past 3 weeks as the construction crew finished up the details. I was happy to leave The Spur as it just was too rough in the evenings.

Creth was managing both places but stayed primarily at The Spur where his talents were needed a little more. The diner was so small it was easy to handle by me and a waitress named Lila. She was no more than 18 with sandy blonde hair she kept wrapped up in a red plaid kerchief and a large curl over her forehead. She was a sweet thing and a hard worker. She said she was earning money for a car but at our wages, she had a ways to go.

The diner smelled new even though George acquired a couple of used ovens and flat tops from a restaurant in Kansas City that was closing. The seats, counters, floors, and tables were all shiny and new and I almost didn't want to dirty the bar counter with one drop of coffee. We didn't serve alcohol, which was a nice change from The Spur and we closed at 4 p.m. giving me enough time to get home before the girls. However, I did have to be up and out the door by 5 a.m. since we opened at 6 a.m. and coffee needed to be hot and ready and the fresh rolls we let rise all night needed baking first thing.

Those mornings were some of my favorite moments of my early years. Lila didn't get in until 7 a.m. so for about an hour and a half the place was all mine. I would turn the key to the front door and hear the fa.m.iliar bell signaling life entering the place, flip on the lights and turn on the ovens. It was quiet except for the dripping of the coffee into the pot and the quick whoosh of the ovens kicking the gas into high gear. Soon after sliding the rolls and loaves into the oven, the small cafe would fill with the most heavenly scent. That, with the coffee and my first cigarette of the day, was the peaceful solace I looked forward to.

Creth and I had been growing farther apart. He would stay late at The Spur and I would rise early for the diner. We hardly saw each other much less communicated. Even our days off didn't coincide. We were just roommates sharing a house. Creth got the girls off in the morning and I saw them safely home in the evening. We co-parented pretty well but any love that was once blooming had eventually died on the vine. This suited me though, as there wasn't any time for fighting either.

Between the two places, we brought in enough money to maintain our humble home and even save a bit here or there. The girls were quickly growing out of their clothes faster than I could mend them, but they seemed happy and in their own little world most of the time.

One fall afternoon the school called me saying Carol had fallen and possibly broken her ankle. I was in the thick of cleaning up the lunch rush so I called Creth at The Spur to go get her and take her to the doctor. He reluctantly obliged but really had no choice since at the moment I was the busier parent. After a quick once over at the clinic assessing a sprain rather than break, Creth stopped to get fuel for the car while Carol sat in the passenger seat and waited. As soon as Creth went in to pay, Carol opened the glove box and found his stash of chew. *Red Man* was Creth's brand and it came in a green bag with large red lettering. You couldn't miss it. Carol quickly snagged a pinch and shoved it into her mouth to see what it was like. She tried stuffing it in her front lip like her dad. She bent over to read-just it not noticing Creth coming back to the car. He jumped in the driver's seat and gave her a firm and swift slap on the back. "How was that, Carol?" She coughed in shock, tried to spit and instead swallowed the soggy, black bulge in response. She instantly turned green and by the time I got home at 5 p.m. she was sleeping off several violent vomiting episodes.

"Why would you have that stuff where she could get it?" I demanded.

"Oh, not you too," Creth fumed, loosening his tie and waving me off with his hand. He still had remnants of sick on his shirt.

"Well, what were you thinking?" I asked walking behind him into the bedroom.

"Nothing! I always have it in there. Why's it my fault she decided to be an idiot?" He threw his tie on the bed and started unbuttoning his shirt. "She won't be doing that again any time soon."

He brushed past me to the closet and grabbed another button-down. "She can get to your cigarettes just as easily so don't be giving me any guff about it. This is not my fault. If anything, I'm glad she did! Now she knows and she might stay away from it a little longer." He threw the shirt around his shoulders.

I didn't know what to say even though I wanted to argue and defend myself. I was so sick of his spit cups all over the house and my ashtrays paled in comparison. He was probably right but I would never admit it. I rolled my eyes and stomped out of the room.

"You know I gotta get back," he said, finishing the last button on his shirt and grabbing his coat. "Wash that up for me, will ya?" He threw the stained and putrid shirt at me. I wasn't prepared for the toss and it struck my face. I had to breathe through my mouth to avoid vomiting myself from the stench.

I didn't respond. There was no time, and it was no use. He slammed the door behind him, and I set to work on the stain at the kitchen sink.

~

Our menu at the diner was always changing depending on what I could get that week. Our standards kept us busy with returning regulars, and tourists stopping through kept the revolving ingredients fresh. Our burgers, french fries, bacon sandwiches, and liver and onions were always popular and oatmeal, eggs, pancakes, and my famous biscuits were loved by the breakfast patrons. Specials came and went like fresh trout or fried catfish, chicken fried steak when cube steak was cheap, and tuna salad on toast when the local A&P had crates of discounted tins.

Ground beef was usually easy to come by, so it went in everything; chili, ha.m.burgers and cheeseburgers, chipped beef on toast and patty melts. Keeping patrons satiated with meat was an important job so when our supplier said they had run out for two weeks, I started to panic. He said he had some offcuts at a discount if I wanted them. No one else took his offer prior to our delivery stop so I agreed. The vendor pulled out a large, rectangular box from the back of his truck parked behind the restaurant and flopped it on the kitchen counter. He flipped up the box flaps and I peered in, not sure what I was looking at.

"Gotcha some tongue and heart in here, maybe a couple tripe and lots of liver," he said matter of factly. He put his hands on his hips looking for a quick reply.

"What can I do with it?" I asked.

"Don't matter none to me. You want it or not? I can't get ya no ground till next Thursday."

"Alright. I'll take it," I said, reaching into my apron pocket for a pen to sign the delivery. He whipped out his clipboard stuffed in his trousers behind his back and thumbed a couple of pages up for the right document. I signed and he spun around and exited the kitchen holding up the clipboard in a nod of departure.

The heavy kitchen door shut solidly behind him and I opened the box top again that had fallen shut. The unorthodox parts were wrapped in clear plastic, but it just looked like a bag of dark, red, slimy meat. This was no time to be squeamish. I could figure out what to do with this or die trying and I'm pretty sure no one died trying to make a heart burger before.

I pulled out the heart and set it with a thud on the steel counter. It was about the size of a basketball with large tubes jetting out in all directions. Next was the tongue... 4 tongues! I instantly thought about one cow with 4 tongues and it made me smile to myself. The rest was liver, no tripe, thank goodness.

I stuffed the bag back around the liver and closed the box flaps then put the box in the refrigerator. Liver was easy and I knew what to do with that. I turned around and stared at the odd body parts before me. We had a few packages of stew meat still available in the freezer, so I took those out and let them thaw. I set up the meat grinder and went to work dissecting the heart. My 7th-grade biology class proved handy; there were 4 distinct parts to a heart. I chopped everything up including the tough and pliable tubes and shoved them in the grinder along with a few cubes of stew meat. When it was all ground it looked just like ground beef. Well, I guess that's what it was, really. Just not the normal chuck and ground muscle most folks were used to.

I portioned it into one-pound balls and tucked them into crates in the fridge then turned my attention to the tongues. 'A lying tongue'. The phrase swooped into my mind not knowing where it came from. Maybe Daddy said it a few times although that's the only part I could remember. Well, these tongues won't be doing any lying anymore. I think I remember seeing Mama boil a tongue once or twice but for how long? No time like the present for figuring it out.

It was 10 a.m. and the breakfast crowd had thinned, and lunch wasn't hopping for another hour, so I filled my largest pot with water and fired up the stove. I got to work trimming the tongues of sinew and excess fat. Once the water boiled, I dumped in a healthy scoop of salt, a few chopped onions, celery, carrots, and the four tongues. I assumed they were a tough cut so a couple of hours would probably be enough time to break down any gelatinous fat.

By lunchtime, they were done, and I took my large, two-pronged fork and laid the steaming logs on the counter to rest. I asked Lila to help me haul the boiling water outside and around the front of the diner to pour on the stubborn weeds that would come up through the sidewalk. This was always a quick way to kill the weeds and the scent of boiled onions and meat brought in more surrounding customers. One such prospect was a young man across the street from the diner that looked up from his work to watch a couple of silly-looking girls dump stock water on the sidewalk.

Across Kearney Rd from the diner was a horse training facility or menage as I sometimes heard the hired hands call it. The boys would often come over on their lunch break for a ha.m. or chicken sandwich or a bowl of soup on cooler days. The fence bordered the road, and it was a pleasant sight to watch the equestrian activities on my smoke breaks. There was a large, red barn on the far side of the pen that opened to the fenced area. A few oaks and black walnut trees were scattered around the pen making it look like a picture I'd seen in a LIFE magazine years ago. It was so picturesque you couldn't help glancing that way when you walked or drove by.

The fence stretched the length of the diner and then some before wrapping around in a circle back to the barn. Beyond that were a few trucks and cars parked in perfect lines. The place was so well manicured you'd think it was going to be on the cover of the next TIME or LOOK.

After we dumped the steaming, scented water on the noxious weeds, I stood up straight and wiped my brow from the steam and sweat that had appeared during the activity. As I brushed fire-red curls from my eyes I noticed that this young man had not stopped staring. It caught me off guard so I quickly looked away and trotted back into the diner. I went in the front door then peered out the window. He was still staring; at what I didn't know since he couldn't see me anymore. Maybe he wasn't looking at me? Maybe he was staring at something past me. Maybe he was eyeing Lila. Well, no matter. I went back to the kitchen to tend to the tongues I had forgotten about.

The heart ground up nicely with the little excess ground chuck I had and made excellent burgers. So good, in fact, that an elderly Jewish woman that often ate at the diner once or twice a month called me over to her table to ask if the burger was heart meat. I was a little sheepish in answering but then was quickly relieved when she said it was the best ha.m.burger she'd ever had. Something about that rich, dark meat sure made the patties tender.

I sliced the tongue and seared it on the flat top and made it into sandwiches with mustard, lettuce, and pickles. Surprisingly, they were a hit. So much so that the word got out and I had a few people come in just for the tongue sandwich.

It was so popular that the young man across the street came in one afternoon asking Lila about the sandwich. I only had enough for a week's worth and the pickin's were getting slim. Luckily, I had enough to muster up one more for this strange gentleman. He came in and sat at the bar. It was close to 2 p.m. and most of the lunch crowd had cleared out. It was just him and an older couple at one of the tables by the window.

"Heard about this 'world-fa.m.ous' sandwich," he said, taking off his large cattleman hat and placing it on the barstool beside him. He rubbed the palms of his hands together and then wiped them on his jacket front.

"Coffee?" I smiled, grabbing a cup and setting it in front of him.

"Thank you, miss," he said staring at me while I poured the steaming liquid. He reached for the cup but didn't divert his eyes. I turned around and replaced the coffee pot on its warmer.

"Looking for a tongue sandwich, huh?" I said, pulling a set of silverware and napkin from their holders and placing it in front of him.

"I hear it's the best in town," he said, taking a sip of his coffee. He winced at the temperature and put the cup down.

"Well, one sandwich, coming up," I said and left the counter to attend to the flat top in the kitchen. I returned in about 5 minutes with a plate overflowing with potato salad, quartered dill pickle and the oval-shaped sandwich cut in two. "Can I get you anything else?"

"Your name?" he said, picking up half the sandwich and taking an unusually large bite. He seemed to realize the awkwardness of it the minute he did it but couldn't do much about it now. He set the sandwich down and picked up his napkin to hide the fact he was chewing large morsels of food.

"*My* name?" I inquired. "Why do you want to know my name?" I filled his coffee cup up to the rim.

"Well," he said, swallowing the last bit of his huge bite. "I've seen you working here for a few weeks and I work across the street. Thought it'd be neighborly if we knew each other by name." To alleviate any embarrassment, he took another bite, a little more manageable one this time.

"Oh, I'm sorry, I'm Virginia, Virginia La.m.b," I said smiling and wrinkling my nose gracelessly.

"Ha!" he exclaimed with a shock. "I'm Bill Byrd. Lamb and Byrd, quite a pair, eh?" He laughed, although I wasn't so sure what 'pair' he was referring to.

I half-smiled. "Well, pleased to meet you, Bill Byrd. I hope you're enjoying your sandwich."

"Oh, it's fantastic! Best tongue sandwich I've ever had. Come to think of it, it's the only tongue sandwich I've ever had so I guess it's the best," he said scooping up the other half and tearing off another bite. It wasn't the most pleasant way one could eat a sandwich but at least he was enjoying it.

"Well, it was kind of an accident, really," I said, grabbing a cloth and wiping down the counter. "The regular cuts were out and this is what was available. At least I'll know what to do with them next time."

"I think you should order this all the time. You sure know how to cook," he said.

"I just boiled it and fried it. Anyone could do it."

"I'm sure but, well," he was sta.m.mering like he wanted to say more but didn't know what to say, so he took another bite.

"You enjoy that and let me know if you need anything else, Mr. Byrd," I said, dumping the last few drops of coffee from the pot and starting on a fresh one.

"You can call me Bill," he said, cautiously waiting for my reaction. "Everyone else does."

I nodded and took the pot to the sink to fill it. He finished his lunch and grabbed the pickle spear as the last bite and plopped some money on the counter. "Thanks so much, Miss La.m.b! Can't wait to be back." He grabbed his hat and sat it back on his head, took a bite of the pickle and winked at me as he turned and went through the door.

"It's Mrs...." But he was already out the door and I hadn't said it very loud anyway.

27

Bill Byrd

"It came to pass, as the ark of the covenant of the Lord came to the city of David, that Michal, the daughter of Saul looking out at a window saw king David dancing and playing: and she despised him in her heart."
1 Chronicles 15:29

Meeting Bill Byrd took up more of my thoughts than it should. I didn't think anything of the meeting at the time, no more than a typical customer. But the next day my mind kept flitting back to that odd encounter. And there really wasn't anything odd about it at all. So what in the world was I going on about? Why did it keep popping back into my mind? I literally shook my head to clear the thoughts the next day as I prepared the breakfast menu. Eggs ready for poaching, scrambling, frying or to reheat for hard-boiled, bacon frying on the flat top, shredded potatoes in a bin of ice-cold water and fruit being sliced and prepped by Lila. It was a quiet morning; one I was not grateful for. I wanted the busyness of the day to occupy my mind. I knew thinking of anyone else that way was not appropriate. Not that I thought of Mr. Bill Byrd in any other way but as a customer but why in the world did he keep coming to my mind?

After the breakfast rush was over and Lila and I finished washing up dishes and prepping for lunch I took a smoke break out back. The front of the diner faced the road and the horse training facility, so I made sure to take my break in the back but a loud yell from in front drew my attention.

I took a long drag off my cigarette and peered around the front of the building. I saw horses bucking and writhing in the training pen and a couple of men trying to calm them, one was Bill. I was more curious as to what was happening, so I kept my cigarette burning and nonchalantly wandered around the front of the diner. I tried to keep a low profile, as if I was just wandering aimlessly on my smoke break but took intentional looks toward the pen to see what was going on.

It seems they were trying to break a beautiful, solid rust-brown stallion. He was a gorgeous creature with a silky, chocolate-colored mane and tail. But he was not having any of the discipline he was getting. Bill had his hands up trying to grab the loose bridle and the other man was trying to coax the horse over to him with oats and treats. Bill eventually got a hold of the steed and the other man quickly came in with the offerings to distract the horse. Bill stroked the stallion's muzzle and patted its crest and shoulder. It seemed to calm immediately and soon enough they were escorting it back into the barn.

I took the last drag of my cigarette and looked up. It was a blue-sky day, warm, but it's funny that I hadn't noticed it until now. I started to wander slowly to the back of the diner when I heard my name.

"Virginia ... Hey there, Virginia!"

I turned around and saw that Bill had come back out of the barn and was now leaning over the fence along the road waving at me.

I waved back but didn't go any closer.

"Whatcha doin?" He yelled across the road.

"What?" I asked leaning my ear his direction.

He waved a hand gesturing me to come over toward him. "Come here," he yelled.

I took the last puff of my smoke and threw it on the ground, stamping it with my shoe and grinding it into the dirt. I looked dow the road in both directions... not a car in sight and sauntered across. I put both hands on the top log of the fence and leaned back a bit to stretch.

"Tough ol' dog, eh?" I said, nodding upward toward the barn.

"Oh, Bearly? Yeah, he's a good one. A little brawny and bitter but we'll get that out of him." He too put both hands on the opposite side of the fence and leaned out mirroring me.

"Just got him in. Owner wants him broke before winter. He'll take some time but he'll come around. Were you watching for long?" He said, hunting for clues, it seemed.

"Just my break." I glanced over at the diner. No one had pulled up so I knew there was no need to hurry back.

Bill Byrd surprisingly reminded me of Creth, only younger and larger. He wore a large Cattleman's hat that seemed to identify him. He had a short torso, a wide belt buckle and the start of a small pooch in front. He had rosy cheeks that almost reminded me of Santa Claus and thick hands and fingers that looked too tight to grip the reins. His smile was infectious though. His voice, wink, and mannerisms were attractive; like he drew everyone in around him with his own personal gravitational field. I too felt drawn in but I didn't really know why.

Bill was leaning back using the top fence railing to hold him steady when his eyes darted to my hand. My right arm made a

90-degree angle in front of my torso and my left wrapped around it holding my right elbow with my left hand. My wedding ring was clearly visible. It was obvious he was looking at it but I felt presumptuous to mention it. He did instead.

Bill Byrd - Early 20s

"Oh, you're married?" He asked and all of a sudden, the clouds seemed to roll over the sun.

I looked up in response. "Yep, that's me," I said with a slight smile and long sigh.

"Not happy about it?" He asked. Was it that obvious?

"Oh, no, no, it's fine... it's okay."

"Just okay?" He inquired, now leaning in closer to me and the fence between us.

"Well, what do you want me to say?" I didn't know where this conversation was going. I was a little annoyed by the questioning.

"Not madly in love and everything?" He swung around and grabbed the fence again in a playful manner.

"Well, I don't know. A couple of kids and several years later and... does anyone know?" I looked down and kicked at the grass. I kept glancing at the diner, almost hoping for a customer now so I could get out of this awkward conversation.

"Oh, you have a couple youngin's. I got 5 myself," he said with as much anti-climactic vigor as exclaiming you had brown hair or wore a size 10 shoe.

"Five?" I dropped my arms in surprise and widened my eyes. "Wow, that's a lot." Part of me felt a little better knowing he was married and seemed happy with the 5 kids and all. But part of me was a little disappointed. I wasn't sure why.

"Well, I don't get to see 'em that often. Their mother don't like me much anymore. Not sure why." He was looking down now kicking the soft dirt of the training track.

"Oh. Where are they?" I asked. This was an interesting web of drama that instantly enticed me.

"Kansas City. She lives with her mom," he said a little embarrassed. "But I take good care of her. I just don't get to see the kids very often."

"So, you're not married anymore?" I asked but not sure why I wanted to know.

"Nope. Divorced last year. But it's alright. I'm doing my own thing and the kids are alright, I think." He kicked the dust on his side of the fence.

I really didn't know what to say and there was an awkward pause. After a few seconds of wondering who was to speak first, I asked, "how long were you married?"

"12 years," he said with an air of frustration, relief, maybe accomplishment, I couldn't tell, like he'd put in his time in prison and was now a free man.

"Wow, that's a long time."

"Yes... too long," he said with a beat-down tone but then quickly rescinded the tone to one more uplifting, "well, to her anyway."

"I've been married nearly 11 myself and I know what you mean. It can get really hard. Sometimes you don't know the person you married after a while. Maybe we never do." I looked down contemplating this thought I had never really had before.

"Ain't that the truth." He looked back toward the barn.

"Oh, I'm keeping you," I said, unfolding my arms and feeling a bit stupid that I just voiced some deep emotions to a stranger.

"Oh, no, no. I just should probably get back to work. You're fine. I should go though. Gotta lot of work today." He looked concerned and furrowed his brow. Then quickly tipped his hat toward me, "Ma'am." He let go of the fence with his other hand and turned to go. I gave a casual smile but the whole encounter suddenly felt odd. I turned too and crossed the street back to finish up the day.

~

A couple of weeks later I was standing high on a step ladder in the diner trying to clean off the top of the fridge when Bill walked in. I heard the ding of the bell but didn't turn right away. I was in an odd position, so I kept wiping until I was sure the grease that had wafted onto every flat surface was cleaned off, at least from the fridge.

Bill walked in and instantly saw my legs. I always wore dresses or skirts that came just at or above the knee and flared out slightly. I regularly had an apron tied around my waist while I worked and stockings that held everything in. Even after 2 kids my figure had not betrayed me too much. I suppose from the backside, my legs probably were the first thing one would see. My nylons were always nude and reaching on my tiptoes to wipe the far back of the fridge made my calves tighten and flex. Apparently, this was my most attractive feature to Bill.

He stopped and didn't move for a moment. I didn't hear the scratching of chairs or squeak of the bar stools, so I looked over my shoulder. Bill was just standing there. He stared at me with a childish grin. When he realized I had stopped wiping and was now staring back at him he looked up at my face and was jolted from his trance.

"Hey there Virginia!" He said in a jovial tone, completely disregarding the awkward stare of moments before.

"Hi Bill," I said, grasping the front of the fridge and climbing down backward from the step ladder. I collapsed the ladder and slid it back along the side of the fridge and threw the sticky towel in the bleach bucket on the floor. I washed my hands and wiped them on my apron. "What can I get ya?"

"How about a lemonade? It's mighty warm out there today and those fillies have me working overtime. I could use a little cooldown." He regained his normal saunter into the restaurant and hopped up on a barstool, setting his hat on the adjacent stool as he always did. Luckily, he never came in when it was busy so no one ever challenged him for the seat.

"Sure thing," I said, turning back to the fridge and pulling out the large glass pitcher of ice-cold, homemade lemonade.

"Nothing beats your lemonade, Virginia," he said, wiping his brow. The weather was getting warmer by the week and even though it was already well into summer, each day seemed to be hotter than the next. My icebox pie and potato salad were the two biggest sellers for lunch and most mornings diners opted for orange juice and ice water over hot tea and coffee.

I too was perspiring quite offensively and tried to hide the fact that my hair was getting curlier and frizzier by the minute. I poured Bill his lemonade over sparkling and cracking ice cubes and he downed it in one swig, jetting the glass out prompting me for another pour. I didn't even have a chance to set the pitcher down before I refilled the tumbler. He took another swig, but this time didn't drain it.

"Whew, It's a scorcher out there," he said, wiping his mouth with the back of his hand. The cliche comment almost annoyed me. I hesitated with the pitcher to see if he would want more right away and then opted for the fridge again. The rush of cool air when I swung open the door was a welcome refreshment. I almost didn't mind if he wanted more lemonade as it required me to access the only cold spot in the diner.

"Haven't seen you in a while," I said, not really knowing what prompted me to inform him that I had obviously paid attention to his absence. The minute I said it, I regretted it.

"Oh, been breaking a stallion the last week. Tough ol' boy. I think he was wild. Fun to get in these wild horses from time to time. You wouldn't think there were many of 'em left but you'd be surprised. There's herds of wild stallions and horses all over Texas and Arizona. I even heard of some on islands off Virginia and Maryland." He took another swig of lemonade. I propped both elbows on the counter, leaned over and put my chin on top of my layered hands to listen. "Hey! Virginia! HA! Whatdoyaknow? Maybe you're a wild horse too?" And I could see as soon as he said it, he felt just as awkward as me with the welcoming remark. He grabbed his glass and took a sip to cover the floundering.

"You love those horses, don't you?" I said, almost mesmerized by the tone he took talking about horses.

"You bet," he said nodding and looking down in confirmation. "They have their own personality. They're amazing. Once you break one, it becomes a part of you. Oh, I know that sounds strange, but it's an amazing connection. Such powerful creatures that heed to our way of life." He felt instantly in his element talking about the horses, as if I had found his spark.

Bill went on telling me about how he came into the business and how Helen, his ex-wife, hated them. She claimed he loved the horses more than her and by the way he talked about both I could see that. But she also didn't seem like a very nice person in general. He mentioned she tried to poison a horse once to get him to come home but the plan backfired and he ended up spending the whole night in the stable with the sick horse, nursing it back to health. He said that was the final straw with her. She said she wouldn't compete with a four-legged filly and he could just go screw them if he wasn't going to be the husband she needed.

I seemed to sense a tenderness in him though. I was never really an animal lover but certainly didn't hate them either. He loved his kids and spoke about them with the same affection as the horses even though he constantly reiterated that he knew the kids were more important. I found myself more interested in the horses too just by Bill's emotional devotion to them. He saw them as not just animals but life-altering beings that were so much more than four-legged carriers.

The days went on and I found myself looking forward to seeing Bill every day. Neither of us worked seven days a week and when I caught myself altering my diner schedule to match his at the stable, I paused. What was I doing? Creth seemed to be in his own world at the Spur and we barely saw each other. The girls were out of school for the summer and occupied their days down at the river or building forts in the woods out off Hwy 69 and Vintage Dr behind the local Scoop Up, an ice cream shop about three blocks from the diner. Each night the girls and I would play cards, read books, or play tickle, as Carol called it, wrestling on the mattress before bedtime. I loved those girls and enjoyed my time with them, but I wondered if Creth was getting any time with them at all. He's the one that really wanted them in the first place. He slept in late and by the time he woke the girls had already dressed and gone. They had learned to cook eggs and bacon at home by watching me at the diner or would often stop by the restaurant for an ice cream cone or hot chocolate, depending on the weather.

It was late August and each day seemed to be getting hotter. I dreamt of the cool of autumn but knew it could still be weeks away. School started in a week and the girls had been driving me crazy. It was a Thursday afternoon and Carol and Dolores came by about 1 pm for a popsicle. That was one great thing about running things around here; George didn't care if we had dinner, lunch or snacks at the diner so long as we didn't abuse the privilege. The girls were sitting in a booth by the window when Bill bounded through the door in his usual way.

"Well, good day to you Virginia!" He bellowed. Throwing his hat on the stool and briskly slid onto the seat beside it. "How's it going today?" He asked, his attention completely oblivious to anything else around him.

"Well, I just gave my girls popsicles, so they're cooling off over there." I gestured toward the window and widened my eyes a bit hoping the motion would prompt him to calm his enthusiasm a bit.

"What?" He said, slowing his movements and twirling around on the stool. He turned to look at them. Carol and Dolores were in their own world. Sugary, red liquid was dripping down Carol's hand, down her arm and dropping onto the table from her elbow. Dolores was neatly licking all around her green popsicle to avoid the drips. They were both in some heated conversation about how horses couldn't tell the difference between apples and carrots.

"Oh, you bet they can," Bill said, avoiding my eye contact and standing up from his stool. He walked over to them. I couldn't tell if he wanted to set them straight or just get involved.

The girls turned and looked up at him as he approached them. He leaned down and put both hands on the table. "Ya see those stables over there?" He pointed across the street and both girls turned and looked, ignoring their melting pillars of frozen sugar syrup. "I train those horses. I'm with those horses more than without 'em. Those are my girls. I know those horses better than anyone and by golly, if you feed Josephine a carrot over an apple, she'll know it!" He stood up straight and put both thumbs through his suspenders mid-torso as if he had won.

"Really? They really know?" Carol asked, still forgetting her popsicle, staring back at Bill.

"You bet ya! Don't *you* know if you're eating a carrot or an apple?" He said furrowing his eyebrows in a question.

"I don't like carrots," Carol said, taking a big suck off her popsicle as her mouth got redder and redder.

"Well, *I* know the difference," Dolores said, neatly licking her popsicle again. "So, of course, they would too. See Carol!" Dolores rolled her eyes at Carol and finished her popsicle wrapping the stick in a napkin she pulled from the canister on the table and setting it neatly in front of her.

Carol shrugged her shoulders as if the argument didn't mean a thing in the world and went back the sticky mess in front of her.

Bill chuckled and turned back to me who had been watching this scenario from the counter.

"Well, I guess that's that," I said, smiling and shaking my head. I had felt a bit embarrassed at first but when Bill seemed amused by the girls I just shrugged and reminded myself he had 5 himself. This couldn't be that unusual.

"Great kids," Bill said, sitting back on his stool and rearranging his hat.

"Yeah, they're not too bad," I said, grabbing a glass and filling it with lemonade. I hadn't charged Bill for lemonade since that first day he asked for it. I probably should have been but he was such a regular I convinced myself that's what I'd do with any regular. I didn't let myself ponder that line of thinking too far.

He took a long drink, set it down and took a deep breath. I expected him to say something after this but only a smile appeared on his face. He looked at me, then down at his glass and back to the girls. There was such an awkward pause in our conversation that I felt I should get to cleaning or wiping or doing something productive, but then Bill spoke.

"They get along with their daddy?" Bill asked, almost as if he was trying to find something to say. I was taken aback by the question. I hadn't really thought of that before.

"Yeah, I guess so. He loves those girls, probably more than he loves me. No, I *know* he loves them more than me." I may have thought that in the past but saying it out loud really made it sound legitimate. Even if I tried to persuade myself otherwise, I knew deep down, children are what Creth always wanted. If he could have had children without a wife he'd have preferred it.

"You're okay with that?" Bill asked, taking another drink to occupy his time while he waited for a pregnant answer.

"I don't know. Never really thought about it, I guess. I knew he always wanted kids and I guess I just assumed the parental role." This conversation got heavy fast. The more I thought about it, the more downtrodden my face must have looked because Bill's expression turned from curious to concern.

His eyebrows lowered and pressed together. "I'm sorry, this is personal. I... I shouldn't ask about such things." He put his glass down and shook his head, looking around the room as if he was searching for another topic of conversation.

The girls finished their popsicles and bounced up from the table, the sugar already hitting their brains, and bounded for the door.

"Hey," I shouted. "Sticks in the trash. Wash your face and fingers."

They jerked back and grabbed their sticks from the table and tossed them into the trash as they skipped to the bathroom. Not more than 3 seconds later they were chasing each other out the diner door.

The diner was silent for a moment. Lila had gone home, and it was just me and Bill. Neither of us moved but I could feel the tension in the air. He was looking out the window at the girls running in the empty parking lot. I examined his profile. He was solid, oval-faced and firm. He had started putting on the middle-age weight around his waist but wasn't necessarily heavy, just tall and husky, like everything on his body was the exact right measurement. He didn't have a big nose or large ears, didn't have crooked teeth, yet they weren't perfectly straight either. His shoulders were symmetrical, and he was about seven or eight inches taller than me. He gave off an air of contentment and satisfaction with the world, even though on the outside it didn't seem like the perfect life; estranged from his wife and complicated parental issues. But he seemed to hold it all together. He was set in his life, yet not quite resistant to better adventures. It appealed to me. Creth always seemed to be wanting more, never satisfied. Always looking for the bigger, better opportunity. Bill, on the other hand, welcomed both opportunity and contentment. I felt content too, right then at that moment. I didn't want it to end.

I was off in my little trance and didn't notice Bill put his hand on top of mine that was resting on the counter. My startled reaction immediately jerked it away before I realized what had happened.

"Oh, god, oh, oh, god... I'm so sorry. I... don't... forgive me." He pulled his hand away immediately and promptly went stiff. He looked embarrassed and was looking down and around his feet.

"Oh, no, I'm sorry," I said, regaining my wits. "I didn't mean to do that. It was just a reaction. I wasn't paying attention." The tension broke and now felt awkward again, not the comfortable awareness I experienced just a few seconds earlier.

"That was uncalled for," he said. I thought he might get up and leave but he didn't. Maybe he was waiting for my reaction. If it was horror and disgust, he could grab his hat quick and make a run for it. If it was a casual mistake, we could laugh about it. But if it was something more... he sheepishly looked up at me. His eyes met mine more direct than ever before.

"I liked it," I finally said. "I just wasn't expecting it."

His demeanor relaxed completely. He gave me a gentle smile and his shoulders dropped. I matched his smile and we just sat there in silence for another couple of minutes. The girls were still outside but in their own world. I too, felt as if I was in my own world in here. It was nice to have a friend, someone that I felt wanted to really know me, understand me, be kind to me. It wasn't that Creth wasn't kind, but he didn't go out of his way to show it unless it involved the girls. This person just wanted to know me for me. For the first time since Mama was alive, I felt special to someone.

"I better get going." Bill got up from the stool and grabbed his hat. He leaned down to rest it on his head and turned back to me. He reached out his arm and his hand touched my shoulder and ran down to my elbow before trailing off. Chills went through my body. I didn't move or make a sound. Something stirred deep in me and I knew it wasn't right but everything in my body wanted more. He winked and walked out the door.

I didn't sleep at all that night.

~

Everything Creth did drove me crazy. The way he got up too late, the way he came home too late, the way he left his socks on the floor and the way he left dirty coffee cups and spoons in the sink every day. I hardly saw the man and he infuriated me. This only added fuel to the fire growing between Bill and me. What I wasn't getting from Creth I easily earned from Bill. Occasionally Creth would come into the diner for a late breakfast but Bill never came in before noon. So far, the two had not run into each other, for which I was truly grateful but I also knew it may only be a matter of time. I had to be very careful in my attitude around Bill when other patrons, Lila or the girls were there, but Bill could usually tell when the place was vacant and that's when he'd show up. We talked about everything while I cleaned the diner for the day. He sometimes stayed and helped me lock up.

Friday afternoons were usually the slowest as people were headed home sooner and the Spur was getting busier the later it got. I never saw Creth on Friday and Saturday because the dancehall was jumping until 2 a.m. It was close to 4 p.m. on Friday and I turned the 'OPEN' sign around to CLOSED' and turned off the outside light. Bill was at the counter with a glass of ice tea, condensation from the ice melting down the sides. I walked briskly around the counter and into the kitchen behind the wall to turn off the fryer and ovens. As I was bending over to adjust the oven racks I felt a presence behind me. I stood up quickly and spun around. Bill grabbed both my shoulders and kissed me. Hard. A tingling sensation shot through my body from my head to my toes. That stirring came on again in full force. He tasted like cool, sweet tea. He smelled like aftershave. His kiss was firm but not violent or aggressive. It was a kiss to let you know how he felt but still hesitant in case it was unwanted. It wasn't unwanted. I melted into his kiss and our lips softened into a more passionate rhythm. My hands slid up his sides and he let go of my shoulders allowing me to wrap my arms around his neck. His lips stayed firmly planted on mine and wrapped his arms around my waist to hold me tighter. It was so different. It was wrong. It felt so good. I wanted more.

He finally broke and pulled away. "I'm sorry, Virginia, I know that's not right." He looked embarrassed again and backed away, his hands coming around my waist as he released me.

"I know," I said. "I want it too." The mood instantly went from passion to shame. "I'm sorry, I shouldn't.... shouldn't have... "

"No. It's my fault, not yours." He cleared his throat and stepped back again. "I should go. I've already done too much." He wouldn't look at me anymore. He turned around and left the kitchen. I didn't move. I heard the front door open and the bell ring once, then once again as it closed behind him. I didn't move for what seemed like hours. Tears welled up in my eyes. Part of me wanted to cry and part of me wanted to be sick.

I finally gathered my thoughts and finished cleaning up. I walked slowly back toward the house reliving the kiss over and over, relishing the feelings of it and the next moment hating myself. What have I done? What could I do about it now? Why did it feel so good? Why didn't I say no?

I laid awake all night staring at the ceiling. When Creth came in sometime around 2:30 am I closed my eyes so he wouldn't see that I was awake but I could tell he was drunk. He always bumped into things and was louder than usual. He flopped into bed shaking the mattress. I turned away from him and finally, thankfully sleep found me.

28

Where There is a Spark

"It came to pass after these things, that his master's wife cast her eyes upon Joseph; and she said, Lie with me." Genesis 39:17

I didn't see Bill for a week after that encounter. I never told anyone either, not that I really had anyone to tell. Lila was about my only close companion and she was much too young to understand such complicated things. Besides, I didn't trust anyone.

Creth seemed none the wiser. We had grown so far apart that strangeness in my behavior went overlooked fairly easily. We hadn't been intimate in months and I wasn't sure whose fault that really was. The stirring in me prompted me to try with my husband but only because Bill brought something back to life in me that had been dormant for several years. It was almost too awkward now. Monday nights were the only time we had as a family and after I cleaned up after dinner and the girls were tucked into bed I took off my apron and clumsily threw it at Creth. He was in the rocker with his paper covering his face and chest. The apron knocked down the newspaper and I was met with an aggravated response.

"Dammit, Virginia, I'm trying to read here," he quickly lowered the paper and threw the apron on the floor. "What you getting at?"

"I don't know. Thought maybe you'd like to come to bed early?" I offered my most sultry voice and leaned against the table.

"Hmph," was all I got as he straightened out the paper and went back to reading. "You go ahead."

This only made me more irritated. I gave a huff and stomped loudly to the bedroom. And although I didn't slam the door, I didn't leave it open. That invitation was now rejected.

~

Another week went by and I didn't even see Bill at the stables or in the training paddock. I knew he drove a red pick-up and I would often wander farther down the street to see if it was parked behind the barn. After about a week and a half, I finally saw it. Where would he have gone for so long? The truck was there. I had to walk about 100 feet from the diner to see around the barn, but it was definitely there. There was no sign of Bill. My mind had been completely occupied by him over the last couple of weeks since the kiss. The taste of his mouth, the weight of his arms around me, the smell of his aftershave. He didn't smell like gin and beer, the normal scents most men exuded. He paid attention to me. He really wanted to know who I was and enjoyed spending time with me for no other reason than because he liked me. That was foreign to me. I was drawn to that. I suppose any woman would have been.

I'd been absentmindedly sucking on my cigarette kicking the rocks into the street and I didn't notice the horse galloping out of the barn and over to the fence. The whinny of the steed brought my thoughts back around. I looked up to see Bill patting down the horse and giving him a good brushing. He didn't look my direction even though I couldn't have been more than 60 feet from him just across the road. He must have known I was there.

"Come on," Bill said to the horse with a few clicks and clucks of his jaw to get the steed moving back toward the barn.

I didn't stop staring and for a split second, I saw Bill's eyes shoot toward me. They quickly shot back toward the horse and he turned to bring him back to the stables. In a moment he was gone. I threw my cigarette on the ground and stomped on it forcefully as if I was stomping my own feelings away. It was childish to be so angry. This was clearly a violation of the marriage vows and yet I was angry it wasn't happening. I should be grateful, but I was just plain mad.

Three days later I was closing up. The girls had gone to stay at a friend's house for the night and Creth said he'd be home late, as usual. Lila asked if I wanted to go to a movie. I told her I would meet her outside the theater in town at 7:30 p.m. I finished cleaning up, turned off the ovens, and threw the last of the towels in the wash bin for the cleaners to pick up in the morning. I took off my apron and tossed it into the bucket when I heard the bell ding at the door signaling a late customer.

"Blazes all..." I cursed. I knew I didn't have to turn anything back on. We had already been closed for 30 minutes, but I hated facing customers with bad news. "We're closed..." I said. My head was down straightening my dress when I came around the corner. I looked up and stopped short. It was Bill.

Both of us didn't move for what seemed like ages. We just stood there staring blankly at the other person. I didn't know if he was here to reject me completely or to confess his undying love for me like some Harlequin novel they had at the local drug store.

He made a few steps forward, testing the waters with me, I assumed. I was behind the counter, but I didn't move.

"How are you?" He asked. He seemed to ask it as if it was the only thing he thought to say even though it was wrought with a thousand other questions in those three little words.

"Hi." I didn't answer his question because I really didn't know how I was; anxious, irritated, aroused, frustrated.

"Did you tell your husband?" Bill asked. He had taken off his hat and was now holding it in both hands by the brim in front of him.

"Of course not!" I scolded. "Why on earth would you think that?"

"I'm sorry... I didn't mean... of course you wouldn't." He smiled slightly and dared to take another few steps toward me. "Have you thought about the other day at all?" He seemed shy not really knowing if he wanted the answer.

I gave a short huff with a smile. "Uh, yeah? Kind of can't stop thinking about it."

"Really? Me too." He said, with the same relieved huff and smile.

We were acting like kids in school, silly emotions, hormones, giddy chatter. What was wrong with me? Both our demeanors relaxed slightly, and he walked even closer still. I slowly walked around the counter and met his eyes. We were just 4 feet away now with a mere bar stool between us. His eyes were so bright, so kind, so welcoming.

"I don't know what to say." He seemed so shy, cautious, nervous. It really was like we were back in school. Bill was close to my age and this all felt new, unadulterated even though that's exactly the opposite of what it was. It felt as if this was how it was supposed to have been in the beginning and I never got that chance. Part of me felt justified to have this as all those around me had experienced.

"I'm okay if you're okay" I said modestly.

He smiled and moved around the stool and came closer to me. He put his hat on the counter and looked around the diner, out the windows to a vacant parking lot then back at me. His eyes traced my face from my hairline to my chin and back to my eyes. He was

just tall enough that I could look up into his face but without cran-
ing my neck. I smiled and he kissed me.

I never made it to the theater.

29

There's Bound to be a Fire

"It came to pass, that when the sun went down and it was dark, behold a smoking furnace, and a burning lamp that passed between those pieces." Genesis 15:17

Each week it seemed Creth stayed longer and longer at the Spur. Some Mondays we didn't even see him because he was off in meetings with George or interviewing new waitresses. I felt his presence more than I actually saw him. He would slip into bed late and I would slip out early. This scheduling dance we did made it impossible to act like a normal family. I felt as if I was raising the girls alone. I would get their breakfast and lunches made early for the day before heading off to the diner. I actually enjoyed being there more than at home. I felt needed at the diner. It was comfortable. It also didn't hurt that Bill was there almost every day.

I looked forward to work, but I also wondered how long the current situation could last. I knew the relationship with Bill wasn't right, but it wasn't like I was having a relationship with Creth either. We had become more like roommates over the past couple of years. I seemed irritated whenever he was in the room. The way he parented the girls, if he was ever around, the way he got dressed, ate his dinner, put on his shoes. It was all irritating. It might have been more irritating because Creth wasn't Bill. Bill was easy, casual, wanted to talk, really wanted to know me. Creth only wanted to know me as far as marry me. Bill seemed to want to know me whether or not he married me. He was genuinely interested in me, my life, and who I was apart from any other ulterior motive. This intrigued me. It made me want to make him know me. Our time together had not been platonic. We escaped to our own world whenever we could but always in the confines of the diner.

I finally felt as though I was experiencing love, real love. My heart jumped whenever he was near and the way his eyes met mine made me feel like the whole world had stopped spinning and everything slowed down. He really looked at me. Creth never looked at me anymore. Between the dance hall and swooning over the girls, I was a lost thread, an entity in the room and the marriage but not real. He passed me sometimes like I was a ghost, only conversing when absolutely necessary.

My heart grew harder toward Creth and ached for Bill. I snapped at Creth and the girls when I really didn't mean to and realized this relationship was affecting much more than my marriage. I wondered if I could leave Creth? Many women got divorces nowadays and it wasn't so much a taboo issue as it used to be although it still was frowned upon. I could get an apartment in the city with the girls or maybe even a small place in Excelsior Springs to be close to the diner. I still loved being there and couldn't lose my job now. Would George still employ a divorced woman, much less one that just left his good friend? That would be a risk, I thought. I walked through several scenarios in my mind. I could just move in with Bill but that would look too suspicious. The girls wouldn't want to do that anyway. Would Creth help support me if I did move out? What if he moved out? I could keep the house and he could visit or take the girls instead of me being the one to visit.

The plans were swirling in my head like a bee's nest. I couldn't really come up with a perfect plan but knew in my heart the wheels were already in motion. Something had to happen soon. I couldn't stand it anymore. I wanted out. I wanted Bill. I wanted someone to want me. The girls had their father, I had Bill, but not really, not fully. I wanted to be in his arms every night, his bed, his life, and I wanted him in mine.

For several months our encounters were getting more passionate. We'd chat over the fence at the stables and he'd help me close the diner almost every afternoon. I learned that Bill saw his kids about once a month when he went into the city. He'd take them to dinner or a show or maybe a drive around the park. Most were still little and just spending time with their daddy was good enough. Helen was so cruel to Bill that he arranged a drop-off with the kids and her mother so he didn't have to see her, although her phone calls loosed her venom on him at least once every couple of weeks. They dissipated some when she started dating a finance manager in Kansas City, Kansas. Bill was grateful that some other idiot, as he put it, was now dealing with her. I got the inclination that he never really loved her. Their parents wanted them to marry and it just seemed inevitable after graduation as if there was really no other choice. Helen, being as fertile as a spring hare, promptly popped out several children in the first five years of marriage and criticized Bill's parenting techniques any chance she got. Being exhausted from the abuse, he found solace and comfort at the stables and eventually got a job training steeds and mares for wealthy families in the area.

The more I learned about Bill the more I wanted to know. We let our carnal pleasures get the best of us more times than I wanted to admit, each time feeling the shame immediately after but relishing in the thought of it happening again. So far, our encounters were all our own. I imagined that the regular patrons who saw Bill there more times than one should, suspected us, but never mentioned it or ceased patronizing the diner. I wondered how long this tryst could continue knowing that the inevitable was on the horizon.

1953

Sunday afternoon in early February the girls were playing in their room and I was finishing up dishes from lunch. Creth banged and hammered on a loose board on the deck after sweeping away the powdered snow that fell the night before. It was cold outside but the old furnace kept the house at a reasonable temperature. Even then I was grateful for the household labor, as the movement also kept me warm.

A rush of winter air blew in when Creth stormed through the door, stamping his boots, allowing the collected snow to shake off onto my hardwood floor and polyester rug. The cold air made me shiver all the way from the kitchen and I turned around, irritated at the sound and the performance.

"Close that door! It's freezing out there!" I stammered, turning back around to the sink.

"Well, of course, it is. Why ya think I'm fixing the step? Don't want nobody falling through. It's slippery." He took off his coat and shook it out, depositing even more snowflakes on the floor and hung it on the hanger then removed his hat.

"You're getting my floor all wet." I didn't turn around for fear of another knife incident.

"I gotta come in, don't I?" He sat by the door and started untying his boots.

"Well, clean it up then." I put the last plate on the drying rack and wiped the soap bubbles from my hands.

"Good God woman, can't I even come in my own house?" His voice was distant but intentional.

"Creth?" I turned around and wiped my hands down the front of my apron. "I... I think I want a divorce."

He didn't look up from his shoes but stopped moving. I glanced toward the girl's room and the lack of silence confirmed they weren't paying attention to our conversation.

Creth put both elbows on his knees and ran his hands through his hair, lifting his head to look at me. His eyes met mine then looked down again and he dropped both hands. I could tell he didn't know how to respond. "It's just a little water, V."

That wasn't it and he knew it. I didn't know if he was trying to be funny, sympathetic, or sarcastic. I rolled my eyes and shook my head.

"You know it's not that." I was silent, waiting for his real response. "We haven't been a married couple in a long time. This isn't working. You're never here and I need something else. I don't know what but it's not this."

He looked around the room not saying anything. A small nod of his head was the only reaction I got. "You married me out of duty and convenience, not love, and you know it. We have the girls and I wouldn't change that for anything, but I need something else, Creth." I made a small movement toward him as if to urge him for a greater reply or maybe just affirmation.

"I told ya I loved ya once. Did I not provide for ya?" His voice was downtrodden, not angry as I suspected. "What else do ya need?" The tone was as if I had shot him through the heart. His speech was shaky, weak, and a little scratchy. "What will become of the girls?"

"I can get an apartment in town and the girls can stay with me and with you, just different days of the week."

"You seem to have it all worked out, then," he leaned back in the chair and scanned the room as if he was looking for something.

"I have enough money from the diner to get an apartment. Can you keep the house?" My tone quickened when I thought he was accepting of the plan. I moved a little closer to him gauging his movements.

He shot up quickly and the act made me startle and jump back. His countenance had gone from grief to violence. His eyebrows furrowed and an invisible wall seemed to loom up between us, one I had never seen before. I instantly felt the cold as if I was standing outside the house all of a sudden. He grabbed my wrist and pulled me toward him.

"Is this the thanks I get?" He growled at me and the blood in my chest pumped ferociously. My breathing quickened and I scarcely noticed that I was shaking. "All I've done for you all these years and this is how you repay me? Get what you want and move on?"

I struggled to free my arm, but his grip tightened. "Let me go. This is *never* what I wanted. You and Daddy wanted this, not me." He stared through me with dagger eyes that pierced my brain. "I want out, Creth. Let me go." My hand had started to go numb and for the first time, I noticed the girls were silent in their room. I quickly glanced at their bedroom door, but it was still closed.

Creth threw my wrist down with a twist that felt as if he sprained it. He turned and forcefully shoved his feet back into his boots and grabbed his coat and hat, threw open the door, and slammed it behind him so hard the door jamb cracked and the door flung back open. I stood there twisting the palm of my hand around my sore wrist and watched him storm away leaving fresh footprints in the snow.

Part 4

30

Kansas City - Alone

"It came to pass through the anger of the Lord, he had cast them out from his presence and Zedekiah rebelled again the king." Jeremiah 52:3

I had wandered into uncharted waters. My days were no longer the struggle of diner needs, children's lunches, and ungrateful husband's laundry. I had tasted freedom, passion, love. And I loved it. I wanted more. I looked forward to the days I would see Bill. I was angry and bitter to those around me when I didn't. I gave up all hope or ambition in making my own marriage work. I didn't care. I just wanted Bill. I knew I loved my girls, but I also thought I loved Bill. No, I knew I loved him. I wanted him all the time. And he wanted to know me. I was drawn to that desire. I didn't even care if Creth found out. It seemed to be a way out almost. I didn't parade it blatantly of course, but if he knew I welcomed it. I almost wanted him to know as a sort of 'see what you made me do' type of attitude. I wanted to show Creth that this is how you love a woman. I wanted him to feel jealous, envious of what he couldn't have.

But I never felt he was jealous. I felt the Spur and all those inhabited by it were more important. I felt Carol and Dolores were more important than me. I was jealous of them. Maybe it was my own fault. I had thought briefly from time to time that maybe it was me. Maybe if I had been more loving, more caring, more affectionate, Creth would care more for me than the other things in his world. But I also felt justified with Bill. I didn't have to try; I was more important to him. No one since Mama or even Daddy had looked me in the eyes like Bill and really cared about what I wanted, what I said, what I needed. I felt so drawn to that that it didn't matter what happened around me.

Occasionally I thought about the repercussions of a decision to leave Creth, but nothing overwhelmed me more than the feeling of love, desire and the wanting to get out. I couldn't see into the future. I didn't know what would become of the girls. It would kill Creth to take them away, but I didn't know of any other choice. Children had to be with their mother, didn't they? We would work something out. I had to keep telling myself that as bleak and messed up as things seemed right now, they would have to get better at some point. I couldn't see the outcome; the future seemed cloudy, uncertain, yet I still felt drawn to a life without Creth, even though I had no idea what that meant.

~

Creth didn't come home for days. I had no idea where he had gone. Snow had been falling for three days straight and I could barely keep up with the shoveling just to get to the mailbox on the street. I closed the diner since most people kept inside during weather like this, but this also meant I hadn't seen Bill. I ached to tell him about Creth and me, but I had no way of getting a hold of him. I dared not call him from the house for fear of Creth finding out. I left his number at the diner underneath the cash register drawer where nobody, save myself, would ever look.

I didn't know if he had moved out and just not informed me or if I was to leave. By the end of the week, the snow had subsided, and a warm spell melted the snow over the weekend. By Sunday only a skiff remained in the shaded parts of town and in geometrically shaped piles where snowplows had pushed and molded the soft ice along the roads and in parking lots.

I was combing Dolores's hair preparing to braid it for the day when I heard heavy stomps on the stairs out front. I stopped and turned toward the door. Creth tried the doorknob but it was locked. He rattled it once more then banged on the door. I quickly let Dolores's hair fall from my fingers and ran to the door. I unlocked it and opened it. Creth didn't look at me but hurried by me bumping my shoulder in a rough fashion as if I wasn't there. He went straight to our bedroom and started making an awful racket. I was so shocked I forgot the door was wide open until the crisp, winter air hit my face and I promptly closed the door.

I gingerly peered into the open door of the bedroom and perked up quick when I saw a suitcase open on the bed. But it wasn't his clothes he was tossing haphazardly into the case, it was mine. I sped into the room with a look of dismay and surprise.

"What are you doing?" I exclaimed in shock. He didn't stop for a moment but kept grabbing skirts and dresses from the closest so violently that the hangers were flicked off onto the floor. "Stop! What are you doing?"

"This is what you want? Then you can have it. Just not here." He didn't stop his movements but went to the dresser and forcibly threw open the top drawer swiping up an armful of stockings and undergarments.

"But what do you mean?" I was scared to stop him for fear of him reacting as violently toward me as he was to my wardrobe.

"You have an apartment in the city. You can go there. You don't belong here." He still wouldn't look at me but instead turned his attention to the suitcase. I felt as if I couldn't move, as if the world was swirling around me and I couldn't breathe. He tucked the fabric in around the sides, slammed the lid shut and pushed the case through the air to my chest. My instinctual reaction was to grab it yet I really didn't understand what was happening. "Get your coat, let's go," he fumed.

"Wait, no," I said furrowing my brows in resistance. "I can't go to the city, I have to work tomorrow, and what about the girls?"

"The girls will be fine. They'll do what they always do, get up and go to school. Now let's go". He walked to the bedroom door and stood in the doorway motioning his head toward the living room. When I didn't move, he finally looked at me squarely in the eyes. "This is for the best, Virginia."

I swallowed hard not quite wrapping my head around what was happening. I walked slowly through the doorway looking down the whole time. I felt my blood get hot and my face flush. I blinked back tears. There was no emotion in Creth's face. I felt like I was staring at a blank wall. I was once behind that wall with him, with the girls, with our life but now I was so far on the other side I felt cold and distant from everything in the room.

Dolores had turned in her chair to watch the ordeal but didn't say anything. Carol was still in bed asleep and hadn't heard the commotion, even though there really wasn't a loud fuss. Creth was calm but angry. There was no yelling or fighting. This was it. This was the way it was to be.

"Say goodbye to the girls." He looked up at me again and then moved to the front door.

"Wait, no, what do you mean?" I spun around to face him with a confused and worried look.

"You'll see 'em tomorrow. Just not today." I saw that he too swallowed hard. As far away from him as I was emotional, I could tell this was just as hard on him as it was on me.

"But..." I gave an irritated huff and put the suitcase down.

"Virginia, I can't be here with you. You gotta go. This is what you wanted, wasn't it? You can go do whatever you wanna do. I won't stand in your way." He opened the front door, and I felt the chill of the air swoop in again. This meant that there wasn't to be a long, drawn-out farewell scene. I was to hug the girls and leave. I knelt down on one knee and stretched my arms to Dolores, she immediately bounced off the chair and ran to me throwing her arms around my neck.

"No, Mama! No, don't go. Where are you going?" She whimpered a little but I didn't hear tears in her voice. She had no idea what was happening.

I pulled her back a bit to look into her eyes. "I have to go away for a bit but you can come visit me. I'm not exactly sure when or where I'm even going but I won't be far. I promise." She looked so confused and lost as if her face mirrored my heart.

"What's going on?" Carol had wandered out from her bedroom, messy hair and sleep-stained eyes. She rubbed her eyes and yawned.

"Mama's leaving," Dolores said turning to Carol. "We have to say goodbye."

Carol shivered from the cold air now filling the living room. "What? Why?" She asked.

"It's just for a little bit I think," I said reassuringly although there was nothing sure about the whole situation. "Come give me a hug. I'll see you tomorrow after school. I'm not going far."

"Your mom doesn't want to be here anymore," Creth finally premised.

"That's not true!" I let go of Dolores and stood up to face him. "I never said that." I turned back around and reached for Carol. She ran to me and I scooped her up in my arms, her legs wrapped around my waist tight. "I love you, Carol," I said in her ear, inhaling the sweet smell of her hair.

"Mama no," she whined, burying her face in my neck. I felt as if I had the strength to hold her like this all day, but the room was getting colder by the moment and Creth made no intention of closing the door. I was to be on the other side of that door when it did. I knelt again and reached one arm out for Dolores. She quickly snuggled in for one last, big hug. Dolores let go first but Carol had a vice grip around my neck. I had to reach back and unlock her arms to forcibly remove her. Now the tears were flooding my eyes and I knew one blink would send them rolling down my cheeks. Carol's eyes had already started to get red and puffy and the sadness in them reflected my own.

"I'll see you tomorrow," I assured them both even though I wasn't sure about it myself. I turned around and closed my eyes. The tears flowed freely from both and I opened them again to look at Creth. He was looking directly at me as if to say, this is your own fault. I walked to the coat rack and grabbed my blue woolen coat that hung to my knees. I silently wrapped it around me and turned back to grab the suitcase. I didn't look at the girls but could see in my peripheral Carol crying in the crux of Dolores's embrace. I stood up straight and walked out the door not looking at Creth.

I walked down the steps and heard the door close behind me followed by Creth's footsteps. I marched through the gate and stood by the car. He came up beside me, grabbed the suitcase from my hand and opened the backseat. He tossed the case on the seat then got in the driver's side and just sat there. I guess all chivalry was now gone. Disconcerted, I got in the passenger side. Before I had even closed the door, he started the car and we drove away from the house in silence.

35 minutes later we pulled up to a brick building on the south side of Kansas City. The silence in the car had been deafening and

I was grateful for the city sounds when I exited the car, not sure of where I even was. It was still a brisk morning, but a few locals were milling around next to a newspaper stand on the corner. I looked up at the brick building. It was 5 stories and appeared to be about 50 years old or so. The stone steps to the front door were faded and chipped and a couple of the top steps seems to slope to the side. Several of the windows had bars across the front while one at the very top was wide open.

The slam of the car door startled me, and I turned around to see Creth grabbing my suitcase from the backseat. He walked around the back of the car and dropped the case at my feet continuing his walk across the sidewalk and up the stairs without missing a beat. I picked up the suitcase and followed him.

He stopped at the entrance and pulled a key from his pocket. He used it on the top lock and a lock just below it. I wondered why bother having two locks if the same key worked in both. Once the door opened, he walked through and held it open for me.

"Where are we?" I inquired.

"You'll see." He nodded in toward the hall but didn't look at me. "Come on."

I walked up the steps and through the door. Inside was a straight hallway that was split by a flight of stairs that went up straight and turned to the left. Creth let the door close on its own behind us and he walked by me up the stairs. It was apparent I was to follow. I glanced around and to my left on the wall was a set of mailboxes. My eyes narrowed on one in the middle with a handwritten 'V. Lamb' on the clear, rectangular window on the post box. As much as I didn't want to admit it, this was apparently now my home.

Creth stood on the first landing waiting for me. I cleared my throat and followed him. I could hear sirens in the distance and someone yelling from a floor above us but couldn't make out the words. A lump appeared in my throat and an arrow of fear shot through me. This was not the home I just left. Is this really what I asked for?

Luckily, the apartment Creth had chosen was only on the second floor. I was relieved at not having to walk five flights of stairs. We turned from the top of the stairs to the right down another long hallway. I watched Creth walk with purpose in front of me. We passed three doors each one customized for its inhabitant. One had a Christmas wreath still attached, the next, a ceramic cat door-knocker and the third simply blank except for a tattered welcome mat on the floor in front of the door. Creth stopped at the fourth door on the left and pulled the key from his pocket again. I hadn't realized there was a couple of keys on this ring when he opened the main door of the building. He jiggled the lock with the key and I heard the teeth give way. The door unlocked and Creth pushed the door open pulling the key from the lock.

I cautiously walked in behind him. He turned once we both were inside and handed me the keys. "One's to the front, the others to this door and the mailbox." I held out my hands to catch the keys as they dropped into my palm. I looked at my hands. I should have worn gloves. Once the keys dropped, he turned as if he was giving me the grand tour.

It was a one-room apartment no bigger than our living room back at the house. My house. I carefully looked around the furnished room. There was one window that was cloudy and dirty, but I could still make out the building across the street. Next to the window was the radiator but the room had not been warmed in several days at least. While it wasn't as cold as outside, it was by no means a warm environment. In one corner was the start to a small section of cabinets that stretched from the floor to the ceiling separated by a counter with a small, electric table-top burner. Next to that was a sink with two faucets. At the end of the counter stood a small fridge followed by a wastebasket. On the opposite wall was a twin bed fitted with a coverlet and pillow. There was a chair against the wall by the door and a table with a similar chair to the right of the window. The room was bare, stark, cold. I wondered if someone had just died here.

"You expect me to live here?" I questioned. My voice quivered with a worried tone.

"You can live here rent-free for a couple months. It's taken care of." He said walking to the radiator. He tried the knob, but nothing happened. He shook the knob and kicked the coils to no avail. "Ah, well, you might have to speak to the landlord about that."

He stood up straight and walked over to me. "This is what you want, right?"

I gave a huff. "No. Not this."

"Well, maybe you can find a better place but for now, you got your wish. I'll look into filing the paperwork this week." He took the suitcase from my other hand and tossed it on the bed. The most irritating squeak came from the mattress in response to the weight. I winced. "Look, you'll figure it out. In the meantime, you don't have to live with me or the girls."

I sighed with a defeated breath. He put a hand on my shoulder and looked at me. "I'll talk to you later." He gave me a pat and left closing the dilapidated door behind him.

Things had happened so fast I didn't know what to do. I stood there in the middle of the room for what seemed like an hour or more. I kept looking around the room as if I was trying to make the apartment better than it really was. A shiver went through me and I realized how cold it actually was in the place. Now that I was paying attention, I could see my breath.

My world had just been shut down. Everything I once knew was no longer. I was on the outside, way outside. Could he do this? I went over to the bed and sat down. The vociferous squeak made my eyes roll. I couldn't take off my coat as it was just too cold. I stood back up and walked over to the radiator. After a few minutes of fiddling with the knobs and kicking the thing, I gave up and went to the refrigerator and opened it. Nothing. What was I going to eat? Did I have any money in my purse? Payday wasn't for another week. Anger started to swell up in me and I thought about all the things I could have taken from the house, but the shock of the situation prevented me from thinking clearly. I was stuck here. I had no car, barely any money and worst of all, I didn't have my kids. I wondered if this was even legal; to take a mother from her children.

I grabbed my purse and searched for my pocketbook. There were some bills and coins. I counted out $13.54. That should be enough to get some bread, eggs, and milk and maybe a cab ride to the diner. But where was the store? I really had no idea where in Kansas City I was. Then the thought struck me, where was the bathroom? I went to the door, opened it and looked out. At the end of the hall was a sign hanging on the wall that said 'Toilet'. Next to the sign a little farther down the wall was a payphone. There was scattered noise in the hall from behind the doors but not one soul to be seen except for me. I turned around and closed the door. I went to the window and rubbed a circle in the dust with the fleshy part of my fist and peered out. Across the street and down at the corner was a small store I hadn't noticed when we first pulled up. I took the keys out of my pocket and rubbed my fingers over them. Fear gripped me. I didn't want to be on the streets by myself, but it was also still mid-morning. Hopefully, the potential dangers of this neighborhood wouldn't be lurking at this hour.

I snatched my purse and tucked it under my arm, adjusted my coat and went back through the door, locking it carefully behind me. I stood up straight and headed for the stairs. At the bottom, I stopped and stared at the mailbox again. 'V. Lamb'. How long had he been planning this? Bitterly, I marched out the front door that quickly slammed shut behind me. I looked up and down the street.

Kids were playing, people were talking. No one had a clue I had just been shut out of my house and family. I spotted the market and headed for it.

The ding of the bell signaled my entrance and the man behind the counter looked up from his newspaper, nodded and looked down again. I went to the cooler and grabbed a bottle of milk. Next, eggs, bread, and cheese. I plopped my stash on the counter and pulled two apples from a basket next to the cash register. The attendant put his newspaper down and started ringing up the items.

"Uh, excuse me," I said. "Where am I?"

He looked at me with an idiotic expression as if I was just released from the mental hospital.

"I mean, where in Kansas City? What part?"

"Oh, you're in Valentine. Pennsylvania Ave to be specific. You okay?" His expression turned to concern but he kept ringing up my items.

"Uh, oh, thank you. Do you happen to know anything about the apartment building on the corner across the street?"

"Nope. Well, I mean, what do you wanna know?" He put the last item in a paper bag pushed a few buttons and the total popped up on the register with a ding.

"Do you happen to know who the landlord is?" I pulled out my pocketbook and took out $2.13 and handed him the money.

"Oh, no ma'am. I don't know that. Is there a problem?" He took the money and deposited it into the drawer.

"Well, I have no heat and I just moved in. Someone else got me the place so I'm not sure who to talk to or what to do." I put my pocketbook back in my purse and slung it over my shoulder.

"Oh, that's not good," he said. "You need heat in this weather. My pal Carl lives there though, he's been there a long while. He'd probably know."

"Carl? Do you happen to know which apartment he's in?" I

picked up the bag and clutched the bottom to avoid any chance of the eggs falling.

"Sure, um, he's 304 I believe."

"Thank you. I'm sure I'll see you again." I gave a faint smile and turned to leave.

"Not a problem, ma'am." He nodded and picked up his paper again.

When I got to the front door, I forgot I needed a key to get in the building. I put my groceries down and rummaged for the key. I didn't know which worked for what door, so I had to try them both before the second one worked.

I picked up the bag, held the door with my foot and went in. I stopped again at the mailboxes and looked for a C. - *last name*. Three rows above my own box was a C. Naylor. Under the name was 304.

After dropping my groceries and putting what little food I had in the refrigerator, I grabbed my keys and went back to the hallway. I walked up the stairs to the third floor and examined every door until I came to 304. I hesitated for a moment before knocking. My heart was racing slightly. I wondered if Carl was nice.

I heard footsteps coming to the door from the other side, heavy, maybe boots. The locks clicked and the door opened. I was looking straight ahead of me and then had to lift my head. Carl was huge. A middle-aged man, balding, with a large belly. He was wearing a white t-shirt about 2 sizes too small. His suspenders were dangling by his sides and it looked like he was swallowing from his last bite of something.

"Yes?" He questioned nonchalantly. His voice didn't match his appearance. His tone was soft and kind and just this one word put me a bit at ease.

"Um, hello. Are you Carl?" I stuttered slightly.

"Uh, maybe. Who wants to know?" But this wasn't a demeaning response. There was almost something comical in the inflection.

"I'm Virginia. I just moved in downstairs and I have no heat. The guy at the corner store said you might know who to talk to about that?"

"Oh, well welcome." He wiped his brow and adjusted his jeans. "Yeah, um, Phil Costen is in charge of the building, but you probably won't find him till tomorrow. He's not around on the weekends."

"Is he the landlord?" I started to get nervous that I might not have heat tonight.

"No, he just manages the place but that's who you need to talk to. I have his number if you want it." He turned before I could answer and went to a small table next to a recliner. There were stacks of paper, an ashtray, old sandwich papers and a glass with brown liquid in it. He rifled through the papers, stopped when he found a small scrap and handed it to me. "Here. Give him a call tomorrow. He should be around."

"Do you have any idea what I could do tonight?" I took the scrap and nodded.

"Man, that's a doozy. Maybe stay with some friends that have heat?" I knew he meant well and couldn't possibly know my situation.

"Oh, that's a good idea. Thank you, Carl." I smiled briefly. "And thanks for the number." I lifted the paper in a thankful gesture and turned.

"Ma'am." He nodded in reply and closed the door.

I returned to the apartment and locked the door behind me. I opened the suitcase to see if there were any warmer clothes. I pulled out a pair of stockings and pulled them on over my existing ones. I tucked my coat in around me tighter, sat down on the bed, rolled to one side and cried until I fell asleep.

31

Time to Go

"It came to pass that there went out some of the people to gather and they found none." Exodus 16:27

It wasn't dark but I had slept most of the day out of pure emotional exhaustion. I managed to organize my meager surroundings and make it through the night, even though the temperature didn't relent. After a quick breakfast of toast and cheese, I hailed a cab outside the building and asked how much a trip to Excelsior Springs would be.

"'Bout two fiddy," the cabbie said.

I nodded and got in. I would have to figure out a better transportation system as this would deplete my finances in a matter of days. Maybe there was a bus route? There had to be. I shook my head. What was I thinking? I can't live like this. I made up my mind to speak to Bill as soon as I got to the diner, if he was around.

45 minutes later I got out of the cab in front of the diner. Noth-

ing here had changed even though my whole world surrounding this place had been turned upside down in the last 24 hours. The place looked dead, abandoned and then it dawned on me. The diner was closed on Monday. I had just wasted $2.50 on a cab ride to a job I didn't occupy on Mondays. There was no point in opening the diner as all the regulars knew we were closed. I cursed myself inwardly for being so distracted and stupid. Looking around at the lifeless parking lot my eye caught movement at the stables. Maybe I could wait there until Bill arrived, assuming he came in on Mondays. I looked both ways down the street, swallowed hard and went around the fence to the front of the barns. Bill's truck wasn't there but a couple of darkies were banging on horseshoes in the tackle barn. There was a bench just outside the barn door that I decided to occupy until he arrived. No one really paid any attention to me even though a slender, fair-skinned, red-head was certainly not a common sight at the stables.

It was about two hours before Bill arrived, which gave me a lot of time to think. Of course, all I did was think of the 'what-ifs' and found myself developing emotions behind actions that had not even occurred. The longer I sat, the crazier scenarios I came up with. What if Bill dropped me right then and there? What if he only loved me because I was unavailable? He never actually asked me to leave Creth. What about Helen? Would she come after me for seducing her ex-husband? Would Creth let me see the girls ever again if he knew I had cheated? Does he know I cheated? Would he be mad if I moved in with Bill? Could I move in with Bill? Would Bill feel he's now stuck with me? What if no one wants me?

My mind was a hurricane of thoughts by the time Bill pulled in the parking lot. He pulled up right in front of me and just looked at me. His face paused for a minute with an inquiring stare before turning off the engine. Then his expression turned to downtrodden understanding. It was as if he knew what had happened. I didn't get up from the bench. I sat there with my coat around me and my purse on my lap, both hands clutching it tightly. He knew something even if it wasn't everything. We had a brief but meaningful conversation with our eyes. He got out of the truck, walked over and looked down at me. He stretched out his hand and I looked at it, then put mine in his. He looked me in the eyes, gave a half-smile and pulled me into him. I immediately melted into his arms. The dam that had kept tears away all morning broke and I sobbed. His pressure on my body brought comfort. My arms were so tight around his neck and his arms so secure around my waist I felt strength from the compression. He didn't pull away until I did.

"Come on, let's talk." He wiped a tear from my cheek with his finger and walked me around to the passenger side of the truck, opened the door and helped me inside.

It was the first time I'd ever been in his truck. It smelled of hay and the sweet pungency of manure although it was not offensive. The leather seats had been worn in places and several rags were bunched in the center of the bench seat. He closed the door behind me and walked around to the other side. The truck was still warm and I invited the comfort like a small child invites a warm blanket at bedtime.

"Tell me. He leave you?" Bill closed the door behind him for privacy even though he didn't start the truck, not that I would have any idea where to go.

"No. I did." I didn't look at him for fear of rejection. I cleared my throat that had become extremely dry all of a sudden. I felt my stomach quiver and my heart race.

"You did? Well, that's... that's, I don't know. Did you do it for me?" He seemed lost for words as well.

"I don't know. I did it for me, I guess." I clutched my purse but eventually turned and looked up at him. "I don't love him, I'm not sure I ever did. We weren't supposed to be married." I scrambled for words of justification. As much as I wanted to excuse the affair, I knew that if I was married, I shouldn't have cheated, no exceptions. I pushed this thought as far away as possible.

"I think I love you, Bill. But... I..." I caught my breath and let it out with slight irritation. "I don't know about you." It was more of a question than a statement. "What we've been doing, it isn't right, we both know that. But, I'm really fond of you and..."

"Fond of me?" He huffed and gave a humorous smile. "Fond of me like you're fond of chocolate cake or puppies or something?"

"No, that's not what I mean, well, I don't know what I mean."

"Virginia, I've told you before how I feel about you. That hasn't changed. I truly feel that I love you."

Those are the words I needed to hear. Creth said them only a few times in our marriage but I didn't know if I ever said them back. I didn't want to lie, even though that was what I had been doing for several months. I didn't know if I ever loved Creth for real. Did I only love him because he had been a friend when I needed one? Because he was the father of my children, the provider... wait, I'd been providing as well. What did Creth offer? At the moment I couldn't think of a thing.

"You do?" I think I knew it, I just needed to hear the confirmation once more.

"You don't know that by now?" He smiled and tilted his head in a soft, kind manner. He leaned across the seat and took my face in his hand and kissed me. "What do you want?"

"I don't know. But not this." I pulled away.

"What do you mean? You don't want me?" His brows furrowed and he pulled back as well.

"No, that's not what I mean. Creth took me to the city yesterday and got an apartment for me."

Bill gave a big sigh and looked down almost defeated. "Well, then I guess you're all set."

"No! I'm not. I hate it. I have no heat. I'm 30 miles from here and the diner. I can't live there. I don't know why he'd do that. Maybe so I'm far away? I don't know. But I can't live there. It's over $2 to get here by cab and I can't afford that. I don't know if he expects me to get a job in the city or if he plans to shut me out of the girls' lives, but I can't do that. I don't know what to do but I know I can't live there." It all came out so fast that I stopped talking quick and just waited for his response.

"Really? He just *left* you there?"

"Yes. And I practically froze to death last night."

"Why didn't you call me?" His voice was of slight irritation but mostly concern.

"I don't have your number. It's at the diner. I couldn't call you from the house, you know that." My heart had resumed its normal rhythm. I was grateful for all of Bill's replies as they validated his feelings the more we talked.

He swallowed and looked down with an expression of concentrating as if he was solving algebra equations in his mind.

"Then you'll live with me. We could leave here. There's a job opportunity in California. Bloodstock Agent. I didn't tell you about it because I didn't want to leave you, but the opening is still available if I want it."

"California? What's a Bloodstock Agent?"

"Bidder. I'd be buying horses for folks. It's what I love, and the job pays really well. Lots of rich folks out there in California. We could make a go of it, you and me." I wasn't sure if this was a statement or a question.

"I don't think I can leave." There was concern and inquisition in my voice. Could I leave the girls? Take them with us? Creth would never allow it. What pulled at me more, the girls or Bill? I honestly didn't know.

"We can take the girls with us. Helen's fine without me and the kids will be okay too. Take the girls, let's do this. I love you, Virginia. I want you to be happy."

He put both hands on mine and squeezed them, giving me a loving smile not only with his mouth but his eyes as well. My head was swimming with thoughts but I pushed them all away and threw my arms around Bill. I held on tight and he embraced me without saying a word.

~

We had planned to leave as soon as the last frost hit. I had been back to the house several times to gather my things, all when Creth wasn't around although he clearly knew I had been there. With each visit, I gathered more of the girls' clothes as well until I was sure we had enough of a stockpile to last a few days. I had been living with Bill and never mentioned the apartment or lack of occupant to Creth, not that I ever saw him. I would meet the girls after school, and they would ask questions but I couldn't bring myself to be totally honest with them. I weighed the costs of taking the girls and examined carefully how I would do it. Should I ask Creth? Should I just leave a note? Yes, I had better leave a note at least otherwise he might assume someone had kidnapped them. I supposed that's exactly what I was doing but do they still call it kidnapping when it's your own flesh and blood?

It was early April and Bill and I had the truck all packed up. We had tied down our meager belongings in the bed with a few furnishings and suitcases. I stood outside the diner with lament, yet comfortable with the plan, I had left Lila in charge and had a note for George all penned out. Lila knew what was going on but for our consideration said nothing to Creth or George. I didn't know what would happen after today but was willing to take the risk. I heard the truck door slam shut and it brought me out of my trance. I looked over to the stables. Bill was watching me. He smiled and nodded a 'come on' motion. I nodded in silent reply and walked across the street. He opened the passenger side car door and I slid in. I stared across the street until we had left the parking lot.

We swung by the girls' school right as the last bell chimed. Parking in front, we watched the hordes of kids spill out of the front of the building. Eventually, Carol and Dolores made their exit, and I was quick to jump out of the truck to meet them.

"Come on girls, we're going on a trip! Won't that be nice?" I ushered them into the backseat of the truck, ignoring their confused looks and questions for the time being.

"But Mama, where are we going?" Carol piped up as she hiked herself in the cab.

"Girls, you know Bill." I tucked my coat around my legs and hastily got into the front seat. Both girls turned and stared at him. "Bill's taking us to California. Isn't that exciting? The ocean! Los Angeles and all the palm trees. Won't that be fun?" My fabricated enthusiasm wouldn't take anything less than excitement from the girls.

"But what about Daddy? Is he coming?" Dolores asked, always the voice of reason between the two.

I gave a sideways glance at Bill and he reached over and patted my hand. "Your daddy is gettin' a little break. You girls are going to love California."

I had left a letter for Creth on the nightstand. I knew he wouldn't find it until we were well past the state line. It took me three days to write it and I still wasn't sure about it. Of course, could anyone be completely sure of telling a good father that his children are going away? I couldn't think about it anymore. We were on the road and this was the plan. However, in the silence of the cab while the girls slept I repeated the letter over and over in my mind. Could I have said something different? Better? He was a good father after all. I had to literally shake my head to rid myself of the guilt.

Creth came in late that night to a quiet, empty house. The house was dark too, which was unusual. He opened the girls' room to find it empty except for a couple of crumpled blankets on the beds. Panic gripped him and he ran from room to room calling for them. Beside his bed, he noticed a large, white envelope. His heart pounded and his mind instantly dreaded the worse. Ripping the envelope apart he saw Virginia's perfect handwriting.

Creth,

I know you're not going to like this, but I have been given little choice. I have taken the girls to California. I met a man. He will take care of us. He is kind and loving. You have been a wonderful father, but I need to be their mother and I can't do that if we choose to continue the life you set up for me. I know this isn't fair… nothing is. But the girls are safe and happy. By the time you read this, we will probably be somewhere in Nebraska. Don't try to find us. I will write and let you know how the girls are when we are settled. I'm sorry I couldn't be the wife you always wanted but maybe now you can have a fresh start.

Take care,

V.

32

Arcadia, California

"It came to pass... that the woman returned out of the land of the Philistines and she went forth to cry unto the king for her house and for her land." 2 Kings 8:3

Arcadia, California was just outside of downtown Los Angeles, east of Pasadena. We got into town on April 15. Bill had set up a hotel for us for a couple of days until he found decent housing. The racetrack was in the center of Santa Anita Park and somewhere in all the crowds was Bill's new job.

The girls must have asked a thousand questions between Kansas and Nevada and after trying to answer them all my mind was hot and jumbled. They didn't understand why Creth wasn't with us, why I was going somewhere with Bill, why I leaned my head on his shoulder or sat in the middle seat of the front of the truck cab next to him. As much as I tried to explain, they just didn't grasp the concept of divorce, separation, and dissolution between two people that they assumed loved each other. The idea was not in their vocabulary. There were tears, arguments and a few tantrums but by the time we settled into the little house off Foothill Blvd it was the first of May and the girls were excited for the mild summer weather instead of the heat of the Midwest.

I wrote Daddy and told him we were in California but didn't quite have the nerve to tell him I'd left Creth. I suspected Creth may have informed Daddy already but was avoiding the conversation, nonetheless. I gave him our address and told him we'd love to visit if we could get up that way, but Bill was busy at the facility and I was active in making our little house a home. I knew we weren't married but everyone else assumed it except the girls and they certainly didn't understand the idea of divorce much less fornication, so I left it alone.

The current situation felt like a bubble I dared not let it burst. If Daddy knew too much he'd try and intervene. If Creth knew where we were there would be hell to pay. I felt as if I were just holding onto my life day by day and enjoying what I could. Bill would come home, throw his hat off and sweep his arms around my waist engulfing me in a big kiss. Then he would tickle and tease the girls until they giggled and ran off. It was a dream I feared would end sooner than I'd like but for now, I was happy, although unnerved most days.

"What's eatin' ya Virginia?" Bill said lying in bed one night after I assumed everyone was asleep. I had been staring at the ceiling, something I did a lot of in Missouri.

"How'd you know I was awake?"

"I know how you breathe when you sleep." His soft, comforting tone made me want to reveal everything to him. His charm, his wit and the way he made ne feel as if yI were the only person in the universe when he was around was intoxicating.

"What if Creth comes for the girls?" My voice was shaky.

"We'll deal with that when it happens." He rolled over to face me.

I turned my head to him and blinked, looking everywhere except into his eyes. He reached out and cupped my cheek. "We'll handle it. I love you and I won't let you come to harm. I love those girls too. I know how it is with an ex. Helen can be a bear but somehow it works out. I just hope the kids are alright. I think they are, but who really knows?"

I really didn't have anything to say. I felt as if he knew how I felt and there was no need for words. I leaned my head into his chest and felt his warmth and breathed in his musky scent. The tenderness drew me even closer and I wrapped my arms around him. He held me tighter and I fell asleep in the crook between his chest and shoulder, warm and comforted.

~

June was hot but not nearly the sweltering heat of Kansas City. Bill loved his job and was an excellent salesman. He bought, sold, traded, and bartered horses for folks all over the county and beyond. He'd come home almost every night with a wild tale or story about some wealthy man that bid $50,000 on a purebred steed or stallion. He loved the rush of the sale and the girls would jump up and down when Bill came to the climax of the story. He was a great storyteller and just seeing him happy and attentive brought me peace. We were doing well, too. We had money in the bank and had purchased another car just for me. The girls were starting school in August and had already made friends with the neighbors. The orange and lemon trees in our backyard provided enough fruit for juice and lemonade and Carol and Dolores had great fun constructing a lemonade stand out front. Foothill Blvd was a busy avenue and there were always folks wandering up and down providing a great business for the girls.

I had registered the girls for 4th and 5th grade in the local elementary school and had to provide guardian proof. They didn't require a birth certificate, so I wrote in Bill as their father. I prayed they never called the house asking for "Bill Lamb". What he didn't know couldn't hurt him and I convinced myself he would have agreed with me for the sake of the girls. As I was filling out their inoculation records that evening at the dining room table I was struck with an odd queasiness. I wondered if the roast chicken I had made for dinner didn't cook all the way through for some reason. I swallowed and sat up, adjusting my torso slightly. Nausea wafted over me and I felt the gurgling of bile in the back of my throat. I bolted for the bathroom barely making the toilet.

Bill shot up from his rocker and rushed to the bathroom door. "Virginia? You okay?"

I knelt at the foot of the toilet and hugged the bowl for a minute waiting for more but no more came. "Whooo... I don't know." I breathed out and let myself rest for a minute. Bill came and knelt beside me rubbing my back.

"Was it something ya ate?" He was concerned, but not for him and the girls and the tainted food they may have also consumed, just for me.

"Well, you all would have ate it too." I moved my legs around and got up on all fours. I breathed out and forced myself to stand up. Bill patted my back and flushed the toilet. I felt slightly better but still woozy. "I think I'm going to lie down."

Bill nodded and guided me to the bedroom with one hand on my back. I laid down on the bed and closed my eyes. The moment I did the realization came to me. What if I'm pregnant?

I didn't share my suspicion with Bill but the next day made an appointment with the nearest doctor. True to my assumptions, I was pregnant. I was about 6 weeks along with a baby due sometime in January. My feelings were torn between the fear of delivery and the deep joy of connection with Bill. I had two kids with Creth but neither felt as if we had made them together: a joint venture or a combining of our love. This felt like love. This felt like something we made together out of love, not obligation. But still, the fear of delivery hung near in my mind. My pregnancies weren't necessarily uncomfortable or miserable, just the delivery. On one or two occasions I even entertained the chance that I might not survive another delivery. I had to force those thoughts away otherwise they would impede my entire day and make me wrought with worry.

I was hesitant to tell Bill. I didn't know if he wanted any more kids and we weren't married, so this posed a big dilemma. The folks at the stables didn't know we weren't married. For all they knew, we looked like a normal American family with a couple of kids. Bill didn't divulge his personal life to co-workers.

After dinner the next day, the girls bolted out the door into the backyard and started yelling and playing. I was finishing up the washing when Bill came up behind me and wrapped his arms around my waist.

"When are you gonna tell me?" His voice was soft in my ear, tender. He kissed my cheek and squeezed me.

"About what?" I didn't look up from the sink, but I knew what he meant.

"About the baby." His hand moved down across my abdomen and circled it.

I stopped washing and looked down. "How did you know?"

"Really?" He turned me to face him. My hands dripping soapy water on the floor. "Your queasy and sick, haven't had your cycle this month and you've pulled away from me."

I shot an embarrassed glance down. "I didn't think you noticed things like that."

"Of course, I do. I love you." He hugged me and I didn't care that my hands were wet. It was just nice to have someone 'know' me. I felt tears welling up inside.

"I didn't know if you wanted any more kids." I pulled away but his hands returned to my shoulders.

"I want your child. Our child." He smiled and his hand brushed my cheek softly following my jawline to my chin. He lifted my chin and kissed me. "Marry me."

One tear crept from my eye and slid down my cheek getting caught in Bill's fingers. I smiled and nodded.

The next day Bill said I should do what was necessary to issue a divorce to Creth. I had no idea how to go about it but forced myself to humbly ask the county courthouse about the proceedings. Family courts were often the preferred route but if I filled out a divorce form stating either infidelity, drunkenness or abandonment, I could get a divorce so long as Creth signed it. I knew I had to state some reason for divorce and me leaving him for another man was not the ideal option. I checked the box marked drunkenness and abandonment and filed the paperwork.

Two weeks later I received a call from the county stating the paperwork had been signed and filed. I had been on pins and needles for so long that the relief of knowing Creth signed them felt like I had been holding my breath the whole time. There was no fight, no argument, no hassle and yet I felt a pang of guilt for stealing his girls away and giving me no grief for it. I decided to write a letter to Creth. I would use the local Post Office as the return address so he wouldn't know exactly where we were, although I couldn't imagine him coming all this way if he did. He hadn't put up a fight so far, why start now.

Creth,

Thank you for signing the papers. I know this is not what either of us wanted out of life but here we are. The girls are doing just fine. Carol started the 4th grade and Dolores started 5th in the local school and kids tease them about their accents. Everyone is healthy. I hope you've found a way to move on. I'm sorry our lives didn't turn out the way you wanted and I'm sorry for leaving with the girls so abruptly but I hope someday you'll understand and find it in your heart to forgive me.

Virginia

There really wasn't any more to say. I didn't tell him about the baby. I felt it would just add salt to the wound. But he didn't even act like he had been wounded? He had signed the papers without a fight or even a struggle. Maybe he didn't care about us anymore. Maybe he had resigned his family? Maybe he had found someone else and started over? Regardless, I slipped the letter in the mailbox and hoped for the best.

There was no response from Creth. Part of me worried and part was relieved. What was he doing? What did he tell people? I couldn't think too hard on that line or it would drive me crazy.

Daddy wrote about every week and begged us to come and see him. I didn't want him to know my situation but knew it was inevitable. At the end of June, we decided to make the trek to Klamath Falls. We pulled into Daddy and Hilda's place around 9 pm and after some hugs, happy tears, and quick reunions we all were put to bed in the loft. Daddy gave me a stern look as we closed the bedroom door but never said a word, at least not that night.

We spent a week with Daddy. The girls enjoyed the gardens and ran through the woods out back. I got to know Hilda a little better and she seemed to enjoy my company more than on previous visits. Daddy and Bill talked while I helped Hilda with supper most nights and although I couldn't make out all their words I was sure it was something to do with "making an honorable woman out of her," and "it's the right thing to do". Bill confirmed this and said it was just a matter of time. Daddy wouldn't hear of waiting and strongly urged us to get married in Klamath Falls so he could be there. He said he couldn't forgive himself for not being there the first time and was damned if he'd miss it again.

We had planned to leave July 1st because Bill had to get back to work. It took a day or two to drive back with the girls but Daddy insisted we stay through the weekend. Bill went down to the courthouse on Tuesday to get a marriage license. I made appointments for blood tests at the local clinic, a formality only at this point. Hilda took me shopping for a wedding dress at a local boutique. It was fruitless to wear white but Hilda insisted on an off-white sheath dress with cap sleeves and a tight waist. I wasn't showing yet and hadn't revealed our secret to anyone. I just hoped and prayed enough time would have passed when I delivered that the obvious timeframe would be forgotten about.

Bill came in the house on Thursday and handed me the paperwork. "Dillard Edward Byrd," it said.

"Dillard?" I shot a glance upward. "Who's Dillard?" My look was concerned and a little repelled.

"Um, that's me." His look was almost apologetic, looking for an approving response.

"Your first name is Dillard? Why didn't you ever tell me?"

"I dunno. Everyone's called me Bill for so long, I don't even think about it except for official stuff like this." He walked over to me, took the papers from my hands and held them. "It's still me, Virginia. That okay?"

"Of course," I gave a little huff and a smile. "I just didn't know. But I 'spect there's a lot about you I don't know." My smile was approving, and he hugged me tight, the papers crinkling on my back. "I want to know though. Tell me everything."

We were married on Friday, July 3 at the Klamath County Courthouse at 2 p.m. Daddy insisted on walking me down the courthouse aisle and passing me off to Bill. The girls were excited, but I think it was just because they got to dress up, even though Carol stripped herself the moment we got back to Daddy's and promptly put on her overalls again. It had all happened so fast that when we finally pulled back into our house in Arcadia it had felt like a dream.

I slowly unloaded the truck while the girls bounded into the house. I stood for a moment in the driveway trying to get a mental picture of my life now. So much had happened in the last 8 months. I breathed deep and let out a sigh. Bill came around the truck and put his arm around my shoulders.

"Happy, Virginia?" He said looking down at me.

"I think so," I said. "Are you?"

"Oh, yes." Then he kissed my head and scooped me up in his arms. I giggled at the silly act but let him carry me over the threshold of the house we'd already been occupying for a couple of months. He shut the door behind us with a kick of his heel, leaving the truck doors standing open.

33

A New Baby

"It came to pass, when the judge was dead, that they returned, and corrupted themselves more than their fathers, in following other gods to serve them, and to bow down unto them; they ceased not from their own doings, nor from their stubborn way." Judges 2:19

Winter in California was a welcome respite to summer even though it was quite mild compared to Missouri. It was nothing like winters in Kansas City with temperatures 20° below zero. We didn't always get snow, but it was always cold. Los Angeles, on the other hand, was a comfortable 70° most days dipping to around 40° each night. We kept our windows open all through November and the girls played in the backyard until it got dark, which unfortunately was only till about 4:30 p.m.

My growing belly left nothing to the imagination, and it was clear I was having a baby in a couple of months. The nausea had worn off, but the impending delivery was giving me nightmares. I woke at least a couple of times a week to dreams of legs tearing out of me, headless babies, and of Creth coming to rip the child away from me. Bill tried to alleviate my fears by constantly assuring me that where we lived offered some of the best doctors in the country. We had informed our doctor of previous deliveries and they were prepared to do whatever was necessary to equip me and the baby for a healthy and safe delivery. Yet, my mind was a torrent of doubt. What if the baby came too early? What if there was no time? Fear paralyzed me if I let myself think on it too long.

Bill in California

I was grateful for Christmas time, however, as it gave me a much-needed distraction from the approaching birth. Bill showered the girls with gifts on Christmas morning. Dolores reveled in her new pink velveteen sweater and matching skirt. Carol was ecstatic over her bicycle with red tassels that waved from the handlebars. I was completely floored to open a delicate black, velvet box revealing a gorgeous pearl necklace. We were definitely doing well and the joy we all received from the gifts made Bill beam with pride. He loved spoiling his girls, including me. We had two nice vehicles, a beautiful home, and all the comforts one could want.

A couple of days before Christmas the post office called to say we had a package to pick up. I retrieved the parcel and noticed it was from Creth addressed to the girls. I thought about opening it ahead of them but declined the intrusion. They were his daughters, they deserved privacy and respect, something I lacked growing up.

The girls were thrilled to have something from their father. Creth had sent Carol a new hunting knife for her 10th birthday in October, quite an impractical gift for the Los Angeles metropolis. For Dolores, he had sent a diary with a key and lock in September. For Christmas, he had sent them each $2, an Alice in Wonderland watch and a Milton Bradley game for Dolores and a Doctor and Nurse kit for Carol. They were in heaven. They had never been so spoiled.

My pregnancy had been easier over the last couple of months but was now entering the extremely uncomfortable stage. I couldn't tie my shoes without losing my breath and couldn't find a comfortable sleeping position, which made rest impossible. We were only 5 minutes from the nearest hospital and all appointments had been promising. The child seemed to be in the right position and my due date was the 20th of January. I could hold out one more month even though the anxiety over delivery was always pending.

The new year came, and we all celebrated by banging pots and pans at midnight. Bill brought home rum punch for everyone, although I was grateful he rarely drank otherwise. Creth almost always drank and it led to short-tempered responses and restless sleep for both of us. Bill didn't seem to have any flaws that I knew of yet

florescent lighting overhead. I was laid flat and an ache in my back began to rouse begging to be stretched.

My eyes slowly scanned the room. Plain, white, cold. Above me was an IV bag with a drip of liquid making its way down a tube. Into me, I supposed. My head felt heavy, but I forced it to one side. Bill was sitting next to me with a magazine in his hands. He hadn't noticed I was awake but the movement of my head startled him.

"Virginia. There you are, my girl." He put down the magazine on a small table next to the bed and leaned closer to me. "How ya feeling? Gave us quite a scare." His hand slid along the bed searching for mine. I felt the warmth of his fingers intertwine with mine and he squeezed my palm. I wanted to squeeze back but couldn't find the energy. I licked my lips feeling life enter me again. I didn't know how long I'd been out or what had happened. I had a baby, that's what had happened, but I already knew this was far more violent than the previous two. Did the child make it? What was it? Did *I* make it? I was alive, wasn't I?

I couldn't bring my brain to form words just yet but turned my head to look the other direction for some sense of barings. The hospital door was closed but I could see people through the slightly open blinds of the window in the door walking hastily back and forth. Bill stood up and made some movement that caused another beep to sound, slightly higher pitch than the current one that sounded out a steady rhythm.

Moments later a nurse came in with a smile on her face. "Oh, are we awake?" I hated it when people referred to themselves in an action they clearly are not a part of. I was awake... at least I thought I was. Everything was still a bit fuzzy.

The nurse checked the IV bag and made some notes on a clipboard. "How are you feeling, Mrs. Byrd?" She didn't look up from her clipboard, but I assumed she must really want to know, for her notes anyway.

I swallowed. "I don't know. I think I'm alright. My baby?" I blinked with more ferocity, trying to will my eyelids to rid themselves of the sleep clogging the corners.

"He's just fine. Healthy baby boy." She looked up and smiled quickly before turning back to the clipboard.

I turned to look at Bill. "A boy?" I involuntarily smiled and breathed a sigh of relief. He put his other hand on top of the one he was already holding and nodded.

"A boy. And he's a big boy too. You did good..." It was as if he wanted to say more but a catch in his voice stopped him and he looked down. He swallowed hard then looked up again and smiled, closed lips with an expression of pity on his face.

"What? What is it?" I could tell there was something more and I needed to know.

"You'll be fine. You just gotta heal, that's all." I could see tears welling up in his eyes and he kept trying to look away so as not to worry me. But now, that's all I could do. If the baby was fine, what was wrong with me?

"What is it?" I turned to the nurse. "What happened? How long have I been out?"

The nurse put her clipboard back into the pocket at the end of the bed and positioned herself beside the cot.

"You lost a lot of blood. There was heavy tearing and damage. We were able to repair it but it will take some time. You received a blood transfusion, and we need to watch you for a few days. You've been out for about 15 hours." She waited for my response unsure if there were more questions. When I didn't answer she continued. "Your baby is fine and in the nursery. He's doing well and your husband has been looking in on him frequently." She patted my arm and smiled; the same smile Bill had just given me. I was starting to get annoyed by the heavy presence of pity in the room. "I'll let you two be for a while. I'll be back." She straightened up, breathed deep and exited.

I turned back to Bill. "Is he really alright?"

"Yes, just fine. It's you I'm worried about. How do you feel? Do you hurt anywhere?" His eyes darted up and down my body as if to detect any additional injuries.

Now that I thought about it, I didn't feel anything anywhere. "Did they give me pain killers?"

"I assume so. You're not in any pain?" He asked.

"Well, I don't think so. But I haven't moved either. Am I still in one piece?" The thought that my lower half may not be there came rushing into my mind. It was an absurd thought but without sitting up, moving or feeling anything, the thought might not be that outlandish.

Bill gave a relaxed chuckle. "Yes, of course. And you'll be fine. You just need to heal. I'm so sorry, darling." His grin changed to concern and there was that pitying smile again. I was getting really annoyed by it.

"When can I see him?" I pushed the pity away and requested further distraction from my own ailments.

"I'll speak to the nurse." Bill got up and let go of my hand. The mild embrace felt as if it was the only thing anchoring me to reality. Once gone, I felt alone, drifting in and out of consciousness. He bolted out of the room and I saw him look left and right in the hall before the door closed behind him. I closed my eyes again. I must have dozed off because the sound of squeaky wheels and the click of heels jarred me awake again. Two nurses along with Bill came into the room wheeling a bassinet with a tiny bundle wrapped carefully in the middle of it.

One nurse came over and adjusted my bed so that my head tilted up. I felt an ache down below but pushed it aside to concentrate on the tiny human. I'd done this twice before so why did it feel so new? I suppose because it had been a decade since I grew the last person inside me, and the familiarity had faded. The baby was asleep but stirring softly. The nurse lifted him from the bassinet and placed him in my wanting arms. He was round-faced except for the small, bowed cone on the posterior part of his head. His perfect lips were pursed in an instinctual sucking motion and his tiny fingers were making their way out of the tightly swaddled blanket, each studded with flawless fingernails. I didn't realize how long it had been since I had held a baby this tiny in my arms and my heart melted with love and wholeness. Bill sat on the bed next to me and put an arm around both of us.

"We'll leave you two alone for a minute, but I'll be back shortly to retrieve him." The nurses left the room and closed the door. It was just the three of us and we were a whole, little family. I was so caught up in the moment I forgot about the girls.

"Oh, where are the girls?" I asked

"They're fine, they're fine. Jeannie, next door, has them. She said to take our time." Bill comforted me with a pat on the shoulder and I intuitively rocked the baby followed by a shhhhhing sound. "Have you thought of a name?"

"I haven't really thought of anything, I guess. Maybe Richard? After my dad?" I looked up at Bill for approval.

"Sure. That sounds fine."

And that settled it. Richard Edward Byrd came into this world on January 15, 1954, and just like that, it felt like our family was whole.

34

❦

Say Goodbye to Your Girls

"It came to pass, when she travailed, that the one put out his hand: and the midwife took and bound upon his hand a scarlet thread, saying, this came out first." Genesis 38:28

Two weeks later I left the hospital, baby in tow, thankful to finally be going home. I almost forgot what home looked like. I'd been so sick of seeing the inside of the hospital along with sleepless nights alone in my room or the occasional heavy-breathing roommate. I craved homecooked meals or at least something I concocted myself. The urge and joy of cooking had not left me, and I relished the idea of creating a menu each week for my growing little family. Rubbery turkey and floury gravy were not cutting it in the hospital, and I tried to pare down my order each day knowing the bill was eventually coming. I longed for the feel of a knife in my hand, chopping vegetables, slicing cheese, and whisking delicious sauces over the stove. I couldn't think of it too long or it just made me hungrier. When Bill wheeled me out to the car. I could almost taste the rump roast I would make that weekend.

Richard had spent most of his first few days in the nursery handed off to me only to nurse or cuddle when visitors came. This was much different than when the girls were born. We could go home right away, or I was already at home and things just went on as normal. This hospital stay, my recovery, the lack of contact with my newborn was unfamiliar and strange. It was as if society was trying to change the way women had babies. Although I knew that if it had not been for the hospital I would have most likely died.

I carefully got up from the wheelchair and sat in the car, baby in arms. I was still sore but getting better every day. I missed intimacy with my husband but knew that scenario was still a far way off. Our focus was Richard. Little Richie, sweet little, red-faced boy. I had a boy. The girls had come to see him only a couple of times after school. Our neighbor Jeannie had been such a doll watching the girls every afternoon when they got home from school until Bill came home from work.

Jeannie had two daughters, one Carol's age and a 5-year old. They all got along beautifully so it was such a wonderful reception to see everyone in the driveway welcoming us home. Carol and Dolores were jumping up and down and waving ferociously when Bill pulled in the driveway. The bump of the sidewalk jolted my lower half making me wince, but I forced a smile. Bill ran around after stopping the car and opened my door, hovering around me as if I was going to drop the baby at any moment. The girls buzzed around me trying to catch a glimpse of their brother and I pushed my way through the small crowd to the door. Bill took off his hat and opened the door, shooing away the girls from my path.

The house smelled like home and I paused for a moment to

breathe in the familiar scent. I looked around as if I hadn't seen the place in months. I missed my kitchen, my comfy couch, and my bed. The girls scooted in around me and raced off in different directions with yelps of happiness and childhood glee. Bill stared at me as if he was waiting for me to make the next move. I walked to the couch and sat down with a relieved sigh. It was good to be home.

I placed the sleeping baby on the cushion next to me and took off my coat. Richard didn't move but merely pursed his lips and cooed softly. This was so nice. Lulled by the peace of the moment, I leaned back and closed my eyes. I could hear Bill rustling around the house but that soon faded, and I was jolted awake minutes later by a shriek. I had momentarily forgotten where I was, shook my head and quickly regained my senses. Richard had woken up and was now wriggling out of his swaddling clothes making an awful fuss.

My breasts felt heavy and tingling and I knew he could sense it was feeding time as well. But this was different. No nurse was verifying my position, the latch, the timing; this was all me. Him and I and we knew what to do. I quickly released a breast and scooped him up. We instantly felt the relief and we both closed our eyes again, letting the comfort wash over us. I leaned my head back and dozed in the comfort of my home to the faint sounds of giggling girls and a puttering husband.

I awoke again abruptly to a fussy baby wriggling in my arms. Guess feeding time was over, yet he did not seem satisfied. The fussing turned to spattered shrieks, then all-out screams. Bill came rushing in when he realized the child was not being consoled.

"What's all the hub-bub?"

"I don't know," I said concerned. I moved him off me and checked the diaper, clean. I swaddled him tighter and held him to me making soft 'shhhh-ing' sounds but nothing alleviated the wailing.

"He hungry?" Bill asked.

"I just fed him, and I thought he was fine. He's getting something because I feel better but I don't know why he's all in a tizzy now." I stood up and quickly remembered my injury. I slowed my movement and rocked him back and forth as I headed for the bedroom. The crying didn't stop and eventually, the girls came in wondering who pinched the baby, a phrase they heard Jeannie say numerous times whenever a baby was heard howling somewhere.

There was a bassinet in the corner next to the bed, something we had purchased before I went into labor and completely forgot about but was grateful it was there. However, little Richie was having none of his bassinet or my touch, for that matter. Bill and I could hardly hear each other over the shrieks, and I worried something must be wrong with him. I didn't remember the girls crying this inconsolably before but I'm sure they must have to some degree.

For three hours I paced the room, checked for injury, fed him, and rocked him until I couldn't keep my own eyes open any longer. I found a position where he seemed to settle slightly, and Rich finally gave up out of pure exhaustion. For a few moments, we both went unconscious.

The reprieve didn't last long. By midnight he was at it again. I knew he was getting milk, was clean, dry and not damaged, at least not anywhere I could see, yet the cries persisted. We were grateful for 6 am because it meant we could call the doctor and at least speak to a nurse on call. She made an appointment for later that morning and I was thankful Bill had a couple of days off to spend with us. He took Rich and let me get some sleep until 9. Fatigue had so overwhelmed me that sleep came quickly, even with the cries and screams from the other room.

A few hours later, the three of us sat in the waiting room again trying to calm a sobbing child among annoyed glances and looks from other patients. I bolted upright when our name was called, desperately wanting to leave the waiting area and get some answers.

The doctor carefully looked over Richard, checked eyes, ears, nose, mouth, heart, lungs, all working fine, and offered his opinion. "I'm afraid your baby has colic." He tossed the stethoscope behind his head and pulled out a clipboard to make some notes.

"What's that?" I asked.

"Oh, nothing to worry about." He didn't look up at me but kept his attention to the clipboard. "It usually doesn't come on for a few weeks but there's really nothing else it could be. Clenched fists, pudgy tummy, yes, yes... all the signs. It will go away eventually."

"But what can I do about it now?" I said, motioning my head toward him in hopes of receiving more eye contact.

"Well, not much, I'm afraid. Babies often get this but keep an eye on him. If he doesn't relieve himself normally or you notice changes in the way he eats, let me know."

"How would I know that? We just went home yesterday. I don't remember him being like this in the hospital."

"They may have fed him formula in the nursery. Common procedure, especially if mom is incapable of providing."

"Fed him? You mean they fed him more than I can give him? How do I fix that?" I swallowed hard and Bill rubbed my back for comfort, but it was only making me irritated. "Why wouldn't they tell me that?"

"Well, it's pretty common, and you *were* in and out of consciousness for several days there. I'm sure they had to supplement." He walked over to the counter and set the clipboard down. "Look, I'm sure this is just new baby jitters. You'll figure it out. Feed him whenever you can. You'll make more milk if he needs it. In the meantime, you're welcome to buy formula or just give him whole milk but it will hinder your milk production. I suggest feeding him every 45 minutes until your milk comes in more. I know it's hard but you'll do great." He came over and put both hands on my shoulders and patted me, offering a patronizing smile. "Congratulations!" And out the door he went.

I stood there more shocked than grateful. "Every 45 minutes?" I stammered, looking up at Bill. "How will I do anything else?"

Bill let out a huff. "Come on, let's go."

He mirrored my irritation, opened the door and ushered us out. Rich had settled slightly but was still wiggling and coughing uncomfortably.

Me with Baby in Lap

Three days later I had barely slept 45 minutes total much less been able to feed Richy that often. I convinced myself things were getting better but with Bill going back to work and the girls taking up all my time the second they got home from school, I was exhausted to the point of delirium. I was short with the girls, agitated at Bill and sometimes lost track of time staring into space as Rich screamed in his bassinet. I felt there was no relief in sight. The girls tried to help but their attention span was about as long as my temper these days and their assistance quickly fizzled with the prospect of tree houses or neighbor friends as a better option.

Bill helped as much as he could but with high demand at the track and late nights with buyers, his help waned too and I realized it was me, only me. 5 o'clock couldn't come soon enough and a dry martini was a welcome friend numbing the exhaustion and making sleep come easier when I was able to get some.

Days blended together and I hardly knew what day of the week it was until Saturday when the girls didn't bound out of the house to school, a routine I was thankful they had down. My attention to the baby was so consuming I felt a twang of guilt whenever the girls were in the house. I couldn't offer them the attention they deserved and felt myself scowl at the baby for disturbing my family. It wasn't his fault, for heaven's sake. It must have been lack of sleep that caused the disdain for the situation. I was truly grateful I had a baby with Bill, but nothing had been the same since Richy came along. I hadn't been healing very fast and even riding in the car was uncomfortable, much less any form of intimacy with my husband.

A few weeks slipped by in a blur and before I consciously realized it, Richard had ceased the incessant crying all hours of the day and night and I could get in a good two to three hours sleep in a stretch. It's amazing what sleep will do for your sanity. Richy was now two months old and had finally switched completely over to formula. Breastfeeding was a battle I relinquished soon after the doctor's appointment as I wasn't about to fight sleep, colic, *and* poor milk supply. Getting into a better routine brought my spirits up; that or the two or three martinis I had after the girls got home. Either way, I was in a much better mood until I received the letter.

I recognized the handwriting immediately. I pulled the envelope from the box with a clear return address from Creth in the upper left corner. My hands began to shake involuntarily, and I shook them violently to each side of me to try and alleviate the jitters. I wanted to tear open the letter but also couldn't bring myself to know what it said. I swallowed hard, my mind racing with the worst possible news. He knew where I was, he addressed the letter directly to our house. Did Daddy tell him? Did someone rat on me? I blinked away all the possibilities and just opened it. The handwritten letter was short. My eyes darted to the bottom where it was simply signed, Creth.

Virginia,

I know I haven't reached out all this time but the whole situation was a shock to me. I understand that you never really loved me, but we did create two human beings together and I feel they should have their dad in their life. I don't mean you any harm but would like to see my girls. If it's okay with you, I'd like to pay to have the girls come out on the train to see me this summer. If you agree, I'll have them take the train on May 30. They should arrive here on June 3. I've included the schedule and will send the tickets should you agree. There is an attendant to assist them along the journey. The whole process should be fairly easy for them. I do miss them so. I hope all is well with you.

Creth

I moved the top paper aside to examine the arrangement, a typed schedule from the Pennsylvania Railroad stating the departure times and arrivals. Could children this young go cross country by themselves? I suppose if there was someone to help along the way. But it was so far all by themselves. He *was* their father, after all, and probably deserved to see them. I'd kept them from him for months and that really wasn't fair.

I couldn't tell if I was trying to convince myself or talking myself out of it. The idea of a summer with just the three of us seemed appealing. I could get settled a little more with Rich and Bill and maybe even have some time alone, or at least enjoy the typical nuclear family, as it was called. I realized I hadn't left the mailbox and was standing in the driveway as the cars rushed by. I nearly forgot I laid Rich down for a nap several minutes ago and only then noticed he wasn't screaming. I didn't know whether to relish the moment or rush in to see if something was wrong. I did the latter.

He was sleeping peacefully, finally pacified along with his blanket and bobby, the small stuffed rabbit we tucked in next to him every night. I couldn't help but stare. His tender lips pursing and sucking at an imaginary nipple while his hands twitched and clenched with involuntary reactions. For that brief second, I was at peace too. I didn't know whether to stay in the moment or actually get some work done around the house. I decided to linger a few more moments then quietly snuck out of the room to try and do both.

It wasn't more than 10 minutes of silent sweeping before the girls burst into the room arguing about whether or not Polly Persons had ever worn braces. I could have shot both of them on the spot.

"Shhhhhhhh!" I demanded in the quietest yell I could muster. They immediately halted and stared at me. "He's finally asleep! Please be quiet!" I loudly whispered. I rushed toward them and shooed them back out the door. "Out!" I said, "I'll bring you a snack if you're quiet."

I shut the door behind them and froze to listen. Surprisingly, there were no sounds from the bassinet. I smiled to myself, acknowledging a little bit of me had returned for a brief second. I hadn't felt like myself in a long time.

I hurried to the kitchen to gather some cookies and a couple of glasses of milk, then tip-toed out the front doors where the girls were waiting on the steps. I sat down next to them and dished out the treats.

"How would you girls feel about visiting your Daddy?"

Carol chugged the milk halfway, shoved a cookie in her mouth and washed it down with the rest of the milk before even looking at me. Dolores stopped as soon as I finished the sentence and her eyes narrowed searching for more explanation.

"What... what do you mean?" Dolores said, resting the cookie on her lap.

"I mean just that. Your dad wants to see you so he's asked to have you come out this summer. Would you like that?" I was searching her face for how she really felt. She wasn't giving anything away. Carol slowed her ravenous appetite and instead nibbled another cookie.

"I want to see Daddy," Carol said through crumbs.

"Me too," replied Dolores.

"Well, let me talk to Bill. We're thinking maybe having you ride out on the train. Would you like that?"

"By ourselves?" Asked Dolores, still curious about the intent behind it all.

"Well, yes. I think you girls are big enough and your Daddy thinks you could do it. I would drop you off and he would pick you up." I waited for their reaction before either accepting their response or trying to convince them further.

"I wanna see Daddy," Carol repeated, and scooted in a little closer to my side. I felt as if she was telepathically trying to feel her Daddy by sitting closer to me.

Dolores looked at Carol then back at me. "We'll be fine, Mama. We can do it."

"Oh, I know you can. You're my brave girls. You can do anything. And then I'll see you at the end of summer, so you can start school." I wrapped my arms around both of them and pulled them in close. "I'll write your dad and tell him."

Bill thought it was a great idea, but I couldn't tell if he thought it was a good idea for us or for them. I sensed he was more excited for the time alone with just the three of us than the idea of the girls spending time with their father. But I was okay with that too.

I longed for some 'us' time, even though we now had a little one. As summer neared Rich became easier to handle and we were all finally getting some sleep.

Creth sent the tickets as promised and on May 30th Dolores and Carol boarded the Pennsylvania Railroad. We all were at the station to say goodbye. This would be the longest I had ever been away from my girls. Bill gave them a squeeze and patted their heads. They both snuggled Rich in my arms and kissed his face and I passed the baby to Bill so I could hold them both fully and tightly. I knelt on the hard concrete and they both wrapped their arms around my neck. I could feel their hot breath on my neck, and I closed my eyes to mentally remember their touch, smell, and feel. At the last minute, Carol said she didn't want to go and started to cry but Dolores firmly took her hand, pursed her lips together and nodded at me confidently.

"We'll be alright, Mama." She said. Carol drew in closer to her sister and they turned to look at the large, heavy train car. A kind-looking lady attendant in a navy-blue pencil skirt and white button-down blouse was waiting on the step with a smile. She moved slightly to the right and held her hand out to the girls, urging them on the train.

I felt a hot wave of fear rise up in me, starting in the back of my neck and engulfing my face. Tears immediately sprang into my eyes and I blinked hard. I swallowed, trying to shove the fear back down. Rich was getting restless in his father's arms, but I forced myself to ignore him. The girls got on the train and I watched them through the windows making their way to their seats. After getting situated, they looked out the window at me and I waved emphatically.

The sound of the train whistle seemed to turn on the tears I had so desperately been trying to suppress. They flowed freely now. The train lurched through all the cars and took hold of the couplings. It began to move ever so slowly. I followed it down the platform with my hand on the window. Carol's face mimicked mine and Dolores looked like she was trying to stay strong; maybe for me, maybe for her sister, I didn't know but I could see this was just as hard on her. I followed the train to the end of the platform and stopped, staring until I couldn't see their faces in the window any longer. Something dark and empty swept over me and I let my emotions take over. I cried all the way home, after all, there was no one to be strong for anymore.

35

Tough Decision

"It came to pass in the days when the judges ruled, that there was a famine in the land. And a certain man... went to sojourn in the country of Moab, he, and his wife and his sons." Ruth 1:1

The house was quiet, something I would have welcomed gratefully just a few days prior to the girls leaving. But now, there was only silence. No laughter of little girls or cries from an infant. Bill was gone all day, sometimes until late in the evening and I was left with the baby. I tried to encourage myself with the notion that bonding with Rich was healthy and good, but I was just lonely. After the girls left, there was no point for their friends to visit, which meant no visits from their parents either. The summer past and I heard nothing from the girls except that they had arrived safely and were going to have a great time according to a quick call from Creth. But as the start of the school year neared, I became more anxious for them to come home.

I gathered my nerves and called Creth. A woman answered the phone. "Hello?"

"Um, hello. Is Creth there?" I said, shaking a bit.

"No, he's not. May I ask who's calling?" The voice seemed firm and direct.

"Yes, this is Virginia. Did I call the right number?"

"Yes, Creth lives here. You're Carol and Dolores' mother?"

"Yes. Are the girls there?" I wasn't sure who this person was and didn't know if I should divulge too much more information.

"No, they're in school."

I paused, trying to think why they would be in school. "Oh. In school?"

"Yes, they started 3 days ago." The voice again was firm yet polite.

"Um, may I ask who you are?" My nerves were starting to be on edge.

"I'm Billy. I'm a friend of Creth's. I sometimes watch the girls." She too didn't offer much information.

"I thought they were starting school here." I now felt odd having a parental conversation with someone I didn't know.

"Well, I can have Creth call you about it later. Shall I take your number?" There was still no emotion in her voice, only directness.

"Yes, I suppose. Yes, please have him call me right away." I gave her my number although I was sure Creth already had it and hung up.

Why would they have started school? Our schools didn't start for another week and I had already registered them. What if he didn't plan on sending them back? Did they want to stay? Who was this Billy person? Were they safe? My mind started composing all sorts of dubious scenarios. By the time Bill got home, I was so worked up that I barked at him for opening the door too loud.

"What's up, Virginia?" He took off his hat and coat and stretched his arms to me but I didn't want to be touched.

"I called Creth today to find out about the girls and some woman answered the phone saying they had already started school back there." He backed away with a puzzled look on his face.

"What?" He made a quick glance around the room before pulling out a dining room chair, motioning me to sit.

I did and continued. "Yeah, I don't know what to do." I rested my elbow on the table and rubbed my cheek in concern.

"Well, did you speak to Creth or the girls?" His eyebrows were furrowed trying to uncover clues to the situation.

"No. No one was there, except this woman. I gave her my number. They better call back." It was 7:30 p.m. in California and 9:30 p.m. in Missouri so I didn't think we would get a call tonight, but I was irritated we hadn't already.

Bill tried to calm me with assurances that someone would call tomorrow and not get so worked up about it, but I couldn't help it. What had I done? Did I give my children away not knowing if I would see them again? Surely a father wouldn't keep his children away from their mother, but that is exactly what I had done to him. Was this revenge? There was so much swirling in my head that I started to feel nauseous. Suddenly, supper didn't sound appetizing and I excused myself to the bedroom to lie down. I asked Bill to watch Rich and get himself something to eat. The stress of the situation made my blood boil and my heart pound, but I closed my eyes and before I knew it, it was morning.

The nauseated feeling had not left though. I still felt queasy and wondered if I was coming down with something or the stress was getting to me. Bill left early and Rich was still asleep in his bassinet by the bed. Eventually, we would have to move him to his own room, now that he could have a room to himself with the girls being gone, but for now, the close proximity to my nearest offspring felt comforting. I grabbed my Pall Malls on the nightstand and headed to the kitchen for coffee. Bill had made a pot before he left, something he was not accustomed to doing but I appreciated the gesture. The coffee was still hot and felt calming as it slid down my throat, warming me from the inside. The blaze of my cigarette and the long inhale rounded out the morning routine but the minute I blew my first puff out into the air, bile rose in my throat and I barely made it to the sink before losing the little bit of coffee I had just drank and whatever remained in my stomach the night before. I threw the cigarette into the sink as I vomited, and the coffee spilled on the counter. The heaving had instantly worn me out and I slid down the cabinets in front of the sink and sat on the floor.

I had but a moment of reprieve when Rich began to cry. I couldn't pull myself up quickly, so I rolled onto all fours and slowly gathered some strength. I paused after standing to confirm I wasn't going to be sick again and judged that I could make it to the crib and back. I pulled Rich from the bassinet and laid him on the bed for changing. The minute the stench of a full diaper hit my nose, I gagged. I quickly covered my mouth but it was too late. Bile and vomit filled my hands and dripped down on the bed.

I quickly grabbed all the blankets I could find and wiped my face and hands. Holding my breath as best I could, I cleaned up the baby, gathered all the soiled blankets in my free hand and carried all to the kitchen. The coffee was still dripping onto the floor creating a puddle where I had just been sitting a moment earlier. I placed Rich in his highchair next to the table and tossed the blankets into the sink. Grabbing a fresh towel, I mopped up the coffee and added it to the pile. I didn't have the energy or willpower to tackle the laundry just yet so I reached for a banana, peeled it, and tore it into bits with my fingers before handing it to Rich. I then sat next to him, crossed my arms on the table and leaned my head down trying to will the queasiness away.

I sharp kick on the underside of the table made me jerk up, not realizing I had dozed for a few minutes. Rich had finished his banana and was getting restless. I dreaded the rest of the day but re-linquished myself to the tasks before me and trudged on. At least I only had one child to worry about now.

By the end of the week, the nausea hadn't gotten better but I also didn't have any other symptoms. I tried to push the idea out of my head but finally realized the sooner I knew the truth, the better. A quick test from the doctor confirmed my suspicions. I was pregnant again. It had only been 9 months since Rich was born and I felt a sense of deja vu from the first time this happened with the girls a decade ago. Why do doctors all assume this is what every woman wants? They offer the news with a hearty 'congratulations' but to me, this was a death sentence. It had taken so long to recover from Rich and the girls had certainly been no picnic that I started to panic on the drive home. So much so, I had to pull over on the side of the road for fear I was going to drive straight into a tree and finish it all right then and there. My hands were shaking as I pulled a Pall Mall from the box and lit it. I inhaled deeply hoping the nicotine would reach my brain faster and offer me the sense of calm I so desper-ately sought. Smoke filled the car and I heard Rich cough a little. I regained my senses and rolled down the window.

From the shock of the news of the pregnancy and not hearing from Creth or the girls all week, I felt like I was living outside my body, or else, trapped in it and couldn't escape. I waved my hand in front of my face, forcing the smoke out the window. I looked in the rearview mirror at my son. "Well, what are we going to do about this?" I was half hoping he would respond with some brilliant in-sight, but he just waved his arms and legs up and down, restricted by the car seat. "Yeah, me too, buddy." I finished my cigarette and let out a deep sigh. At least I made it home that afternoon.

I didn't tell Bill about the pregnancy that day. Instead, I focused my attention on why I hadn't heard from the girls. I waited until

Bill got home that evening and decided we'd call them together. The phone rang several times before someone picked up.

"Hello, is Creth there?" I said confidently, Bill leaning in close to my head to hear the conversation.

"No, he's out." The voice sounded familiar, but I couldn't place it.

"Do you know when he'll be back?"

"Next week, I think. May I ask who's calling?"

"This is Virginia."

"Oh, hello Virginia. It's Merle. I'm here with the girls while Creth's hunting this weekend." Merle was Creth's sister. She and his other sister Muriel often watched the girls when I lived there when we had to be at the diner or dancehall. She was so helpful when we needed extra hands.

"Oh, hi. Um... Are the girls there?" I knew it was late, but I thought I'd chance it.

"Well, yes, but they've gone to bed. I can have them call you to-morrow." She sounded hurried as if she wanted me off the phone as quickly as possible.

"Yes, please do. I haven't talked with them in months and I hear they started school out there." I was fishing for information, but she didn't seem to catch on or else wasn't willing to give any.

"Yes, and they love it. I'm so glad they're here with their father," she stated judgmentally.

"Well, that's good, I guess. I'm glad they're happy. Will you please have them call me tomorrow?"

She agreed hastily and hung up the phone.

I hung up the phone as well and turned to Bill. I could feel tears welling up behind my eyes and he gave a sympathetic smile and reached for me. I gave into the embrace and let the tears fall, partly for my girls, partly for the unsure situation before me.

Saturday came and went and there was no phone call. I tried call-ing Sunday morning but there was no answer. I knew the girls were safe. Maude and Merle always took good care of them and I knew Creth would too. I just didn't know why all this secrecy and reticence was happening unless it was out of pure revenge. I wouldn't give up though. I had made my mind up about that.

About the other thing, however, I was extremely indecisive. I still hadn't told Bill and I had to be at least four weeks along by now but no chance of showing for some time. Rich took up my days and by the end of them, I was exhausted. I couldn't imagine adding another infant to the mix. But it wasn't just the idea of another baby, it was the delivery. My pregnancies were not that bad, save some morning sickness here or there, but the deliveries were hell. I was scared I wouldn't live through another. I barely lived through the last. But what could I do? I started praying for a miscarriage, even though I really hadn't prayed for anything in my life. Occasionally, Bill insisted we go to church, but I never had a desire to pay God any mind. He certainly had done nothing for me in my life and here I was faced with another horrid predicament.

I had heard about women ending their own pregnancies but only through gruesome tactics and failed attempts leaving children deformed or women with serious infections. I didn't want to risk harming myself further, but the risk of another delivery made the prospect awfully tempting. The longer I waited, the more traumatic it would be. If I could induce a miscarriage maybe my body would expel the situation by itself. But I didn't know the first thing about inducing a miscarriage much less a full-on abortion. I knew I didn't want any more children but beyond that, it was the fear of dying a painful, agonizing death that provoked me further. But would an abortion be any better?

The next week I left Rich with Jeannie for a couple of hours and headed to the library to learn all I could. Not surprisingly, there was not a lot of information on self-inflicted abortions. I did find a few topics of self-induced miscarriages dating back to the 1700s using strange methods such as swallowing gun powder, consuming opium or tansy oil or throwing oneself down the stairs. Unfortunately, none of those elements were highly accessible unless I were to fall down the stairs at the city hall building. Our own home was only one story, and I knew the two steps into the house wouldn't suffice in the least. Anyway, I didn't think I could force myself to fall. The body naturally wants to protect itself from harm and the instinct to catch myself would probably kick in.

I left frustrated and irritated. Jeannie still had Rich for another hour or so and I wandered home slowly. We only lived 8 blocks from the library, and this was enough time to think about my options. The books did say trauma to the vaginal area or a punch in the gut is often enough to cause a miscarriage but good lord, I'd already had enough trauma to that area for one lifetime. What if I did it very carefully? I had heard rumors of rusty hangers but the visual of that made me gag. It would have to be clean whatever I used. But could I go through with it?

I passed Jeannie's house before reaching my stairs and glanced in the window. She was washing dishes at the kitchen sink and Rich was asleep on the floor, surrounded by pillows and blankets. Swirls of maternal instincts swept over me and my eyes became heavy with tears. I blinked them away and quickly went next door before Jeannie saw me.

I walked in, shut the door behind me, locked it and looked around. A knife would do too much damage. A pencil probably wouldn't reach. Then my eyes landed on the sewing basket on the floor next to my rocker. I went to it and rummaged through the cloth, yarn, scissors and... knitting needles. They were soft-tipped, about 12 inches long and offered smooth aluminum. I had several pairs, mostly straight with a flat stopper on one end. I pulled up a couple of sets and examined them. I figured the smallest would do even though I really had no idea what I was doing.

I took them to the sink and poured rubbing alcohol all over them then set them on a clean towel to dry. My heart was pounding but I pushed the fear aside convincing myself this was better than the alternative. Bill wouldn't be home for a few hours and Rich was asleep. It was now or never.

I gathered a few towels from the closet and laid them out on the bed allowing several layers above the coverlet. I retrieved the needles from the kitchen and caught sight of a bottle of gin on top of the refrigerator. I set the needles down again and grabbed the bottle, taking a large swig. The movement was so fast the gin spit back up in my face and dribbled off my chin. I coughed from the sheer strength of the stuff, wiped my mouth and replaced the bottle. Grabbing the needles again I headed to the bedroom.

The sun was streaming through the window and I felt this needed a more ominous environment, so I closed the curtains, which blotted out nearly all the light. I didn't need light since I couldn't really see what I was doing. I pulled off my skirt and laid on the bed. I couldn't ignore the pounding in my chest and temples. I had no idea if this would work but I had to try. I wished I had brought the bottle of gin in the room with me and realized this is how people performed surgeries before ether. I supposed if you got drunk enough you could endure about anything. But I made up my mind that any more alcohol and I wouldn't think straight to perform the procedure.

I breathed a few heavy breaths as if I was about to go deep-sea diving and maneuvered the needles where I assumed they needed to go. I did have some familiarity with women's anatomy but honestly had no idea what I was poking at. A couple of sharp pains shot through my body as flesh resisted but then the needle went further on its own. I felt no resistance but my abdomen seized and clenched with deep pain. A few more quick jabs and I pulled the apparatus from me. There was blood but not as much as I imagined. I laid there a few more minutes not knowing if I had done anything but cut my womb. My heart was still pounding and now tears were building. I let the emotion overtake me and curled up on my side and let myself cry. I felt hot liquid on my thighs and jumped up. I ran to the bathroom and sat on the toilet. I watched as bright red blood dripped slowly into the bowl. The doorbell rang, suddenly startling me from the position and I realized I had been sitting there for over 15 minutes. I stuffed a wad of toilet paper between my legs, regained my composure and pulled on my skirt.

I shot a quick glance at my face in the mirror before exiting the bathroom but couldn't look myself in the eyes. I felt ashamed, disgusted, bruised and weak. With a quick brush of my hand across my cheek, I hurried to the door. It was Jeannie with Rich.

"Oh, good. You're home. He's been crying for the last 20 minutes." She forcefully handed me a hysterical Rich and grabbed at the bag slung over her shoulder. "I'm sorry I couldn't keep him longer. Did you find what you needed at the library?" She was trying to be polite, but I could tell she was just making conversation until I released her.

"Um, yes, thank you." I tried to collect myself and responded again. "Thank you so much for watching him. I'll take him from here." I forced a smile and retreated from the doorway as she waved and hopped off the porch back home.

Behind the closed doors, I bounced Rich in an attempt to calm him, but I felt that his behavior matched my own. I wanted to cry and scream as well. So I did. We stood in the living room shaking, crying and wailing. This odd response from me actually alleviated his own action and he was more enthralled with my reaction than whatever caused the upset in the first place. I eventually put him in his highchair, handed him some Cheerios and set to the task of cleaning up.

The towel on the bed was only lightly soiled with a smear of bright red blood, which instantly brought me back to a few moments earlier and the primitive operation. Despite only a small stain on one towel, I still threw them all into the laundry basket. My abdomen gave a sharp pang as I tossed the heavy fabric, and I gave a verbal 'oof' clutching my mid-section and pausing. The pang subsided and I picked up the needles. One was perfectly clean, the other wet and sticky with blood. I walked out the back door and promptly placed them both in the garbage can, slamming the lid down. I swallowed hard and headed back to the house, another tightening in my mid-section making me stop and hold my breath. I almost forgot to breathe again when the pain subsided, and I continued back into the house.

For two days I bled constantly, womb contracting trying to rid itself of the intrusion. Luckily, Bill was at work during the day and I chalked my symptoms up to the flu. By Friday that week, the bleeding had almost stopped, and I prayed the event was successful and over with. However, I decided right then to give up knitting for good.

Part 5

36

Always Moving

"It came to pass, as they journeyed from the east, that they found a plain in the land of Shinar and they dwelt there." Genesis 11:2

Each day got a little easier after the 'incident' and I tried to push it farther from my mind whenever something reminded me of it. When the emotion or image of the procedure flooded my mind, I would try and justify the act with the alternative. It was just a little blood, I'd think. I might have died had I gone through with the pregnancy. Bill knew something wasn't quite right but never asked. I caught small but hesitant glances from him for a few weeks after but he never prodded and I never confessed. I'm not sure I was glad about that or not. Keeping something so heavy to myself seemed almost too much to bear at times, but then I would push the thoughts away, bury them with the unborn child that would never be. No, I couldn't even think like that. There was no child. PERIOD.

At least once a week I tried to call the girls but never could get through. Billy always answered and the girls were always gone. They would never call me back. I wrote a few times but never heard a response. Once, I got through to Creth.

"Oh, hello." He said nonchalantly.

"Well, it's about time," I stammered. "Where have you been? And where are the girls?"

"Virginia, let's not do this. You know they're fine." His tone was patronizing.

"No, I don't know that. How would I know that? I haven't spoken to them in 6 months!" I could feel my blood pressure rising as my heartbeat faster.

"Fine, I'll have them call you later." His voice was now rushed as if he was trying to get me off the phone as fast as possible.

"No, that Billy woman always says that, and they never call. Who is she, by the way? And why is she always at the house?" My focus shifted and I seemed determined to accuse in any way.

"That's none of your business."

"The hell it is. Those are my children." I started wondering if my temper was going to cause this conversation to be cut short.

"Listen, I've taken out the proper paperwork. We think the girls would be best suited here. You have a new baby, and they are a handful. I know you never wanted them to begin with. Just let me take care of them. You don't have to do a thing." His tone mellowed as if he was trying to make me think this was best for all but inside, I was so shocked I was speechless.

"What do you mean, paperwork?" I sat down at the kitchen table at this revelation and my tone went numb.

"It's all done. I have sole custody of the girls. They love it here. Maude and Merle take the girls during the day and after school and we're gonna be moving to a 40-acre farm here before winter. It's all done, Virginia." He paused but I could hear a hard swallow on the other end.

"How can it be all done? Don't I have to agree to this?" The pounding was getting fiercer and I felt like I wanted to hit something... or someone.

"Well, not when you abandon your children, it's pretty easy. Especially when one parent is here and the other is 2000 miles away." He said accusatorily.

"Abandon them? What are you saying? This was your idea to take them away!" I stood up again and shook my fist to no one.

"And good thing too. From what I hear it's been pretty rough on them." He could tell I lost the upper hand and had no rebuttal.

"What are you talking about?" I could hear my voice increasing in volume and ferocity.

"Now listen. It's all done. Next time you come out we'll schedule a visit. Gotta go now." And he hung up the phone.

I stood motionless with the phone receiver in my hand for what seemed like an hour. What had just happened? Just like that, I had lost my children.

Rich was asleep and Bill wasn't home. I scanned the room looking for comfort from someone. There was no one there. No one to feel my pain, my shock, my heartache. For the first time ever I felt like two giant holes had been torn into my heart. Regardless of whether or not I wanted children in the beginning, I had them and I loved them, deeply. A flash of a bloody towel raced through my brain and I instantly thought this was fate. I didn't deserve children, any children. If I could so casually get rid of one, what right did I have to have two... three? No, I again pushed the thought away, but it was burning in my mind so hot I had to shake my head to get the thoughts to stop.

Like magma bubbles and shoots from a volcano, my eyes welled with tears and I ran to the bedroom and sobbed. It all came out. I created this. I did this. I hated all of it at that moment. I just wanted to die. Why didn't I die? Why was I going through all this? My emotions were all over the place and I couldn't contain my heartache. With each sob, I felt a piece of my heart spill onto the bed.

I laid there until it got dark outside. I had stopped bawling but hadn't left the bed until I heard the door open and Bill drop his bag and boots on the floor. I wanted to move but couldn't find the energy. Bill hollered for me but I couldn't answer. He searched until he got to the bedroom, which was dark. He flicked on the light to which I flinched and hid my face in the pillow.

"Here you are. What's up, Buttercup?" He came over and peered in the basinet where Richy was still asleep then sat on the bed and patted my back.

"They're gone." It was all I could muster.

"Who's gone? What's happened?" His tone was concerned but comforting.

I swallowed hard and used all my strength to sit up, face stained with tears and eyes red and swollen. "Creth. The girls. He took them."

"Well, I know but what do you mean?" His eyes furrowed and his tone sounded more worried with my vague answers.

I was slightly irritated he couldn't just read my mind and understand without so many words. "He... he got permanent custody of them. We can't have them back. He said I abandoned them." I couldn't look him in the eye for fear he would see who I really was at that brief moment.

"What? Why would he do that? *How* can he do that?" He said defensively.

"I.... I just can't talk about it right now, please?" I felt too weak to even get mad anymore.

"It's alright. If you're not up to it, let's not talk about it now. How about I take you out? Huh? Would you like that? Maybe a nice steak dinner at *Rosario's*?" He tried to lift my face to him for guidance and acceptance.

I knew I had to make dinner anyway and nothing in me had the gumption, so I obliged. If I didn't have to talk and didn't have to clean up, I was all for it. I nodded and he patted my shoulder.

"Good. Now let's get you fixed up. We'll feed the boy and be on our way. Want Jeannie to watch Rich? I could go over and ask her?" He stood up and tried to make the scenario as normal as possible. I couldn't tell if it was for his benefit or mine.

"NO!" I quickly shouted. My maternal instinct wasn't having any more babies taken away from me today. "I mean, no," I said more collectively. "Let's take him, please?"

He gave a pursed-lip smile with a casual nod and wink. We got ready and left. I think I had a steak; I don't know. I don't remember much about that evening.

~

I called at least once a month but never got the girls on the phone. I hoped at some point by chance they'd answer but it seemed as if they were never allowed to answer the phone. During one of my monthly calls, Billy informed me that she and Creth had married and I was to refer to her as Mrs. Lamb. They had moved to this 'farm' Creth spoke about on the phone but had not changed their number, a little thing I was grateful for. Even if I didn't know where exactly they were, at least I could call.

Richy was growing and by the spring of 1956, I had another two-year-old running amok in the house. I hadn't worked since we moved to California and missed adult conversations. I could feel my days dragging on in lonely silences. Jeannie had gone back to work full time as a teacher and I really didn't get to know any of the other neighbors.

Occasionally, Bill would take me to a work dinner or function and told me to get all 'spruced up'... look my part, he'd say but I felt he hadn't really 'seen' me in a while. Maybe it was the parental thing. I'd become too involved in being a mom that I neglected my wifely responsibilities. I had been cautious after the 'incident' not to be intimate anywhere close to when I could conceive, at least to the best of my abilities. Maybe Bill was noticing and pulling away himself. We use to be able to talk about this but with him being gone all day, sometimes until 10 o'clock at night and leaving first thing, it left little time for conversation, much less intimacy, in any way.

Richy was a happy baby after the colic wore off. He was active, into everything and adventurous, but after Dolores and Carol, he was a breeze. We'd spend our days cleaning, walking to the park or library, or taking a drive around the Arboretum, that is until Bill came home one day stating he'd sold my car.

"What? Why would you do that?" I heard my resistance, but it was not met with the same urgency.

"Oh, well, you don't need it. Besides, Luke from the barn needed a vehicle and we could use the money." He didn't look me in the eye but rather went to the kitchen sink to wash his hands. "What's for supper?"

I was floored that this information was not of more importance, or at the very least the shock to me was not even considered. "I don't know. I didn't *drive* to the store to get anything." I knew it was a lie but I needed some validation.

"Oh come on now. I could smell it a mile away. Your cookin' always brings me home." He patted my bottom and peeked in the oven where a whole roast chicken was crackling and shining with juices. "Yeah, that's what I'm talking about." He inhaled deeply as he stood up straight and closed the oven door.

"But what if I need to go somewhere? What if something happens to me or Rich?" My mind was scrambling to come up with other scenarios of why I would need a car on a daily basis.

"Oh, Joe's fine. He'll be fine and if you really need me, just call." Bill often called Richard, Joe as a nickname. "I'm only 15 minutes away. But I think you'll be fine and just think, we'll have a little extra money. How about $25 for whatever you want?"

Bill was big on nicknames. Ever since we watched *Our Miss Brooks* on the television back in Missouri in 1953, Bill was hooked. The spunky redhead, which we only knew by reputation and screenwriting since we had a black and white television, reminded him of me and since her first name was Connie, he got to calling me Connie and then just plain Con.

Our days at home meant a lot of time in front of that television where Richy would watch *Dragnet* and run around saying in the best enunciation he could that he was Sgt. Joe Friday, although it came out as Srgg. Joe Fizzle. Bill got such a hoot from it that ever since he called him Joe.

"$25 bucks, huh? Is that all I get? How much did you get for the car?" I had succumbed to the fact and that this was just the way it was regardless of how unvalidated and irritated I felt.

"Never you mind about that. It'll be good." He patted my shoulder and sauntered off to the bedroom whistling.

"I'll need more than that for groceries and such," I hollered after him. "I haven't gotten a lot lately. Been having to penny-pinch. Ya think I could get maybe $80 for the month?" My voice ended in a higher tone pausing for an answer before setting the table.

"We'll see." He mumbled something I couldn't make out. "You need that much?"

"Well, if you like roast chicken and pork chops, yes." I set plates and utensils down, mumbling frustrations to myself.

He came back out with a fresh shirt, sat at the table and I promptly served him. I watched him eat oblivious to the tension between us. My monthly allowance was going down little by little each month even though Bill said everything was 'fine and dandy' at the stables. I was able to stretch a chicken for three days, something I learned at the diner, but Joe needed milk and wouldn't eat a lot of things I prepared. I felt I was back to being a short-order cook, but for a 2-year old.

~

Christmas came and I begged Bill for a few extra dollars to get something for the girls. I felt this year was the reverse of last, with me now sending gifts to *my* children in another state. Bill gave me $10, which barely covered the shipping. So I made some candy sticks and wrapped them up in a mason jar topped with colorful fabric and a ribbon. I packed them neatly in straw and sent them on their way praying they'd arrive in one piece.

Rich was almost 3 now and more active than ever. However, I was getting bored at home and asked Bill if I could get a job.

"Not if you're just working to pay someone to take care of Joe. That's pointless." He spoke to me as if my opinion really didn't matter and that I was foolish to think such a thing.

"But it'll give me something to do. I can't stay cooped up here all day. How about just a couple days a week? I can find someone that won't take all my paycheck to either watch Joe here or at their house. Or I can swap with them. I've taken Joe to the park a few times and met some other moms there. Maybe we can swap?" I said non-defensively so as to coax a more serious conversation.

"Well, what do you think you'd be doing?" His eyebrows furrowed but he looked directly at me. Good, I had his attention.

"That office building down on the corner of 3rd needs a cleaner a couple times a week, just for a few hours but I think the pay is decent. Would you mind?" I continued to wipe the table and tidy the kitchen so I wouldn't be accused of not putting in my 'fair-share' around here.

"Hmmm. Guess that'd be okay. Will there be someone else there?" I was surprised at his response and paused a bit, having my rebuttal ready instead of an answer to this question.

"Um... I don't know. Probably, it's after hours though, ... but...

but not too late. I'll be home or I won't leave until supper is ready." I swallowed hard. I was perturbed it was getting so difficult to talk to him.

"Well, as long as your duties around here don't slip, I guess I don't mind it. Who'd be watching Joe?"

"Um... not sure, but I'll let you know, and you can meet her as soon as possible. I'll figure it all out. Don't worry. And thank you." I smiled and walked over to kiss his cheek. He turned and my lips landed on his.

"I know another way you can thank me," he said and swiveled to face me wrapping his arm around my waist and rear end. He pulled me close and urged me to lean down for another kiss.

April 1958

"Con, how'd ya like to move to Oregon?" Bill boisterously shouted when he came in one evening. I'd been working at the Carson Accountant Firm for the past year cleaning offices and such every Monday and Thursday evening for about 3-4 hours. It wasn't much but it brought in a few extra dollars and trading babysitting with the gals from the park for free made it so I could keep all the money. Bill got on me a couple of times saying that the taxes he had to pay to support my job weren't worth it but otherwise he didn't complain too much and let me keep it.

"Move? Why?" I looked up from my chicken stew with a curious and confused look on my face.

"Got some good news about a job up there. A client wants me to take a stud up for breeding and willing to pay pretty good for it. There's a training facility up there that's looking for my kinda work. Figured we could swing by and see your pop and what Oregon has to offer. Getting too expensive here anyhow." He'd manage to come in, take off his coat and boots, pour himself a glass of milk, wash his hands and sit at the table all while relaying this new information.

"Whoa." I hadn't moved a muscle the whole time he communicated this and now that he sat down, I broke from my frozen state. "Wow. Well, um... really?" I winced, realizing all the roots we had laid in California already. I liked my job as it gave me a sense of worth as if there was someone or at least something that needed me more than my 3-year old. I had found a couple of friends and we'd organized poker days where we'd gathered at different houses and played cards while drinking martinis. The kids would run around outside or be confined in front of the TV on rainy days. It was a beautiful respite that helped me feel that my own situation was not unusual, and my opinions were validated. All of this flashed before me thinking we had to move.

"When are you wanting to do this?" I asked turning my attention to the stew, collecting bowls, and filling each one. Joe bounded into the room with a toy car shouting 'vroom-vroom' as the car sailed through the air in his hand.

"Pop up here, Joe," Bill said patting the chair next to him. "How'd you like to go on an adventure?"

"Yes, yes!" Rich exclaimed and bounced on the seat as if he had batteries installed at full strength.

"He needs the stud by July so I had a thought; what if we got everything packed up and made our way to Missouri before we actually had to be in Oregon, Baker to be more precise? I know it's completely out of the way, but I thought we could visit the girls, maybe see if we can persuade them to go with us, or at least try and convince Creth." He put a hand on Joe's shoulder to calm his bouncing so he could better grasp my reaction.

"Oh really? Truly? That would be wonderful." I was so caught up in the last statement that the idea of moving became a distant issue.

"Well, it's all settled then. I'll tell Pete we'll take the job and make the arrangements. Why don't you write to Creth or see if they'll answer your call and arrange that? I'm thinking next month. Maybe mid-May we could go visit, see the families and all that nonsense and then head for Oregon. I feel good about this Con. This is a good move for us." He inhaled deeply when the chicken stew was set before him and told Joe it was hot and to be careful. I wasn't sure what just happened but remembered that a lot of events in my life seemed to just happen to me, rather than me making them happen. Is that what I did? Just went along with what everyone else wanted. Did I care? I liked my life here and felt I had a purpose but at least I could see Daddy and hopefully the girls. I was not looking forward to the long drive but the reward of seeing the girls again was enough of an incentive. I was determined to not only write a letter to Billy and Creth but to call first thing in the morning.

~

We had packed up as much as we could take and loaded it into a commercial moving van headed for Oregon. We went the other direction in our truck loaded down with camping supplies, food, basics and a few valuables we didn't trust the moving company to transport. It took us 3 days to get to Missouri and Joe was a bear through it all. He had to be constantly entertained and when we pulled into Maude's place, Creth's sister, at 11 pm we were exhausted.

I had written the girls and called and finally got through to Creth just 1 week before leaving. He said it was alright to visit but that's it and reiterated the fact that he had full custody. I said I just wanted to see them.

When we arrived, Maude said we had just missed the girls as they went camping with their father for a week in the Ozarks. My heart sank. I didn't have a shred of strength left and all I wanted to do after the long drive was sleep. The added drain on my emotions was just too much to bear and I burst into tears. Bill held me tight and patted my back trying to console me. Maude breathed deep and pursed her lips in agitation, turned on her heels and left the room. Joe clung to my leg scared of the unknown environment, as well as my reaction and I just sobbed.

We stayed 3 days with Maude, made the rounds to various family members, tried to put on a good face and be cheerful but inside my sorrow was turning to anger at each explanation of why we were here when the girls were clearly not at home. Coming up with tailored excuses was taxing and all I wanted was to get out of my surroundings. I asked Bill if we could just go and he obliged.

2300 miles back across the country we drove and sometime in July, we pulled into our temporary living quarters in Baker City.

Bill had arranged for the stud to be transported to the stables in town. We hadn't even hung up clothes when Bill insisted he had to be at the stables the day after we got there. "Already lost too many days here," he'd said, rushing around the small 1-bedroom apartment the next morning.

Baker City was a small, podunk town on the east side of Oregon. Bill had promised I'd be able to see Daddy, but he was still in Klamath Falls, a good seven hours west of here. I figured now was not the time to bring up another road trip.

Our moving van was being held at an RV rental facility and I wasn't sure I wanted to unpack in this temporary home. I did my best with the furnishings provided and set up house as best I could. Joe slept on the avocado green couch in the living room. Bill and I shared the small bedroom complete with a dresser, nightstand, and full-size bed.

Bill worked every day that first week and seemed distracted when he was home. I figured it was just the stress of a new job, but the neglect was getting to me. I tried to push it away so as not to burden him with one more thing, but the loneliness was isolating. I tried to occupy my time by wandering around town and learning more about my new home. I called Daddy and asked if he wanted to come visit but work was keeping him busier than normal. He hoped he and Hilda could make the trip in a few weeks.

We'd just been settling into our new life, hoping for a more permanent residence when Bill came home announcing we were moving again.

"What? We just got here," I said, adjusting the contents on the small dining table to accommodate mealtime.

"Look, you know this wasn't permanent and I got some business up in Aberdeen Washington, now so we just need to go." He sounded irritated that I was even questioning him.

"Wait, what is happening? You never told me this wasn't permanent." I set down the plates and situated myself in the chair across from him determined to get some straight answers. "Did this job not pan out? Were you fired?"

He inhaled deeply and let it, out searching for the words. "No, it didn't. I expected something it's not and ... we just need to go where the money is." He sat back and swallowed hard. I almost thought he might be tearing up. I reached my hand across the table and grabbed his.

"I'm here. I'll go where you go." I gave him an accepting smile and patted his hand before letting go. "We'll do what you think is best."

"Thank you, Con. That means a lot to me." He returned my faint smile.

For a moment I had let my guard down rather than allow my frustration and confusion to take over. I felt sorry for him in some way. I hadn't had a chance to set down any roots in Baker City but in less than 3 months we were packed up again and heading for Aberdeen.

37

I Was One Way and Now I Was Different

"It came to pass when the people removed from their tents, to pass over Jordan, and the priest bearing the ark of the covenant before the people... that the waters which came down from above stood and rose up upon a heap very far from the city..." Joshua 3:14

Our small house in Aberdeen Washington was humble but warm. Bill continued to work in the equestrian industry and I quickly got a job cleaning medical clinics in town. I tried to keep myself busy with work but the girls and the general state of my emotions clouded my thoughts day in and day out. It became routine to call Creth every Sunday night, but no one ever answered the phone. I sent letters, cards, and gifts when I could but never got a response. My heart would say a prayer that they were safe, but I wasn't really sure who I was praying to or if I even believed in that stuff. I just felt that if I didn't, I was giving up the last shred of being a decent mother.

Rich was growing and getting into everything he could all the time. The ghost of another child running at the same pace through the house would flash through my mind unintentionally and I would have to blink hard to bat it away.

~

One evening in the fall of 1960, we got a call from Missouri. It was a collect call and as all the hairs on my neck stood up, I felt this was not good news. It was Billy. I was shocked that she was calling *me*.

She said that Creth had had a heart attack and died a couple of days ago. The words echoed in my ears and rang through my brain. I know she said some other stuff after that, but I didn't comprehend. I instantly thought of the girls.

"Can I talk to the girls?" I interrupted. She paused and seemed irritated I had been short with her.

"No. They're fine. They're at my sister's place till I get things figured out," she said as if she had just put down a loyal dog. "We'll be fine. I just thought you should know. Well, goodbye," and she hung up the phone. I held the phone long after the dial tone started to beep.

Just like that... Creth was gone. *till death do us part...* was the only thing running through my mind.

I was quiet for a few days after that. I even tried to call back multiple times to get the girls but to no avail. It was just so odd. Creth... gone. I felt there was so much unfinished business between us and for some reason, I felt that we would someday get it all straightened out. But that never happened. My last connection to my daughters was now gone and they were being brainwashed by some other family. Would they ever know how much I loved them? How much I missed them? How I wanted to make it all right? Was this the end of any hope of that relationship?

I spoke to Bill about it but all he could offer was condolences and a reprieve of, "Well, at least you're not committing adultery anymore... according to the Bible, and all."

This left little comfort. There was so much unfinished between us, between me and the girls. It felt as if multiple balls were flying through the air trying to stay afloat and one just dropped into blackness.

~

The days dragged on and turned into weeks. We were adjusting to our life and Rich was growing. I thought of the girls every day and wondered how they were fairing without their dad. I would still try and call every week but would get no response.

The stables in town were small but profitable. But I never would know which Bill I would get when he came home at night. It could have been a great day with favorable clients or a lousy one with cranky patrons taking out their personal frustrations on the staff. Regardless, we always got the leftovers. Bill was always tired and never really interested in my day, even though I gave up trying to communicate months ago. But I was always grateful for a spark of happiness.

The biggest spark came when Bill announced that Duke and Don were coming to stay with us. Bill had five kids with Helen - Wayne, Ken, Karen, Duke, and Don. Duke and Don were the oldest and had written their dad saying they wanted to get out of the house but because they weren't of age yet, their mother insisted they still live with a parent. Bill gladly welcomed them. I could see his face light up, imagining three of his boys living under his roof. All I could imagine was the food bill.

Duke and Don arrived in 1961 and we had just barely gotten them settled in school when Bill insisted on another move. This time to Port Angeles, Washington. Again, another horse transport but this was more personal. The owner wanted Bill for his personal stable hand and promised him a pretty penny.

In June 1961 we packed up once again and moved the seven hours north to Port Angeles, a small fishing and logging town on the Olympic Peninsula. I had never seen a prettier place and secretly begged the nameless, faceless entity I had been praying to that I could stay.

Don, Duke, Rich, and Bill - Aberdeen Washington

Duke was a strong, tough guy that immediately tried to prove himself to me. He wouldn't hug me but insisted I shake his hand when they first arrived. Don looked up to his brother and Richy looked up to both. I was worried Rich would feel left out or that we had shifted part of our time and affection to two new children, but his response was a welcome retreat. He thought the world of those two boys and they showed off for him every chance they got. Bill just sat back and laughed, I had never seen him so happy.

This, along with the landscape, made Port Angeles an easy move, even though I felt we hadn't lasted long enough anywhere to really grow roots. Bill's job was doing well but I was noticing he was coming home earlier and earlier every day. Occasionally he would come home for lunch and never go back. One morning, I decided to head out to the stables with some hot coffee and a donut. I borrowed Duke's car, which Bill bought him as soon as he could drive although *I* was still lacking a separate vehicle for myself.

The stables were located on a large farm up Draper Valley Road. It was easily a 100-acre farm with dozens of horses and several stables. The dust settled as I turned off the car and a loud shriek came from the stables. I jerked up with a start to see a young, blond woman stagger playfully out of the barn with a giggle. She was followed by Bill sauntering after her also laughing and smiling. I honked the horn and both their expressions vanished.

"Con!" Bill shouted with a wave. "Whatcha doin here?" He quickly walked over to the car but the woman stood where she was with a wary eye. He opened my car door and reached for my hand, pulling me out of the vehicle.

"I thought you might like some coffee and a donut," I said hesitantly, trying to deduce the situation in front of me.

"Well, ain't that nice of ya. Come meet Marilyn." He took the thermos without absentmindedly and put his hand to my back to guide me to the introduction.

She was about 29, thin, pretty... not me. She reached out a weak hand and shook mine reluctantly as Bill introduced us. "This is Con... Virginia," he said, correcting himself.

"His wife," I added with a fake smile.

"Nice to meet you," she said casually. "I'll talk to you later, Bill." And she smiled again, nodded and strode off toward the main house with a slow glance behind her.

I looked at Bill with all the questions a wife should have but never said a word. He chuckled nervously and quickly shoved the donut into his mouth. My response was a look that said, 'yeah, you better come up with an excuse, quick.'

He motioned for me to sit on the bench outside the barn and finished his donut as I poured the coffee.

"Well?" I said. Although we hadn't been the epitome of marital bliss, there were just some things we could tell by looking at each other.

"Oh, that? That's nothing. She's the owner's niece and comes to help once in a while. Doesn't even live here." He tried not to look me in the eyes but inhaled deeply and took another sip of coffee.

"Well, so long as you haven't been doing what I think you're doing," I said.

"Why? Ya jealous?" He said poking me in the ribs with his elbow.

"Don't you just forget how you and I got together," I said with an air of warning.

"Oh, now, come on. You don't think..."

"Yes, I do think. And don't you forget it. You better behave yourself up here." I was faltering between being mad or playful but didn't want that playfulness to come across like Marilyn's. He chuckled and finished his donut while I took in the peacefulness of the farm. I missed the farm life. It was hard but it was honest. Moving so much made settling down seem like a faraway dream. There was no point in assuming we were going to be here for long even though I really felt like this could be home.

I stood up, held his face in my hands and kissed him. "Remember the family name," I whispered with a smile, patted his cheek and left.

Bill Byrd and Little Rich

~

One Sunday morning Bill bounded into the kitchen exclaiming we were all going to church. He had been talking to a guy in town about this church called Open Bible. I thought all churches were supposed to be 'open bible' but I didn't want to cause an argument. I felt like Bill was trying to get something from other places that he couldn't get from home but I wasn't sure what that meant.

Regardless, I refused to go, insisting that if God really wanted me to go to church he wouldn't have made it so early on a Sunday morning. Bill pushed a bit but in the end gave up and took the boys. Well, now I *really* didn't want to go... an hour of peace and quiet in the morning? How could I have given that up?

My strong-willed stubbornness refused to admit it but I began seeing a positive change in Bill. I figured it was just because he was around those 'church folk' and shoved it to the back of my mind. Each Sunday he consistently said, "Okay, we're going to church," and every Sunday I just waved him off with a hand, sat down with my coffee, and enjoyed my cigarette in the peace and quiet of my home.

That August Bill said there was to be a special speaker at the church and would I please go with him and the boys. I asked what made this guy any better than the regular one. He didn't know, only that he wished I would go just this once. He assured me that if I didn't like it, he wouldn't ask again. I felt this was my out. I knew I would hate it and if I didn't have to hear about it again I would put up with it once.

I insisted we sit in the back. I didn't need anyone *seeing* I was actually in church. Who knows the ridicule I would get in town, even though we really hadn't been in Port Angeles long enough to know anyone. Bill, on the other hand, knew quite a few people. He smiled and shook most people's hands at church with a hardy 'Hello' and such. I felt embarrassed in my own skin. I couldn't wait for this to be over.

We sat like any normal, American family in church. Duke, Don, Rich, Bill and I, neatly dressed in our Sunday best, me screaming on the inside. Every fiber of my being was rejecting this. But why? Was it church or the fact that I had to go? I felt so much of my life had been controlled and ordered, yet the more I thought of it, the more I realized that I had chosen this life. I had left Creth and chose to be with Bill. I made the decisions that led me to where I was today.

I refused to stand during the singing. I was never a good singer and singing songs I had never heard before or at least trying to be cordial seemed sanctimonious. Once everyone sat back down again, I tried to tune out, thinking about the roast I wanted to make for dinner, the grocery list I was compiling in my mind, and how to ration the milk this week for the boys that drank the stuff like water.

The preacher was an older man, typical. I thought, what will this guy have to say that I haven't already heard? He got up and just smiled at us. A little too long in my opinion. I wondered if he was a little touched in the head and just as I broke the moment by turning and looking at Bill for clarification, he spoke.

Did you know that God loves you? Really loves you? Not for what you've done, but for who you are? I know I've spoken on this many times but sometimes it's just a good reminder of how simplistic Jesus is. How he really just loves you the way you are. I am reminded of that little children's song, "Jesus Loves Me" and how precious it is to just be reminded how He loves us so much.

Have you ever felt that you've done so much wrong you couldn't ever be forgiven? How do you think David felt? He committed adultery and murder yet was called a 'Man after God's own heart'. How far have you drifted? Have you tried to do life on your own terms? How's that working out for you? Do you feel as if any moment the hammer is going to come down again on you? Like you're just trying to keep all the balls in the air? What would happen if you dropped them?

That's what Jesus is asking you to do, today.

Okay, he had my attention. I was convinced that Bill spoke to the preacher ahead of time and told him what to say. There's no way this was a coincidence. I wanted to scowl at Bill but my pride resisted the urge.

The truth will set you free, and what is that truth? That you were made in the image of God.; that He loves you and it's not like any love you've ever known. He said he would never leave you. Have people left you? Have people let you down? Jesus says He will never let you down. The Bible says in Psalm 139 that the Lord knew us in our mother's womb and His thoughts toward us are precious. He wanted you so bad that after all He created, the earth, the sky, the stars, He thought the world needed you as well. He wants you. He has always wanted you. He wants you today.

I felt tears well up in my eyes but I wasn't about to blink and show my weakness to others. I forced my eyeballs to stay open. God wanted me? No one really wanted me... at least not for long. How long have I wanted someone to want me?

But what about all the horrible things God did in the Bible? I was sure he was angry with me. I had not lived a good life. Surely he wanted someone else more?

I know what you're thinking... the God of the Bible can be fierce, wrathful, vengeful. How could He possibly be a God of love and kill all those people? Well, this is where Jesus comes in. For thousands of years people have been struggling to follow God's laws to no avail. It's almost impossible. Thousands of animals died for other people's sin because the Bible says that the wages of sin is death. Since we cannot be sin-free, something or someone has to die. Before Jesus, this was the only way to get God's attention, to be clean before Him.

But Thank God for Jesus! He is the way, the truth, and the life and He is the only way to be completely set free. And it's a one-and-done. He paid the price for all our sins, both past, present and future. God used a perfect sacrifice, once and for all. This is why we don't sacrifice animals anymore because we don't have to. Jesus died and rose, paying the ultimate price for us. Why? Because that's how much He wants us. He wants us so bad that He couldn't bear being separated from us any longer. He made Jesus die in your place so you don't have to. And because of this great gift... it IS a gift you know... something that is free, you don't have to worry about your life, your eternity, your actions. Now, of course, knowing what He's done helps us WANT to live a better life, but even when we mess up, and we will, He has already paid for that too! What an amazing thing that is and when you really wrap your head around it, there is no greater joy, peace, freedom and gratefulness.

And what do you have to do? Simply receive it! Have you ever received a gift before? I'm sure you have, we all have. Did you have to do anything for that gift? No. A gift is free for the taking. Here, have it. Is a gift forced on you? No. But you do have to hold out your hands and take it in order to benefit from it.

Here is Jesus, holding out His gift to you. Will you take it? If so, what does that mean? It means no condemnation ever again. No guilt, no shame. Now, the world might condemn. You can't rob a bank and receive no condemnation from the world for it, but God won't condemn you. Again, it's really knowing and acknowledging what He's done for you that prompts us to live a better life. To constantly be reminded of His grace and forgiveness. To truly know that you know where you're going when you die. Do you know for sure?

"No!" I said out loud to my own surprise. Immediately people turned and looked at me with similarly shocked faces.

Then let's be sure. You can know for sure. You can have a completely different life with a God that loves you, wants a relationship with you and will never leave you or be done with you. Do you want that kind of love?

If so, please stand and come to the front and we'll pray with you.

I don't know where the boldness came from or if I was even acting in the physical sense but I shot up off the pew like someone had put a pine cone under me and I knew I had to get to that altar. Whatever it was I needed, I knew it was there and I wanted it. Pride be damned... I wanted what Jesus gave. I wanted Jesus because He wanted me.

Bill quickly moved his legs aside letting me by. I saw one other person get up as well and make their way to the front but I felt I couldn't get there fast enough. If this was real, I wanted it. As I bolted to the front I felt something like heaviness unwrap around me as if someone just took off a 50-pound blanket from around my shoulders. Immediately I was lighter and was able to move much easier.

I made it to the front and collapsed. I didn't even care if the whole audience was watching. All that matters was that Jesus wanted me.

Thank you for coming. If you're ready to have Jesus be your Lord, take all your sins, lead you in a freedom you've never known before, pray this with me....

"Father, I have sinned. I am not worthy of Your love but through Jesus, You have given me a way out. I acknowledge your gift of eternal life. I confess my sins and believe You are Jesus, the Son of God, raised from the dead and I now ask you to come live in me. Thank you for forgiving me and saving me."

I couldn't say the words fast enough. The minute I finished repeating the preacher's words that 50-pound blanket that I left in the isle was nothing to the feeling I now experienced. It felt like the weight of the world, all the heartache, torment, rejection, suffering and pain totally and completely lifted from me. There was nothing on my shoulders. I closed my eyes and just wept. I saw the abortion wiped clean, I saw the adultery flooded with white, I saw the anger and bitterness washed away and all that was there was Jesus. Pure white, shining so bright that none of the bad things I had done could ever be seen again.

I was so overcome with thankfulness that I couldn't even leave the floor. Bill and the boys went home and I stayed just thanking God for about 3 hours until the preacher touched me on the shoulder.

"Here, Virginia. Take this Bible. God wants you to know that there is so much more to know about Him. He is so excited to be on the journey with you. He wants you to know Him more. Take this and learn." He handed me the Bible and smiled again.

I took hold of the Bible, which now seemed so much more precious. Thanked him and got up. My knees were wobbly, but I heard a voice that said, *'I will steady you... walk with me!*

38

Joy and Heartbreak

"It came to pass, that, as I made my journey, and was come nigh un-til Damascus about noon, suddenly there shone from heaven a great light round about me." Acts 22:6

Everything was the same and yet nothing was the same. We got up, made breakfast, headed to work, fed the boys, went to bed, yet something had changed. It felt like everything before that Sunday was a different life and now everything was new.

I went home that night after the life-altering experience and Bill sheepishly asked how I was. I couldn't contain myself. All I wanted to do was talk about God, learn about Jesus, and read that Bible.

"Sheesh, Con, didn't think it'd do that to ya," Bill said after he finally got a word in edgewise. I couldn't stop talking about what the preacher had said.

"But did you hear what he said? Did you know all that? Is that what you've been hearing this whole time and didn't tell me?" I felt like there were sparklers popping and fizzing inside my soul that couldn't be quenched.

"Well,.... yeah? But the way you make it sound seems so much more real." He grabbed the Sunday paper and flopped down into his chair.

"Was it like this for you?" I asked, wondering if everyone had this type of conversion and if so, why didn't more people talk about it.

"Well, no. I was saved as a kid and I guess it's just something I've always known to be true." He crooked the corner of the newspaper to respond to me, shrugged and flipped it back.

"Bill, I just don't know what to say. I've never felt like this before in my life. I didn't even know all this. Why wouldn't you tell me?" I sat down to face him.

He flipped the corner down again. "I just thought you knew. Or at least didn't want to hear it. You never came to church with us before and I don't think you were raised in the church. I didn't want to pester you with it."

I leaned forward and put my hand on his knee. "I'm glad you did. I'm sorry I didn't listen. Thank you." I smiled and let my gaze linger.

He smiled back but furrowed his eyes slightly as if I had never said those words before. I probably hadn't. I breathed deep and got up. I reached for my cigarettes in my front pocket, took one out and lit it, inhaling deeply. Then clutching the Bible, the preacher gave me, sat in the chair next to him and opened it. The book fell open to 1 Corinthians 6:19 and I read, *"What? Know ye not that your body is the temple of the Holy Ghost, which is in you, which ye have of God and ye are not your own?"*

I stopped. Looked at my cigarette and what I was inhaling into my lungs. This body? This body is a temple? I froze for a moment then jumping up, I ran to the kitchen and jammed the cigarette into the sink.

Bill, startled, looked up. "Land sakes, Con, what was that?"

"I'm done. I'm done smoking." I couldn't believe I just said that. I had smoked since I was 17 and it had become a part of me. But I knew God wouldn't want me to do this.

"Ya are?" Bill said skeptically. "How ya know that?"

"I just am. If this body is a temple of the Holy Ghost, then I'm done." I turned to him and asked, "What's the Holy Ghost? That's a good thing, right?"

Bill laughed, folded his paper and put it down as he got up. He came to me and put both hands on my shoulders. "Yes, that's a good thing. It's the Spirit of God. There's three parts, like an egg; the Father, the Son, and the Holy Spirit, or Holy Ghost. You've heard of that, right?"

I had. I nodded and exhaled. There was nothing I wanted to do more then get back to that Bible. If this God were now 'in me' I wanted to know as much as I could about him.

~

The next few months were interesting. I expected Bill to be just as enthusiastic as I was, but he reminded me I was in the 'newborn' phase, drinking in all the milk I could get. I wasn't quite sure what that meant only that I was like a child, soaking up all the amazing information, knowledge and revelation God would give me. And He did. He gave to me willingly, graciously and freely. I had never known such grace. Even on days when the boys were frustrating, beating on each other and Bill came home from a week of bad clients, I couldn't shake the unbelievable gratefulness I felt.

It really didn't matter what was going on around me, I felt safe and secure as long as I was leaning on God for everything. I read through the entire Bible in 3 months and although I didn't understand most of it, God was teaching me to trust Him and that revelation would come in time.

Out of the blue in 1963 I got a letter from Carol. I didn't recognize the handwriting but saw it was from Missouri. I tore into it with trepidation and anticipation. There were four small pages of writing both front and back, so I quickly scanned to the last page and saw Carol's name.

I ran to my bedroom so as not to be disturbed, curled up on the bed and read.

Mom,

I hope this letter gets to you. Dolores and I have been living with Billy on the farm. It's a wonderful place with lots of places to explore. I just graduated from Excelsior Springs high school and am thinking of trying college. Dolores is much better than me at most things but I can shoot a gun like nobody's business, thanks to Daddy.

I'm writing to you in the hope to see you someday. I hear a lot of things but I have to know for myself. I miss you all the time. Billy is not you. She's sometimes cruel and harsh but I try and stay out of her way as much as possible. I miss Daddy too. Nothing is the same now that he's gone. He used to take us on camping trips but Billy doesn't.

I remember someone saying you came to see us during one of our trips but left before we came back. I wish you had stayed. I cried for days knowing I missed you and thought you just didn't like us anymore. I really hope that's not the case but I have to know for sure. If you don't want to see me, I'll understand but I thought since I'm an adult now I would at least try one more time.

If you want to know a little bit about me, know that I am 5 foot 5 inches, dark brown hair that I wear in a bob, as it's all the latest thing right now. People say I'm too skinny but I think I'm too fat but I do have a few boys that seem to like me so I guess that's saying something. I like school okay but prefer to be outdoors. I love to hike, waterski, fish, and ride my bike around the farm and into town from time to time.

If you want to know about Dolores, she's about the same only with lighter-colored hair. She's more the indoorsy type and boys really like her.

I don't know if she likes them or not. She sometimes treats me like I'm 10 years younger than her rather than just 18 months.

Well, I won't take any more of your time, if you've bothered to read my letter this far. But know that I love you and I hope you still love me. I don't believe all the things they say about you and I'd love to see you sometime. Let me know if that's ever a possibility.

Love, Carol

Tears had already begun streaming down my face when I read that she missed me. My emotions were torn between gratitude that my daughter still loved me and thought of me and the horrible things she must have heard about me. But she wanted to see me. That was the best news. Someone obviously told her our address, but I hadn't called in a few months. This was definitely the time, or at the very least, the perfect time to write back.

I immediately searched for paper and a pen to respond. I wanted to say so much but I also didn't want to scare her. I tried to make my letter as comforting as possible, which meant rewriting the thing 2 or 3 times. In the end, I told her that I absolutely loved her and missed her more than anything. There was a lot she didn't know and that I would love to have the chance to tell her. I welcomed her to our home anytime. I ended the letter with our phone number and encouraged her to call.

The space between those letters seemed like an eternity but I heard this small voice encourage me that everything would be alright and to be Jesus to everyone and in every situation.

Not more than 5 days later I got a call. Carol's voice was the sweetest thing I had heard in a long time.

"Hello?" I answered and positioned the phone on my shoulder as my hands were covered in soapy dishwater.

"Mom?"

I dropped the phone and yelped. Quickly, I grabbed a towel and used it to pick the phone up off the floor. "Hello? Hello? Carol?"

"Yes, it's me!" She was precious. Every fiber of my being wanted to crawl through the phone cord and hold onto her.

"Oh, I'm so glad you called!" I'm sure she could hear the excitement in my voice.

"Yeah! I just got your letter so I'm calling. I hope that's alright?"

"Of course. I'm so glad you did." I secured the phone again on my shoulder and finished drying my hands before sitting at the kitchen table, the pig-tailed phone cord draped across the room.

"Are you okay?" I asked.

"Yeah. Just sitting here trying to think about school but I don't really want to. I enrolled in some classes, but I really don't have the motivation." Her voice was sweet, and it was hard for me to consider her a woman although that's exactly who I was talking to. This was not a little girl anymore and a part of my heart grieved that I had missed so much of it.

"Well, you are more than welcome to come out here anytime."

"Are you sure? What about Bill? Are you two still together? I mean, I guess you are cause you're there for him, right?" I couldn't tell if she was resentful of that or not.

"Yes, he's here and your little brother Rich, who's 9 now. And Bill's two older sons have come to live with us, Duke and Don, although I think they are considering moving home with their mom in a year or so. But don't let that stop you! We have room, or we'll make room, or we'll figure it out. I'm sorry, I'm talking too much, aren't I?" I quickly shut up for fear I would scare her off.

"Oh no, not at all. Daddy says I could talk the gate off its hinges if he let me." She huffed a little laugh and I chuckled.

"It's so good to hear your voice, Carol. You just don't know what it means to me." I paused but she didn't speak. "I... I never meant to leave you girls. I love you both so very much. I hope you know that."

I was hesitant but I felt that if I didn't share now I wouldn't know when I could or if I even would have a chance.

"Can I come see you?" Her voice was timid but sure of herself.

"Of course. Anytime. Uh... what are... or when are you thinking?" My mind raced at possible options.

"Well, I really don't want to go back to school and Billy doesn't care much even though Dolores says I'll regret it. But can I come in the next few weeks? I've saved some money for a train ticket." She sounded as if she was asking, hopeful and nervous all at the same time.

"Oh, yes, of course. I would love nothing more!" My heart skipped in my chest.

"Great! I'll talk to Billy and see when I can get the ticket. I.... love you, Mama," she said hesitantly but as if she had wanted to say it for years.

"I love you too, Carol. I'm so happy. I have so much to tell you and I can't wait to hear everything about you." We said our goodbyes and hung up the phone. My hand lingered on the phone handle for a while reliving our conversation. Nothing could have made my day more complete.

Then Bill stormed in the door. "Well, that's done," he shouted, slapping his hat on the table and kicking his boots across the room. "Damn stable owner gave me the boot." He huffed and slumped in his chair.

"What do you mean?" I shook off the emotion from the last conversation and joined him in his frustration.

"Chuck Banner, Charles, told me he just didn't have enough work for me. I thought things were picking up but I guess not. Darn it all. I thought this was a good move this time." He was frustrated but I was a little relieved as Bill wouldn't be around Marilyn as often.

"What are you gonna do?" I asked

"I don't know. I was gonna talk to a guy in town that used to own some horses. I think he's got a business in town. Maybe he's got some work for me.

Fred Hayward owned 8th Street Motors, a car dealership in Port Angeles and agreed to let Bill work for him part-time. Bill met Fred at a coffee meeting after church and loved his spark, vivaciousness, and fire for selling. He told Bill he'd make an excellent car salesman. Fred promised Bill that if he sold cars half as well as he sold horses, he'd be making a killing. The idea of sales, even though it wasn't horses, intrigued Bill so he started working at the lot a few days a week until he'd done so well, Fred decided to hire him full time.

But it wasn't more than three months and Bill was back to his seesaw attitude every day. I never knew what I was going to get. It was either feast or famine in the car dealership business. Some days he'd come home after selling three cars in one day and on cloud nine insisting we celebrate by going out to dinner. The next week he hadn't sold a car in four days and was convinced we were going to starve. As often as I could, I would tuck a few dollars away in my jewelry box just for some sense of security and control. I couldn't tell Bill no when he wanted to celebrate, and I couldn't cheer him up when times were tough. The emotions almost gave me psychological whiplash, like riding a roller coaster up and down. One minute it was exhilaration, the next you felt as if your stomach was going to drop right out beneath you.

Luckily, I had learned how to stretch a meal with my days at the diner when things got tough. It was a fun and interesting challenge to make one chicken into a meal for five people and then have a bit leftover the next day for lunches.

The one constant was this new life I was living albeit secretly. Bill knew I had completely quit smoking and drinking and was reading my Bible several times a day but he seemed almost annoyed by it. My pride wanted to well up and exclaim, "well this is YOUR doing," but I didn't. Not sure why... just something inside that kept the anger away.

Regardless of what happened externally, I felt safe and secure internally, or in my spirit. Something I had never had before. It was as if the entire world could come crashing down around me and I'd be safe. But yet, externally, life went on.

Carol came out in the spring of 1964. Seeing her get off that train was a sight I will never forget. Her dark hair bobbing on her shoulders; her smile that just filled the space with joy; her enthusiasm for life and her thirst to know things was insatiable.

She bounced off the train and looked around. The moment she spotted me her smile widened the length of her face and she came running. Every fiber of my being exploded in joy, excitement, and nervousness. She threw her arms around me and hugged me so tight I thought I might choke, but I didn't care. I just wanted her. Tears filled my eyes and I let them. There was no place I'd rather be and deep down I thanked God that He had given me the opportunity to enjoy my daughter once again.

When we pulled away from each other, her eyes looked like mine and she blinked heavily, wiping her tears but not ashamed of them. To look in her eyes; to see this woman before me was surreal. The last time I saw her she was just a girl, a child. Now, she was a woman and such a beautiful one, at that.

We wrapped our arms around each other and headed for the car. We laughed, shared, cried, and just bathed in the presence of one another. My heart was full and I was so grateful.

Carol stayed for two weeks. We caught up on a lot. Every question answered, every doubt erased, every sin confessed. I wanted to be honest with her. I needed her to know that it was not her fault; that I desperately wanted to see her and her sister and that it had been torture to go through life not knowing for sure what was happening.

Carol said that Dolores didn't believe I really loved them and that I had truly abandoned them. I was sure that's what Creth wanted them to believe. No doubt he was angry, jealous, and hurt over what had happened, and he had every right to be. I always wanted to ask Creth's forgiveness but really didn't know how. I asked for Carol's instead. She gave it freely and graciously. This was part of the unfinished relationship I so desperately wanted and needed. The time we spent together was so precious. During the couple of week's stay, Carol got to know Rich, Duke, and Don, all of whom loved her to pieces, especially Rich. He couldn't get enough of his big sister. No one showered him with more love and attention, and he looked up to her like a queen.

Which made it so much harder when she had to leave. I was determined this was not the end and Carol knew it too. To both of us, this was a new beginning... a different beginning and one we were sad to leave at the moment but hopeful for the future. Rich grabbed her around her waist and clung for dear life. He begged her not to go. She reluctantly pulled his small arms from around her and looked us all in the face with tears streaming down her cheeks. She got on the train in July and after a tearful goodbye, we parted.

~

Duke graduated in the spring of 1965, Don was 15 and Rich was 10. Keeping these boys fed was a chore but something I actually enjoyed so long as we had the funds for food.

Duke joined the Air Force soon after graduation and Don was entering his senior year. Rich just started the 4th grade and the absence of just one mouth eased the strain of food consumption in the house a bit. Bill was torn when Duke left and even though they both put on a brave face, I could see the heartbreak especially in the last hug that lasted a half a second longer than normal. It was nice to have Duke for a few years and we wished him well in the life before him.

Don graduated the next year and decided to move back to southern California with his mom and siblings. The heartbreak repeated all over and once again, we were back to just the three of us.

Things were actually going quite well for a while. Carol and I spoke frequently on the phone or when I could afford the phone bill but mostly, we just wrote to each other about every other day. I hardly heard from Dolores, but Carol filled me in on the goings-on back in Missouri. Carol was trying to save up enough to move out to Washington despite the push back from the family. I suspect many of them spoke negatively of me and wondered why on earth she would ever want to go be with a parent that 'abandoned' her. I think at this point she knew the truth and if that's all God would allow me, I would take it.

My relationship with God deepened as well and I felt I just wanted to know more and more about Him. My spirit yearned to rest in His peace every day regardless of what was going on around me and knowing Bill, it could be anything. Sure, he still went to church, but God didn't seem as real to Bill as He did to me. I didn't know why. I mean, I thought he'd known about this Jesus since he was little but yet, it had become old hat. To me, He was as alive as anything. I felt His presence when I woke up and when I went to bed and it comforted me something great. I was always hot-tempered but since God showed up, nothing in my soul or body wanted to lash out anymore.

~

Carol finally got enough money to come out and she arrived on the train in February, 1966. We fixed her up the hide-a-bed in the living room and Bill worked on getting her a car from the lot. He was so proud when he came home announcing he'd found the perfect one.

"It's a bug!" He said, throwing his hat on the hook and touseling Carol's hair to her disdain as he waltzed across the room. He gave me a peck on the cheek and inhaled the evening's dinner aroma. "Smells great, girls. What's cooking?"

"Stew. What you do mean it's a bug?" I grabbed a towel to clean my hands and Carol straightened out her short, dark bob.

"A Volkswagen! Baby blue. Got the guy down to $400. Think you can swing that, Carol?" He slumped in the dining room chair and started untying his boots.

"$400? That's pretty good, I mean, I guess? Is it?" Carol was shocked Bill had found her a car so fast.

"Well, tell you what, if you can't pay for it all at once, I'll spot you the money and you can just pay me back when you get a job." Bill kicked his boots off to the corner and grabbed at a piece of white bread stacked in several slices on a plate in the middle of the table.

"She might have one. Pam at Crestview might have a job for her. Carol knows a little nursing and they need someone up there," I said, placing butter, knives, and big spoons on the table.

Rich bounced into the room and pounced on Bill who immediately scooped him up for a hug. "Hi, Papa. Sell any cars today?" Rich asked, not really caring about the answer.

"Sure did." Bill's mood was always contingent on whether or not he sold a car that day. I could instantly tell what kind of a day it was the second the car door closed from outside. A casual close meant it was a good day. A slam meant the opposite.

"Well, thanks, Bill. I'd love that and am real appreciative! It's nice to have someone in the car business," Carol said with a smile, looking to me for approval. I nodded and smiled.

~

Carol stayed with us for about four months until she was able to get a small apartment a block from the Crestview Nursing Home. She liked the fact that she could walk to work on sunny days and yet had the option to drive on rainy ones.

We had the best conversations She told me all about her childhood on the farm. She said she never received any of the gifts I sent and while it made me sad for a moment, it was in the past and there was nothing I could do about it now. Yet, I *was* doing something about it. I was making up for it. *We* were making it up and it felt so good. The only twinge of guilt I had was that I could not share this time with Dolores as well. Carol said she and Dolores went down separate paths. Dolores was very prim and proper, and Carol was more tomboy-ish. Dolores was dating and had met someone named Eugene, but everyone called him Abner. She was convinced she was going to marry him, but Carol wasn't really interested in that yet.

She recalled how much she loved the farm and how close she got to her dad. He taught her to shoot a gun, hunt for rabbits, and experience fox hunting with hound dogs. She never quite got along with Billy and vice versa so they just tolerated each other. Her yearning for a real mom was strong and was finally being quenched. We found strength in each other and her thirst for the things of God grew my own faith and later that year Carol found the same Jesus that found me just a year earlier. There was nothing greater than knowing your children are walking in the truth.

Carol would come over for dinner every Sunday and we'd chat throughout the week occasionally being requested to pray over this car or that car in the lot that just wouldn't sell. There were more and more days of the slamming door scenario and I noticed Bill getting more distant each day. I wanted to ask about it but the timing was never right. I would ease into conversations but was met with annoyance and frustration, so I just patted his shoulders and said quiet prayers under my breath.

July 6, 1966

I had come home from an afternoon at Carol's apartment. We had had so much fun fixing it up, enjoying each other's company, and really learning about the God that changed our lives. I had stopped at the market and my arms were full when I clumsily made my way into the house, holding my purse strap with my teeth and shutting the door with my foot before dropping the groceries on the table.

The second I did I heard a crash from our bedroom like someone just threw a chair through the wall. I jumped and threw my hand to my chest. The wail that came from the room sent all my nerves on end and a chill shot through my body. I ran to the bedroom door and opened it. I saw Bill on his knees, fists pounding on the bed. I quickly scanned the room to a fist-sized hole in the wall. I immediately dropped beside him and put my arm around his waist. He was crying, no, weeping. I had never seen this emotion from him before. He was pounding the bed, weeping, crying 'no - no - no'.

"What?" I said. "What is it? Is it Rich?" I looked around quickly but didn't see Joe anywhere. My insides started to panic. "Bill, what... what is it?"

He released his clenched fists and slid his hand back and sat back on his heels.

"It's Duke. He's dead."

"What?" Everything in my body screamed that this was a mistake, a horrible mistake.

"He got shot. He's dead." Bill spoke blankly, his face stained with tears.

I didn't know whether to ask for clarification or just sit there. I chose the latter. He leaned his head against the edge of the bed and sobbed. I clung to his side and just cried with him.

I learned later that Duke had just graduated from boot camp in Alamogordo, New Mexico at the Air Force Base. He and some buddies had been going out to some ranch on their days off, riding horses and target practicing. His buddy Dan had bought a new pistol and was showing it off. He loaded a round into the revolver, flipped it shut and it went off, striking Duke in the head, killing him almost instantly.

I don't know how long we sat there on the floor but the cream was room temperature when I finally got a chance to put it in the refrigerator. Rich didn't understand. To him, Duke was this invincible tough guy. Slick hair, black leather jacket, loved by everyone. Why is it always those ones that die young?

I couldn't make any sense as to why this had happened. An accident. A crazy, tragic, fluke accident. Although the future looked unclear and I hadn't really heard anything from God, I still felt a deep-seated peace. I prayed very hard that night that God would comfort Bill and Helen and the siblings, including all the stepsiblings and half-siblings. One person's death touches so many others.

I don't know if you're ever the same after losing a child. I know it felt that way when I lost the girls, but I knew deep down they were still alive. It gave me a bit of comfort to know that hopefully somewhere they were happy. I was grateful we got to spend a couple of years with Duke, but it gave little comfort to Bill.

He didn't go back to work for a week after the news. Duke's body was flown back to Southern California and Rich, Bill and I flew down for the funeral. I knew we probably were overdrawn in our account buying the plane tickets, but Bill didn't seem to care, and I wasn't about to question the purchase.

39

The Endless Wandering

*"It came to pass that, when the sun went down and it was dark, be-
hold a smoking furnace and a burning lamp passed between those
pieces." Genesis 15:17*

Nothing really goes back to normal once you've lost a child. The
days after the funeral turned into weeks and Bill continued to mope
around the house, ignoring his son, his wife, and his job. I gave him
four or five weeks before approaching him with concern.

"Bill," I said cautiously one evening after he came in, dropped his
hat on the chair, and slumped at the dining room table. "Is there
anything I can do?" I set a glass of iced tea down in front of him, but
his gaze didn't change from that faraway look as if he was daydream-
ing through the tablecloth, the table, and past the foundation of the
house.

"Bill? We have to do something." I poured myself a glass of iced
tea and sat at the table with him reaching a hand out to touch his

arm. The minute I did he jerked it away and his trance was broken bringing his eyes up to meet mine.

"What do you mean?" He said in a monotone.

"Those creditors called again today. I don't know what to tell them and I don't have any money to pay them." I knew this was a sensitive subject but the longer I procrastinated, the worse the finances would become.

"What's this?" His eyebrows furrowed as if he was truly surprised.

"Bill, you haven't sold a car in a month and I haven't been able to pay the bills." I chose my words carefully. "We have to do something."

"We'll go to Mom's. She'll know what to do." The trance resurfaced and he mindlessly picked up his iced tea and took a very small sip.

"Mommy Byrd's? In Ohio? We don't have the money to pay the bills. How are we going to find the money to move?" This complete change of direction came out of the blue and was not a solution I had ever seen on the horizon. Lima, Ohio was all the way across the country, must've been 2500 miles or so. There was no way we could just pack everything up and leave, especially now that Carol was here.

"Mommy Byrd will know what to do," Bill said. He just sat there nodding his head, convinced this was the only solution.

I didn't say anything more for the time being but got up and began supper. I thought we could revisit this at another time, yet I had no idea when that would be.

I got my answer soon enough when Bill stormed through the door the next day stating that he had sold the house.

"What?" I was in the middle of stirring a roux into the evening gravy when Bill slapped the purchase and sale contract down onto the kitchen table. I quickly dumped the rest of it in and turned off the stove, wiping my hands and throwing the towel down with similar vigor.

"Yep! It's all done, Con. We're out of here in a couple of weeks." He took off his coat and hung up his hat with as much calm and determination as if he had just sold a horse.

"But Bill, it's our house. Why wouldn't you talk to me about this first?" My mind was reeling, realizing I probably couldn't do anything about it and as frustrated as a mad hornet that he had done such a thing without consulting me first.

"Con, I can't do it anymore. I can't live here with those memories anymore. We've got to make a fresh life, a fresh start somewhere else. Somewhere that's not here. I'm reminded of Duke every day and I need some better counsel. Mommy Byrd can help. And maybe we can make a good life in Ohio, I don't know, but I have to try. I just can't make it here. I'm no good at work, I've run us into the ground, and I just can't think straight. Please, Con, say you'll be with me in this." After pacing the living room, throwing his hands up in the air and then back towards the kitchen he finally looked up at me with scared and hesitant eyes pleading for approval and acceptance.

Somewhere deep inside, the still, small voice reminded me, *I will be with you. I will never leave you nor forsake you.* Instantly, I was flooded with peace even though on the surface I was irritated and frustrated that we had to move one more time. I had really started to like Port Angeles but knew that my place was with my husband.

We sold nearly everything we had to pay for moving expenses, packed up the remainder, and left for Lima Ohio. Somehow, the separation between me and Carol was not as painful as I thought it was going to be. We knew where we belonged and that we would never truly be apart, but it was still heartbreaking to watch her in the rearview mirror on the corner of Hancock and Laurel Street waving a tearful goodbye.

~

Mommy Byrd certainly had answers and they all had to do with leaving me. Bill's mother never approved of me and always considered me the 'other woman'. She would constantly take jabs at my parenting style, cooking abilities, or wifely duties by suggesting that Helen had done it this way or that way. Clearly, I was not welcome, and the quicker we got out of bunking with her the better. All we could afford was a mediocre two-bedroom apartment. This small town was not known for its booming job market and Bill struggled to find work. He finally found a small manufacturing job with the Ford Motor Company in town.

The attitude about Duke was disturbing. It was almost as if Duke had never existed. Mommy Byrd and Bill never spoke of him and I tried my best to avoid her as much as possible.

Rich attended Lima Senior high school for his freshman year but never really made friends. We both felt as if we had been walking on eggshells for over a year, not just around Mommy Byrd but Bill as well. He seemed to be distracting himself with one thing or another. From carefully following the horse races in the local newspaper to schmoozing with employees to get a raise or a day off, Bill never really addressed reality as I saw it. But, slowly, money started to come in and we were able to pay off some debt.

December of 1967 came the wonderful news that quickly turned bittersweet. Carol had called saying that she was in love and was going to be married. She started attending a small church in Port Angeles and met Lillian Weiler, a good friend of mine for the short time that I lived in Port Angeles. Lillian and I had talked about Jesus, the Bible, and other niceties of daily life all the while knowing she had a nice looking, single son. Carol met Jerry Weiler and the two quickly became friends. After a few months of dating, Carol wasn't sure if Jerry was ever going to ask her to marry him so instead of waiting around forever, she calmly suggested that she move back to Missouri to be around her family. Sitting in her apartment one evening reading the newspaper, Jerry casually asked if she married him, would that keep her here. Naturally, she said yes, and the wedding was set for February.

Unfortunately, we had just barely begun to make ends meet and there wasn't a spare penny to left to travel back for the wedding. It was one of the hardest things I ever had to do. When Carol got married in February, I cried and cried the entire day. I had missed so much of her life. I had missed her growing up, I had missed her graduation, and now, I had missed her wedding. I knew she was happy, and I wanted nothing more, but I was still so heartbroken I couldn't be there to share any of these monumental life moments with her.

Carol called to inform me of the good news and we just cried and cried, cries of joy for the event, cries of sorrow for the separation. I wished her well on her honeymoon and hung up the phone. I felt like I had closed the pages of a book in someone else's life only to return to my reality. Although we had food on the table, we never had enough to make it out of that apartment.

As much as Bill wanted me and Mommy Byrd to get along, it just never happened. I was an outsider, the other woman, and, to top it all off, a hypocritical Christian. She couldn't see past mistakes or faults and had no grace for anyone that wasn't blood.

Bill finally realized there was no room for me in his mother's life and in September 1968, we again packed up everything we had in a 1954 Dodge truck and pulled a homemade camp trailer the long way back across the country stopping in California to visit Bill's remaining children before finally settling in Klamath Falls, Oregon.

Daddy had worked for the Klamath Falls school district for 25 years and was eager to enjoy his retirement. Rich finished his freshman year in Klamath Falls and in 1969 we moved again, this time to Lakeview, Oregon where Rich finished high school. Shortly after graduation, Rich left for college and it was just the two of us.

Bill got a job as a used car salesman in town and worked for five years making a meager wage but barely enough to get by on. I got a part-time job at a local café doing what I loved but each night, the lines on Bill's face got deeper and he seemed to have aged overnight.

One evening he complained that his feet felt numb and when he took off his shoes realized that he had stepped on a tack at work that had driven itself into his big toe without him knowing. The toe had turned purple and we quickly rushed to the doctor. Several tests revealed that Bill had diabetes. He was a big guy, loved his food, but didn't take care of his health. Knowing he was winded and began to sweat from the simple act of removing his coat, hat, and shoes every night now made sense.

The doctor gave him a slew of pills that he had to take every day, which alone wore him down. By 1974 he was going to the dealership less and less. My income was becoming the more stable wage of the house, but it just wasn't enough. We decided to move again, this time to Ontario Oregon. Bill said he could get a desk job at a dealership and the cost of living was a bit less. We were stretching our meager dollars thinner and thinner and when I couldn't imagine they could go any thinner, they became see-through.

Our move to Ontario was uneventful but at least our apartment was a little bigger than the one in Lakeview. I quickly got hired at a diner in town but was treated like a freshman in high school, as if I knew nothing. So, I put my head down and did the work for the paycheck. The job that Bill had moved for didn't pan out and he sat at home more often than not, depressed and getting sicker by the minute.

I was able to work my way up at the diner and finally got a raise. It wasn't much but it was enough to keep us afloat. The highlight of my week was calling Carol. We couldn't afford to stay on the phone for long but the time we spent was precious. She was headed out on a trip around the world with her husband and would call me when they came back, whenever that was. Before she left we prayed over the phone that Bill and I wouldn't move again. I couldn't take the constant moving and relocating and felt it was wearing us both down. Carol agreed and prayed that this would be the last place Bill and I lived.

How true those prayers turned out to be.

40

Till Death Do Us Part

"So they poured out for the men to eat. And it came to pass, as they were eating of the pottage, that they cried out, and said, O thou man of God, there is death in the pot. And they could not eat thereof." 2 Kings 4:40

"Con... Con!" Bill cried in a congested and struggling tone from the bedroom. "Con!"

I came running from the kitchen, hands dripping with dishwater. "What Bill? What's wrong?"

"Can't breathe." He grabbed his chest and beat it as if forcing it to take in air.

"What do you want me to do? What can I do?" I knelt beside him as he sat on the edge of the bed.

"Call an ambulance." His voice strained; eyes shut tight trying to withstand the pressure in his chest.

Exactly seven and a half minutes later, the emergency team was strapping Bill down on a gurney, hauling him to the Boise VA Medical Hospital 50 miles away. I had to follow in the truck. My friend Lucille agreed to come along with me.

Lucille had lived in Aberdeen Washington and was a friend from years earlier. I knew she was a Christian long before I found the Lord. Since then, she had become a mentor, confidant, and friend. She had moved to Ontario about ten years earlier and since I'd moved, had become the closest friend I ever had.

We would pray constantly for Bill, our children, and God's will and sometimes just bask in the quiet peace God had provided through all the turmoil. She accompanied me not just that first time to Boise, but the six times that followed over the next year. Each time we would learn something more about Bill's condition.

Pulmonary fibrosis....

Congestive heart failure...

Diabetes...

What could be next? Each time there meant more pills and drugs coming home. The nightstand looked like a nurse's station and pretty soon Bill could barely make it to the kitchen and back.

"God doesn't heal diabetes," Bill said one evening.

"What do you mean?" I looked up from my Bible reading. "Yes, He does!"

"Not for me. I've done too many bad things in my life for God to heal me." Bill's eyes were filling with tears but none of them left his lids.

"Bill, that's not God." I put down the Bible and looked directly at him. His eyes kept to the ground.

"I figured something like this would happen. I'm not a good dad. I let my kid die. I stole you away from your husband. I haven't been good to you, Con." Now, a tear dropped and landed in his lap where his hands were resting, open.

"I wasn't good to my customers. I haven't been a good man." His head dropped farther.

My eyes started to well up and I felt the Lord say, *go.... this is your husband. I will give you the words.*

I left the chair and knelt down beside him reaching for his hands and holding them tight. The tears let loose in my eyes as well and Bill just sobbed.

"I'm not a good man but I don't want to die. I'm scared to die. I don't know if God will have me." His sobs were fierce.

"God loves you, Bill. He died for all those things. If you believe it, He will have you... He DOES have you," I said, looking up at him. He wouldn't look at me and I knew it was shame.

"I don't care what you've done. God doesn't care. He just wants you to know He loves you. I love you. I don't know what the future holds but He does, and He doesn't want you sick," I desperately pleaded with him.

I grabbed his hands and prayed. I prayed more fervently than I ever had before. I felt angels holding up my prayers and although I don't remember what I said, Bill nodded his head, wiped his eyes, and held me. I remember him whispering 'thank you'.

April 20, 1977

Less than a week after that prayer the ambulance came again for Bill. Lucille and I followed, and they put Bill in the VA hospital room he had so many times occupied in the last year. We sat by the bedside praying, begging God, interceding for his life. I called Carol and asked her to pray.

She and Jerry had their first baby in January of that year and once again, I couldn't be there. We cried over the phone when I admitted that I needed to be here for my husband. She didn't understand then. There's nothing like having your mother with you when you give birth to a child. The circle of life. With cries in the background of my new grandbaby, we agreed in prayer for God's will to be done.

Early the next morning after a rough night of sleeping on couches and chairs in the hospital waiting room, I checked on Bill and decided to find some coffee. Lucille stayed with Bill. It was just after 5 am and the only place open was a coffee shop a block away.

In that ten-minute walk, I felt very close to God although I was very confused. What had my life become? What was the point? I accepted Jesus, yet nothing really got better? I felt more at peace; maybe that was it. Were we still to suffer even though we had turned our lives over to God? Didn't He pay for this already?

The Lord spoke to me and said, *I am with you in the storm. Stay close to me. The trials of this life are for a moment and don't compare to the joy I have in store.*

This alone kept me going. I had never known peace like I had after I gave my life to God. I often wondered what my life would have been like without Jesus. Different? The logistics of my life may not have been but the peace certainly wouldn't be there. I was an angry, frustrated, hard-to-control woman and God had softened me. He tenderized my heart to be more compassionate. That had to be a good thing.

April 21 - 77

Dear Carol and family.

Lucile and I are having lunch on the grounds at the hospital so will write a line and also tell you this, if two of you agree down here on earth concerning anything you ask for, my Father in heaven will do it for you. Matt 18. 19 — L. B.

When I got here this morning there was such a peace in Bill's room, he had a good nights rest and the Dr. told me he would most likely take him out of intensive care tomorrow. He has lost 24 lbs fluid weight and they plan on stopping IVs when the bottle is empty he has now.

God has answered prayer in a mighty way in his behalf.

We know this was a last ditch stand of the enemy, and a real trial of Lucile and my faith, after we had fought the battle night and day for two and ½ months and were so sure that Bill would come out of that bedroom any moment walking, leaping and praising God, rather than being carried out on an ambulance stretcher.

But the God of all grace, who hath called us unto his eternal glory by christ Jesus, after that ye have suffered awhile make you (me) perfect, stablish strengthen, settle you, to him be glory and dominion for ever and ever Amen; 1 peter 5-10-11

The word from the Lord was such an encouragement also La martha sent me a prophecy about a year ago, which

God had given her that has truly been a ~~sustaining~~ sustaining force. Dolores called late last night, she has been so concerned that I might not have money for gas etc, but God promised to supply "all" our needs and He is doing it day by day. We are still looking for Ananias to lay hands on Bill and the scales fall from his eyes. Take care of yourselves and sweet baby, who can tell what a day will bring forth—

Love that face
Mama

April 26, 1977

Walking back from the coffee shop, instant anxiety flooded me out of nowhere. I walked faster and almost jogged into the hospital lobby. I was tapping my fingers against my coffee cup all the way up the elevator. The doors opened and Lucille was standing at the nurse's station. She turned to me with tears running down her face. She shook her head.

I didn't feel the hot coffee hit my shoe or the hard floor catch my body. The next thing I knew, Lucille was waving her hand in front of my face and an overweight nurse was trying to help me.

He was gone. Bill had died just after 5 am... moments after I left the hospital for coffee.

Why? Why did I leave? Why didn't I stay? He was scared. Lucille said he was scared. She was with him, but it should have been me.

Bill's lungs filled up with fluid faster than they could get it out, they said. He'd basically drown. I couldn't imagine the pain. The fear.

"He knew Jesus," Lucille said to me. "I believe he knew Jesus."

And that's all that matters. Why did I feel such peace? On the surface, my head was spinning. What was I going to do? Bill was gone. I had now outlived two husbands, regardless of whether I was married to Creth when he died or not. Yet, I didn't feel alone. Everything on the outside should suggest I would be alone, feel alone, have nothing. Yet for all the surface grief, there was also this deep, solid comfort. Something assured me I would never be alone again.

~

We buried Bill the following Saturday. Don and Karen, Bill's kids came up from California for the funeral and Helen sent flowers. Rich came home from college and stayed with me for a couple of weeks before he had to go home. Everyone left and the house was quiet... cold and quiet.

I tried to maintain my job at the diner and soon it got to be too much for me. That fall, I got a desk job with the local newspaper and while I missed cooking, I didn't miss being on my feet all day.

Walking home from work one evening after the cold had set in of winter, I lost my balance and fell on the sidewalk, breaking my wrist. A few passerbyers got me to the hospital and now that she and Jerry were home, Carol said she was coming to get me. She and Jerry moved most of my belongings into a storage shed in Port Angeles and I moved into the spare room in their home. I finally had the downtime my heart needed. I didn't leave my bed for 3 days.

41

Thursday - Hope. Friday - Peace

"And it came to pass a long time after that, the Lord had given rest unto Israel from all their enemies round about, that Joshua waxed old and stricken in age." Joshua 23:1

I actually didn't leave that bed for almost 12 months. When I did, I was dizzy. The doctors had determined that my blood pressure was way too high. I don't know if it was the years of holding my breath figuratively, waiting for the next shoe to drop? I don't know if the pain of anguish and loss was finally manifesting itself physically. I don't know if I had been holding it together for everyone else in my life and now I was in a place of safety and security, where I didn't have to keep it together and my body was finally expelling all the guilt, strain, and suffering.

Whatever it was, I couldn't stand up for longer than five minutes.

My head would spin. I was dizzy and on so many blood pressure pills it looked like I downed the contents of a Tic-Tac bottle every day.

Carol was patient, sweet, and accommodating. It was peaceful to live in a home where I didn't feel the earth was going to crumble beneath me. It was also comforting to know I didn't have to move every couple of years. I was here and no one was telling me I had to go anywhere, do anything or take care of anyone. Even with a two-year-old running through the house, my joy was complete.

I finally got to have the relationship with my daughter I so desperately missed and her with me. We would sit for hours studying the Word, praying for each other, our families, and our country. I mentored Carol and ministered to her as she ministered to me. This blessed me and we cherished our time together.

I was grateful to Dolores, who found it in her heart to forgive me, called on a regular basis and would come to visit occasionally. I was thankful my son, Rich, found a woman he loved and had settled down in Portland. While not all of my children were close, all were connected and that gave me deep satisfaction.

Over the next couple of years, I regained my strength and moved into a small apartment in Port Angeles. The Lord restored to me the years I had rebelled and gave me the strength to minister to others. The overwhelming grace and forgiveness I was given was easily shared with others as I offered my testimony over and over. I was asked to speak at several conferences, conventions, women's meetings, and assemblies.

I was never wealthy, at least not with money, but the Lord supplied my every need. I never worked again, but Jesus was my husband. I would receive checks in the mail from random folks. The Lord provided my rent, my car, my gas, my food, and my livelihood. I wanted for nothing. I watched my grandchildren grow up and had great relationships with them. My son had a boy of his own, Cory, and he and Carol's daughter, Tammy, would often spend the weekends with me. I was surrounded by love, my family, and God's unending grace.

I rested in these quiet years that the Lord had reserved for me. He had made beauty from my ashes. He had restored my faith. He had made Himself known to me and I was eternally grateful. Nothing was wasted. He took all my sorrow, all my grief, all my pain, all my faults, and all my mistakes and made me beautiful in His eyes.

Me in my apartment in Port Angeles

I never remarried. Jesus was my source. He always had been, it was only me that had chosen to try and do it on my own. I was nothing without Him. He was everything. It was when I laid everything at His feet that he truly showed me Himself.

I enjoyed years with my children, traveling, visiting Missouri, remembering my life before Jesus. We laid my father to rest in 1985. He and Hilda moved into my same apartment complex in the early 1980s and Hilda passed shortly thereafter. Richard Cunningham died suddenly of a brain aneurysm at 85, clear of mind and secure in his salvation.

I lived in that apartment longer than I had ever lived anywhere else. It became a refuge to the hurting, a respite for the weary, a chapel for the needy, and a place of learning for the hungry.

God had given me my family back even after all I had done, all I had lost, and how far I had run from him. He gave me friends such as my son-in-law's mother, Lillian, who became a wonderful, Godly friend to me during my time in Port Angeles, both when I was there years ago and the years I spent after I returned. I had value, but not in anything of myself but because Jesus loved me. I was His right-eousness and because He loved me, I could offer love, forgiveness, and grace to others.

The week of July 5th was a wonderful week. The sun was shining on Wednesday and Lillian, Carol, my friend Marion and myself all took a short drive to Lake Crescent, just outside of town. We en-joyed lunch at the lodge, beautiful weather, and good friends. God is good.

Thursday of that week the Lord was ministering to my spirit. I often wrote scripture and tucked it away, in my Bible, in drawers, in letters, under my pillow, and even in my refrigerator. I was never going to forget the goodness of God. I was hopeful for the future but peaceful in the present. I felt compelled to write this on a Post-It™ note, **_Thursday - Hope, Friday - Peace_**. I tucked it under the doily on my dining room table.

Friday, I was doing what I had been doing for the past decade, ministering, praying, fellowshipping with my friends. My friend Marion had come over for prayer and coffee that morning. At least once a week we would gather and just bask in the goodness of God and His faithfulness. Oh, how things had changed. I was well, whole, forgiven, saved by His amazing grace.

I felt chilly, so I told Marion, "I'm gonna get a blanket." Those were the last words I ever spoke on this earth. I stood up and dropped. Marion rushed to me and held me in her lap on the floor of my apartment, my refuge for the past 15 years. I turned to her, saw Jesus, smiled, and closed my eyes.

I died on Friday, July 8, 1994. But my spirit had never been more alive. I was finally with Jesus. I had run the race; I had fought the good fight. I did what He wanted me to do and now, I was more alive and more at peace than I had ever been on this earth.

I was only 72 but I had lived several lifetimes. God doesn't call us home because He needs us, He calls us home because we have fulfilled our purpose. My purpose didn't really start to be fulfilled until I was in my 50s, but God uses all of us and He has the patience for us in spite of our stubbornness and rebellion.

Genesis 41:13 - It came to pass and He restores unto me...

My story is not unique. There are millions of people who go through life thinking life is just happening to them and they adopt the 'why me' attitude. But God wants us to get out of ourselves and realize there is a greater purpose exactly where we are and He loves us enough to not leave us there. He never left me. He wanted me. He wants you.

Things have come to pass in my life that have not been the will of God, but He can certainly take those broken pieces and turn them into something good. That's what He did with my life. God graciously welcomed me into His family and I am eternally grateful.

Now it came to pass, when Jesus finished commanding His twelve disciples, that He departed from there to teach and to preach in their cities.

And when John had heard in prison about the works of Christ, he sent two of his disciples and said to Him, "Are You the Coming One, or do we look for another?"

Jesus answered and said to them, "Go and tell John the things which you hear and see: The blind see and the lame walk; the lepers are cleansed

and the deaf hear; the dead are raised up and the poor have the gospel preached to them. And blessed is he who is not offended because of Me."
Matthew 11:1-6

My gravestone - I am not here. I am in glory.

...It came to pass

Epilogue

Epilogue

Carol married Jerry Weiler in 1968 and had one daughter, Tammy. They live in Port Angeles Washington. Tammy and her husband Tim have two children, Alexander and Caleb.

Dolores married Abner in 1962 and have three children, Jana, Kelly and Randall. They have four grandchildren and four great-grandchildren. They remained in Missouri and currently live in Lawson. Dolores visited Virginia every few years and Virginia got to spend time with her grandchildren.

Richard Byrd moved to Portland and married Carolyn. They had one son, Cory. Cory and his wife Dierdre live in Cleveland Ohio and have one son, Dean. Richard visited Virginia often and she got to spend time with her grandson.

Bill Byrd's other children, Wayne, Don, Ken and Karen grew up and had families of their own. As of the publishing of this book, only Karen and Ken are still alive. Helen moved to Tennessee after Bill died and passed away some years later. Karen still lives in Tennessee and Ken lives somewhere in Ohio.

Mitzi married Jim Brassea and lived in Missouri her whole life. They have one daughter, Jamie and three grandchildren. Mitzi passed away at age 89 on November 28, 2020.

Vern married Marie and become somewhat estranged from the family. They have two children. Vern passed away sometime in the 1990s.

Virginia lived the remainder of her life in a small apartment in Port Angeles, Washington. She lived above her dad's apartment and had close contact with him until he died in 1985. She ministered to hundreds in her latter years, spoke at conventions and led many to the Lord with her ministry and testimony.